# LEADERSHIP

*and the*
*Culture of Trust*

# LEADERSHIP

## and the
## Culture of Trust

### GILBERT W. FAIRHOLM

PRAEGER

Westport, Connecticut
London

**Library of Congress Cataloging-in-Publication Data**

Fairholm, Gilbert W.
    Leadership and the culture of trust / Gilbert W. Fairholm.
        p.   cm.
    Includes bibliographical references.
    ISBN 0–275–94833–1 (alk. pap.)
    1. Leadership.   2. Corporate culture.   I. Title.
HD57.7.F35   1994
658.4'092—dc20              93–42804

British Library Cataloguing in Publication Data is available.

Library of Congress Catalog Card Number: 93–42804
ISBN: 0–275–94833–1

First published in 1994

Praeger Publishers, 88 Post Road West, Westport, CT 06881
An imprint of Greenwood Publishing Group, Inc.

Printed in the United States of America

The paper used in this book complies with the
Permanent Paper Standard issued by the National
Information Standards Organization (Z39.48–1984).

10 9 8 7 6 5 4 3

# Contents

# Preface

Three seminal ideas have changed the way we think about managing our complex economic and social organizations:

- Leadership based on shared values that build mutual respect, freedom, justice, unity, and happiness
- Shaping a culture within which mutual work is done based on mutual, interactive trust
- Using power to get out of their association in the organization what leaders want for the group and for self

Together these three ideas have reconstituted our ideas about the nature of leadership, the organization, and how to work with stakeholders—the many suppliers, customers, clients, constituency groups, and communities (in addition to the traditional core of immediate followers) who have a stake in the leader's success.

In other books I have treated the ideas of values leadership and organizational power politics.[1] Here my focus in on shaping unified cultures characterized by high trust. I believe this kind of cultural context to be essential to the idea of leadership. Indeed, without a unified trust culture, leadership as it is now defined is impossible.

The leader-follower relationship is essentially a voluntary association. Followers need not respond to our leadership as employees (subordinates) must to their manager's orders. Gaining the use of follower talent, time, and creativity means leaders must induce them to *want* to do what needs to be done. Leaders cannot force creativity or commitment. Followers give these essential aspects of collective success.

I have come to realize that leadership is a process of building a trust environment within which leader and follower feel free to participate toward accomplishment of mutually valued goals using agreed-upon processes. This book is about how leaders define and shape cultures characterized by shared values that enhance and respect the individual, encourage mutual trust, and empower all members.

## NOTE

1. See Gilbert W. Fairholm, *Values Leadership: Toward a New Philosophy of Leadership* (New York: Praeger, 1991) and *Organizational Power Politics: Tactics of Leadership Power* (New York: Praeger, 1993).

# Acknowledgments

Many people share in an activity of any magnitude. In this case, I am indebted to the many, many authors of other books and articles—and to practitioners I have worked with and observed—whose ideas and insights have found their way into this book. Many of the ideas have become so much a part of my thinking that they are reflected throughout this book, whether or not they received direct citation. I am indebted to them for their wisdom and recognize their leadership in my life.

Not the least of these exemplary leaders that deserve recognition and a part in anything others find worthy in this book are the members of my family: Barbara, Ann, Paul, Daniel, Scott, and Matthew. They are and have always been examples of the best of leadership and of all else good.

# LEADERSHIP

## *and the*
## *Culture of Trust*

# Introduction

It is clear that much of current American culture works against internal unity and cohesion. Multiple competing cultures and subcultures with attendant different value systems are challenging our cultures from within and without. We are now in a situation in America where most organizations try to cope with multiple diverse value systems espoused by each of their stakeholder groups.

Leadership in this cultural environment is difficult at best, impossible at worst. It stretches our collective imagination to suggest that one person can, by dint of individual personality or capacity, bring together a group of diverse individuals and groups to produce anything. The task is simply beyond the capacity of any one leader. This is especially true when effort is also directed to respect, honor, and preserve largely intact each cultural subset's unique values, customs, and traditions.

There is little hope that acceptance of multiple and diverse internally competing value systems will produce stable, effective, responsive economic, social, or governmental organizations. The likelihood is that all that will be produced is balkanization. There is even less hope that a situation of unrestrained cultural diversity will result in a cure for our social ills and restore a nurturing culture most Americans can accept and to which they can conform.

The need is for leadership to focus and direct individual action; even though the individuals in the organization try to maintain their diverse cultural features. Present models are inadequate to the task. This book suggests that these past models, in fact, are part of the problem.

## THE LEADERSHIP CHALLENGE

Part of the present leadership problem is that we have thought of leadership in terms of the individual leader. We have advocated a leadership model characterized by a charismatic individual with special traits of character or special skills. And we have charged this superleader solely with the task of shaping our social organizations and institutions.

Another part of the problem is that our models for social change are faulty. The conventional wisdom is that to change individual leaders need only to change the formal structural or work process systems within which people live and work. For years we have understood change as a function of altering external, environmental factors. We think that new programs, new parties in office, new equipment, computerization, different procedures, rules, or laws, will affect a change in the quality of life of individuals and an increased standard of living for the general society.

This approach, of course, does work, but at great cost of personal freedom. The only way that this kind of change works is if leaders closely supervise their followers. Externally imposed change is effective only if we exercise close control over co-workers. This change model is coercive in nature. It denigrates the individual worker, treats them as interchangeable parts, "cogs," in the organizational machine. And present models see change as a leader task. We change as the organization leaders see a need, whether or not workers want to, are ready, or are capable of the proposed change.

There is, of course, another change model. A better, more fully successful method to change the organization or a work system is to change individuals first and let them change the formal structure. The whole organizational development movement is predicated on this change-the-individual-first model. Unfortunately, not all leaders have adopted this model. Even though it is more sure and longlasting, it is also slower and less predictable.

Increasingly, today leaders are coming to see their role in change as a task of creating a trust culture to undergird both personal and institutional growth. Once leaders have created and generalized this unifying cultural background they can allow co-workers to change the organizational structure or system because they share common aims. The trust culture provides a unifying context within which leader and followers work and focus effort toward agreed-upon goals, values, and vision ideals. The combined impact is to force the formal structure to change. Collectively the sum of individual changes is to change our circumstances as an organization, a community, a nation, the world.

The leadership mechanism for this kind of change is shared vision and values and a culture that trusts members to behave according to these shared values. It is not laws or rules that change society. Rather, it is the cumulative result of individuals who change in conformance to a shared vision and shared values that changes the organization for the better. These people then will obey rules and regulations because they believe in them. This change model focuses on teaching and sitting in council with co-workers about goals and outcomes and then stepping back so as not to constrain follower behavior as they implement shared goals.

## LEADERSHIP OF TRUST

This book is about the leadership of trust. It describes cultural leadership that produces a homogenous organization where work can be done collectively. Leaders aid this cultural change process when *both* leaders and followers define, shape, and maintain, in this era of diversity, organizational cultures that value reciprocal trust between leaders and their followers. They do this so both individuals and organizations can develop and mature along congruent lines.

Seeing leadership in these terms is different from past models. It has been an American tendency to see leadership in terms of the personality and capacity of individual leaders. Leadership has been seen as something the leader is or what he or she does alone. This model is really a managerial model keyed to position or role in an authoritarian hierarchy with the manager at the apex of the structure.

In reality, leadership is an expression of collective, community action. Leadership is something that happens as a result of leader and stakeholder collaborative action. Leadership is not a starring role. True leadership describes unified action of leaders and followers (stakeholders) working together to jointly achieve mutual goals. It is collaborative.

Shaping a culture in which group members can trust each other enough to work together is the first leadership task. It creates the context within which leaders can lead, followers can find reason for full commitment, and both can achieve their potential.

Unfortunately, there is little available to emerging leaders to guide them in developing a trust culture. There is a spate of recent research on managing culture. There is also a very small and older literature on trust as a tool leaders may use to enhance their leadership. In neither body of literature is the role of leadership emphasized. This book tries to fill this gap.

## FOCUS

Three ideas—culture creation, trust relationships, and leadership—form the basis of this book. It begins with a brief description (in Part I) of the kind of culture leaders need to exercise leadership. Chapter 1 is important in setting the stage for the rest of the book. It provides an overall introduction to the importance of the leadership task of creating harmonious trust cultures within which we can perform leadership—as well as all other organizational tasks—with some assurance of enduring success.

Leaders need to understand the underlying culture within which they work. They also must shape the culture to meet changing needs. Shaping a culture conducive to their vision for their organization may be the quintessential leadership task. It is a transforming task aimed at keeping the cultural surround continually responsive to the organization's vision and the needs of a changing, evolving follower core. It is shaping an organizational situation where followers can and want to work together to gain mutually desired goals. Indeed, leadership is successful—maybe, even, possible—only as this goal is attained.

Parts II and III explore specific and critically important leader tasks of shaping, maintaining, and changing culture. These analytical and descriptive parts define culture creation and culture maintenance and change as tools leaders use in attaining their (and the group's) aims. The task of creating a culture engages leaders in a wide variety of actions to build trusting, cooperative, unified, committed organizational teams. Each of the various elements of culture are interrelated. All are essential to success. They are described and placed in context in chapters 2 through 6.

Part IV discusses trust formation and its relationship to the overarching culture. Part IV focuses on this second critical element of leadership, trust. The leader's special role is in shaping trust cultures that fully recognize organizational needs, while also recognizing human needs. These chapters focus attention on issues associated with creating a pattern of values to guide both individuals and organizational vision that compose the foundation of mutual interactive trust.

Chapters 7 through 10 present a new model of trust, this most important, but rarely discussed element in organized relationships. These chapters relate our willingness to trust others to an eventual reality. This trust-truth model suggests that real trust can only be in the truth; the eventually proved reality of a future situation we accept as "fact" now. To be trusted, one must make a connection between present action and a future situation that, with the passage of time, the trusting person proves to be true.

These chapters also relate trust to most of the significant features of organization, such as shared values; productivity; problem solving; communication of meaning, commitment, and leadership. They define a trust culture as an essentially healthy organization that focuses on leadership based on shared values, voluntary individual performance within the cultural constraints, and in terms of team structures and relationships.

Part IV also provides insight in helping the reader understand the idea of trust and relate trust to factors of integrity, action, and personal character and judgment. Also introduced are some factors in the culture that may constrain the full exercise of trust. Part IV describes some cautions leaders and others need to be aware of as they try to build trust cultures. Traditional organizational structure, authority relationships, communications patterns, divergent selfish interests, and the complexities of building trust are related to the task of creating trusting environments within which leadership can take place.

Parts V and VI focus on the critical element of leadership in a trust culture. They introduce several ideas occupying the attention of leaders today as they concentrate on creating and maintaining harmonious trust cultures.

Part V reviews some leadership skills leaders may need to be successful in a homogeneous trust culture. Other chapters in Part V deal with team building, with its attendant technologies of empowerment, strategic thinking, and innovation; all very prominent today, as are ideas such as inspiration, conflict resolution, and helping employees gain a sense of personal ownership of the organization's work goals and tasks. Chapters 11 through 14 place these popular tools in context of a harmonious, trusting culture and define success of these tool in terms of this context. Part V also elaborates on the need for vision setting and shaping employee values so they accept the challenges of shared governance of their common enterprise.

Chapters 15 through 18 focus more on the third major element of this book—leadership. These chapters apply culture maintenance and trust management to current issues, such as multiculturalism and managing for total quality. Part VI also deals with some constraints on culture leadership that leaders must account for in their work of forming and maintaining cultures conducive to trust relationships. The chapters in Part VI present cautions that leaders must be aware of as they practice leadership—perhaps the most significant activity in today's and tomorrow's world.

# PART I

# HARMONIOUS CULTURES: THE FOUNDATION OF LEADERSHIP

Of all the new and pressing problems the chief officers in our large-scale organizations face day-to-day one stands out. It is the challenge of creating and maintaining an organizational culture that fits the nature of the work done *and* the character and capacities of its growingly diverse work force. This is a problem of integration of worker and organization so the system meets the needs of both. It is at the center of the challenge facing leaders in the coming century.

Leadership is not so much a function of the individual leader as it is a condition of the culture. While leadership may be spontaneous at times, most often it is a result of specific, planned actions by individual leaders to create organizational cultures characterized by internal harmony around values and ideals the leader and follower share or come to share. Leadership is the task of creating harmony among the disparate, sometimes competing, organizational—human, system, and program—factions. It is a task of culture creation more than of development of charisma. It is an expression of community. It is a task of generalizing values and principles of action in ways that all stakeholders will find acceptable and energizing. This acceptability is more important than, say, creating standard operating systems.

Leaders are identified, flourish, and grow in situations where they and their followers share unifying values, ideals, and goals. Leaders are successful when they unite individuals in collaborative action without losing too much of the individual freedom they and their followers want. Leadership is not so much what individual leaders do as it is what leader and led do collectively.

Leadership is the exercise of values that give preference to democratic participation in the joint enterprise. For Americans, these values are found in our founding documents and give context to values such as liberty, respect for life, unity, justice, and happiness (Fairholm, 1991). Much of the problem we see in our social, governmental, business, and other organizations today is a result of an overemphasis on individual freedom. We seem to value individual freedom (some might say license) more than collaborative, cooperative interaction.

The problem with many organizations—including our nation—is that too few people understand or care about overall organizational goals. They see the world through myopic, single-issue eyes. They want to realize their specific goals and give little, if any, heed to general institutional ones. Many people value personal independence and difference over collective interdependence. They celebrate individual difference, not collective action. The effect is to thwart leadership.

Chapter 1 introduces the reader to the other half of the leadership equation: the homogeneous, harmonious culture within which leadership can take place. Chapter 1 raises the question of unified cultures and places this need in the context of leadership effectiveness. This chapter makes the case for shaping unified trust cultures as a preeminent leadership task; an essential aspect of leadership itself. It defines leadership as a function of inducing people who are essentially free to constrain their freedom and to conform to group values; that is to become willing followers of leaders.

Leadership is a collective activity. It is only when the group is united and functioning in harmony that leadership is a part of the interactivity. Defining leadership solely as a function of individual charisma or talent is faulty. Experience does not confirm this hypothesis. Rather, leadership is an interactive function of a leader and several followers jointly engaged. It takes place in situations (cultures) where leader and led are united on value terms and trust each other enough to risk self in participation in collective activity. Chapter 1 begins the development of this essential "other side" of leadership.

# 1

# Where Have All the
# Unified Cultures Gone?

## INTRODUCTION

A few years ago many people joined in asking the question, "Where have all the leaders gone?" True, visible, active, dynamic leadership is scarce in American society and many of its institutions. Indeed, it is hard today to even begin making a list of authentic nationally recognized leaders. We find depressingly few people whom others acknowledge as leaders in government, business, social, or religious realms. Those that do come to mind are often older and represent a former time.

One reason for this lack is that we have asked the wrong question. It is not sufficient individual leaders that are lacking. Rather, the missing element is the context—the culture—that makes leadership possible. Leadership takes place in a context of *mutual trust* based on shared vision, ideals, and values. Leadership is in part the task of building harmonious, collaborative teams as well as the task of leading them. Few present local, regional, national, or global organizations can boast of these qualities and characteristics, hence, the dearth of leaders.

These qualities describe the leadership environment, a unified, harmonious culture characterized by mutual trust that allows leadership to take place. We need to remember that the leader-follower relationship is a voluntary relationship. The key to leadership is in an organizational context in which leader and led share values and vision. Leadership takes place within a context where both leaders and followers can be free to trust the purposes, actions, and intent of others. Leadership can only take place in such a climate of mutual, coordinated action based on a common vision. These organizations place follower development as a

*Followers – leaders!*

high priority, for after all, leadership is impossible without followers (Hunt, 1991).

Unless the organization creates and sustains a follower core, leadership cannot take place (Fairholm, 1991). People follow leaders because they choose to. Followers are volunteers. People do not follow because of an imposed authoritarian, structural relationship. They do so out of choice because they think the relationship will enhance them in some definable ways. We follow leaders who care for us; empower us; represent desired goals, methods, or objectives. We follow people whose values and ideals match our own.

People do what others want for one of two reasons. First, they share the need; they agree with the proposed actions. Second, they comply because of some external compulsion; that is, they are induced to comply. In the absence of shared reasons that let followers volunteer to enter a relationship, leaders must manage and control followers in what most people would describe as restrictive, even, punitive ways. If shared vision, values, and ideals are missing, then leaders must induce followers to follow. They do this by imposing external controls: restrictive rules, detailed procedures, close supervision, audits, reports, spot checks, or any of a myriad other managerial controls to force compliance.

The real question we must ask—and answer—if we want to reestablish leadership in our homes, our groups, our businesses and governmental organizations, our societal institutions, and the nation and world is not where have the leaders gone. The critical question is where have all the homogeneous, mutually trusting, unified groups gone? The real purpose of organizational culture is to create a climate and condition of mutual trust within which all persons can decide (want) to grow and develop to their full potential as leaders and followers. It is only in this kind of a shared trust culture that leadership can evolve, develop, and flourish. And it is in this kind of culture where leaders can empower followers in the fullest measure.

## THE IMPACT OF CULTURE ON LEADERSHIP

Culture is a powerful force. It directs the life of members both as individuals and in their relationships with others within the organization. Strong cultures act as intellectual and emotional paradigms that can block acceptance of alternative cultures (Barker, 1992). Cultural paradigms can isolate the individual member from other cultural associations—from co-workers, from family, from church, from the larger community. They also can unite individuals into strong coalitions of mutually interdependent teams. The key to attaining this latter result is the strength of mutual trust present in and characteristic of the culture.

Finding a common values basis for interaction is the preeminent challenge of leaders today. The task, however, is not so daunting as it may appear. Most people share certain principles and truths in common. These principles and values transcend culture, race, religion, and nationality. They represent something more than mere preference or belief. They provide a common bond on which we base our trust of another person.

Values are the settled beliefs we have about what is true or good or beautiful for us. They guide our actions and judgments of what is good, right, and appropriate. Values represent those truths all or most members of a community share and know they should seek after (whether they do or not) because they are good for them and will result in greater material, moral, or spiritual development. Commonly shared values are the foundation of trust between individuals. Shared values also form the basis for mutual trust between groups, whether nations, communities, or organizational cultures.

*values*

Just as values shape culture, so too does the culture shape leadership. The leadership style adopted by leaders (though not necessarily consciously) grows out of their ideas and feelings about the nature of humankind. Some agree with Thomas Jefferson's view that some—the managers among us—see followers as children and love them with paternal affection. Others—leaders—see followers as adults whom they can prepare and then leave to govern themselves. For still others, these two views are excessively optimistic. Yet experience with self-governance teaches that people respond to training, counciling-with their leaders, and the opportunity to lead themselves (Fairholm, 1991) with greater trust, loyalty, and commitment.

*exp*

Common values build trust, and trust is the foundation of cooperative action. The kind of leadership that grows out of shared values only flourishes in a climate within which individuals can accept the individuality of others without sanctioning all of their behavior or words. In a climate of trust, individuals can give open, candid reactions to what they see as right or wrong. In trust cultures there is little manipulation, few hidden agendas, no unreasonable controls, nor saccharine sweetness that discounts real problems. Instead, there is a congruency in concepts, conduct, and concern; a unity appropriate to group membership that does not risk individuality. Without trust, cultural values can become strictures, impeding individual and group progress.

The problem with most texts on management (and even many older texts on leadership) is the focus on the mechanics of control, not on cultural values supporting trust relationships. The mechanics of control is, of course, necessary. The risk, however, is that this focus might ignore the underlying skills and traits that rest on fundamental concepts without which no system of techniques, procedures, mechanics, and follow-up can possibly work.

It does little good, for instance, to develop elaborate organizational and work flow charts if the people who inhabit the real world symbolized by these charts do not trust each other or really communicate with each other. It does little good to strive to achieve goals if leaders allow themselves to be too much at the mercy of their moods so followers see them as ambivalent administrators whom they find unpredictable or capricious about the goals mutually embraced.

## THE IMPACT OF TRUST ON CULTURE AND ON LEADERSHIP

It would not be unfair to characterize the current political and social climate in America on one level as a general lack of trust. Some Americans do not trust our political and social systems and their leaders (Hart, 1978; Barber, 1983; Lipset and Schneider, 1987; Mitchell and Scott, 1987; Heise, 1985). While several recent events (not the least of which is the Watergate episode and our quadrennial presidential elections) have worsened the problem of leader trust, this suspicion is a part of our national culture. Americans have always had a sort of love-hate relationship with their leaders regardless of whether they represent our social, political, or our economic institutions.

It is a traditional American cultural custom to distrust our leaders. While some would suggest there is a crisis of confidence today, history reports a continuing series of such crises. In the creative years of this nation, Abigail Adams expressed her (and many other women's) dissatisfaction with any new political systems that did not permit women voice and representation. Other crises issues and events pepper our history. These crises have involved differences about revolution, national place, freedom, equality, union, and many other powerful ideas.

More recently, we can point to multiple events that have raised questions of trust and confidence in our political system and its leaders. Civil rights, the Vietnam War, Watergate, Iran-Contra, corruption, incompetence to lead, the savings and loan crisis, the decline in American industrial productivity, and recession have perpetuated and widened the confidence gap some citizens feel toward their leaders. Some blame the gap on leadership deficiencies (see Hart, 1978). Others blame the gap on systemic shortcomings in a 200-year-old Constitution (Bailey, 1980). Still others see the root cause of our distrust of our leaders in a decline in values and ethics (Scott and Hart, 1979). The uniform formula for change is to alter cultural features.

From an organizational perspective, the problem of culture creation and maintenance is one of leadership. Creating the kind of physical and psychological environment necessary to get others to *want* to follow them taxes leaders' abilities on all levels. The task of creating an organizational culture that engages both the emotions and the best efforts of members and coordinates them into a unity is daunting. Nevertheless, it is *the* central leadership task. And it is, essentially, a problem of developing trust.

The process of gaining trust relies first on having or securing some accurate real (truthful) knowledge of the person or situation. Armed with this knowledge, we can extend our trust to the other person or to some thing. Trust once given then opens opportunities for us to gain experiences with that person or thing. These experiences are the means by which we gather and analyze additional data to further build trust or to diminish it. That is, we increase trust by the acquisition of more true knowledge about, let us say, a person. We diminish it by the same process: acquisition of information that belies our initial perception of the truth about the person that formed the basis of our initial trust actions. We increase or diminish trust by this process of incremental development of information about the true reality of a person.

This kind of intimate knowledge acquisition about another person or some thing forms the basis of a lasting trust. It is encouraged by a culture that values trust per se, that honors the individual, and that fosters cooperative interaction. Trust takes place and is favored by leaders only as they act to create and maintain a cultural situation in which individuals can feel safe enough and confident enough in the situation to take the risk to unite with others. Leadership is as much—maybe more—a task of building unifying trust cultures as it is charisma, communication, or crisis management.

We may ask the question, where do leaders get the strength to lead in this way? What are the sources of strength allowing leaders to emerge and to endure over time and in the face of problems, competition, and recalcitrance of followers? Perhaps the best answer to this question is: "from their own cultural foundations." Leaders gather strength from their inner conviction that their vision values are correct, right for their followers, true for them and the group led.

Added strength for leaders comes from the support of their followers within the culture as they come to share the leader's vision values, accept the cultural constraints defined by those values, and participate actively in accomplishing the joint vision. The vision becomes a kind of defining moment in the life of the leader and the organization. A defining moment is when one receives insight that illuminates an aspect of self or an idea or a concept and makes it a part of one's self-image and self-definition.

## VALUES LEADERSHIP AND THE TRUST CULTURE

Culture impacts on leadership in specific and direct ways. Unless the culture is supportive of leaders, leadership based on common values is impossible. Culture determines a large part of what leaders do and how they do it. Much of Peters and Waterman's work in *In Search of Excellence* (1982) is about organizational cultural factors that impact the leader's skills, knowledge, or abilities. Culture determines organizational practice and confirms that set of practices. In actuality, leadership is a consequence of organizational culture and culture a result of leadership (Wildavsky, 1984).

Leadership takes place in an organizational cultural setting that fosters and honors the funding values characteristic of American society. Many values come to us from the past. Most Americans adhere to values such as respect for life, liberty, justice, unity, and happiness. As one or more of these values are central in the organization's culture, we can practice leadership—as opposed to management or something else (Fairholm, 1991). But, plainly we cannot use these values as the basis for leader action outside a culture that fosters and encourages them or one where trust is absent.

## INTEGRATING VALUES IN CULTURE

Culture is conventional. We can define individual success in organizations in terms of fit with the prevailing culture. We realize a fit when individual behavior conforms to prevailing values; when it becomes conventional. Ultimately, all culture is convention. It is putting design and shape into the common environment, beginning in the mind. A culture is a self-contained system of values that we see as conventional. Conventions are rule-bound, internally complete, and values-laden. Conventions separate, distinguish, and isolate a culture from other cultures—to value some things as opposed to others.

Values are enduring beliefs that a specific kind of conduct or a particular state of existence is personally or socially preferable. Values are prized and cherished. They are part of a repeated or repeatable pattern of behavior. Individuals freely choose values from among alternatives after reflection. Values are positively affirmed and acted upon.

An individual's values are part of a system, or set, of variously rated values that guide one's life and actions and that make that action conventional, predictable. Most people's values are similar to those of people around them. Values constitute a network of known and shared understandings and norms taken for granted and provide a substrata of commonality in organizational life.

Values guide day-to-day activities in organizations. Ott (1989) equates values with beliefs, ethical codes, moral codes, and ideologies. For him they mean the same things as organizational culture. Indeed, Deal and Kennedy (1983) suggest that organizations become meaningful to members only after leaders infuse them with values (see also Selznick, 1957).

Values are an important part of human experience. They can be personal, professional, organizational, or societal. Values define both what ought to be and what is in our lives (Schein, 1985; Sathe, 1983). Cultural beliefs inside our organizations cover a wide range of topics (Lorsch, 1986). At the core is the values system of its top leaders. These values often find voice in a vision statement or commonly accepted focus around which the organization and its leaders act. The vision is the leader's values version of what the organization is and what it should do and become. It sets the direction and limits of the organization's capabilities. It is the crux of the leader's core beliefs about the work, the workers, and the organizational possibilities.

Organizational values are at the heart of the organization's culture. These values and the culture that gives values context direct and open some possibilities and inhibit other possibilities. They need to be set, maintained, changed as needed, and constantly kept relevant to present action and plans.

Culture is an individual and collective human phenomenon. Leaders need to understand and use the corporate culture to ensure member commitment. People commit when appealed to in terms of their values, needs, beliefs, customs, and practices. A common set of values binds people together in a culture. Conflicting values between employees affects work behavior and attitudes. They disrupt and may even destroy a culture.

America is in the midst of significant cultural and organizational change. Statistics abound about the decline of American manufacturing dominance. Service industries are on the increase. Our economic position internationally has deteriorated. German and Japanese dominance in world economic arenas has overshadowed America. Japanese dominance in management theory is also a factor (for example, participatory management and Total Quality Management).

Technological innovations are changing the nature of the work done in organizations. The work force is becoming more diversified. Past organizational attitudes and values cannot serve today's or tomorrow's worker or leader. These factors require that leaders give attention to organizational culture and to efforts to make substantive changes. Leadership is, thus, a values displacement task.

Values permeate organizational life. They define it. They are a main cause of the sense of permanence most organizations enjoy. And, they are a prime cause for the difficulty many people—leaders and workers alike—experience in changing organizational structure, process, or systems of work. Yet, most people ignore values in their analyses of organizational life.

Values define the organization, prescribe its purposes, and provide the basis for measures of success. Values are powerful paradigms prescribing organizational rules and regulating worker actions. We do not develop a trust culture as a byproduct of routinely developed and changed programs. Trust is not a new program nor a result of a series of "new programs." People will not continue to offer their commitment to leaders who continually present new programs—which are really rehashes of the same basic paradigm—to accomplish the same task. Rather a trust culture is best illustrated by programs that implicitly or explicitly prioritize values and are conducted consistently in terms of those values.

# PART II

# CULTURAL LEADERSHIP

We can make several assumptions about culture. First, it exists. Every organization and group that endures for even a modestly short time develops a culture. Each culture is largely unique. It is a socially constructed concept. Second, it provides members with a method of understanding events, symbols, and messages formed within the organization and unique to it. Third, culture is a kind of lever for guiding group behavior. And, it is a control mechanism approving or prohibiting some behaviors and conditioning others.

Organizational culture is distinct from organizational strategy, structure, and work processes. An organization's culture provides the implicit context within which the organization and its members function and perform their assigned tasks and interrelationships. The success of individuals and new systems is a function of how they relate or fail to relate to the extant culture and not to the explicit utility of the new person or technology. All organizations are definable in cultural terms.

Of course, there is value in looking at organizations from the perspective of their physical facilities, their structure, the systems of work flow, and the tools and equipment used by workers. While important, that is not a complete picture. Organizations are about people in interaction. They are about the collective values people hold regarding the common enterprise. Organizations are about how much members trust each other, if indeed they trust others at all. They are about attitudes and emotions and their impact on effective performance of the group tasks. Organizations are definable best in these terms and in ideas such as change, trust, cohesion, conformity, and adaptability. In a word, they are about culture.

The culture creation task for the leader is to build both a formal, structural system to organize people and material and an emotional foundation that supports the values and future vision leaders have for their organizations. This task asks leaders to consider both internal (intrinsic) and external (extrinsic) aspects of the organization as they build trusting teams capable and willing to engage in the work to attain the shared vision. Both structural and emotionally charged elements of organization are necessary.

The chapters in Part II develop both general and specific definitions of culture from a leadership perspective. They relate organizational culture to the cultural ideas we have developed about traditional social institutions. These chapters extend the larger community culture to the specific needs of organizational leadership. Chapters 2 through 4 devote attention to details of definition and to specific elements of culture that leaders need to understand to do their work. They also provide insight into the need (the requirement) of evolving the culture to keep pace with change.

Chapter 2 discusses the general concept of culture in the literature of sociology and relates it to organizational cultural models. It notes the impact that features of culture have on life as we live it in America and the power the larger umbrella culture has on our present-day organizations. This chapter focuses the reader's attention on the values foundation of organizational culture. It notes the importance of values-setting to leaders as they lead their followers. Also identified are several important aspects of the leader's role as the prime shaper of organizational culture.

Chapter 2 also breaks down the idea of culture into its component elements. The main components of culture that define it and prescribe its nature and character are elaborated. While cultures differ, all cultures are composed of assumptions and expectations that set the tone for both worker involvement and program priority. These assumptions help members ascribe meaning to their interactions.

Cultures recognize and honor some follower behavior and penalize other behavior, and they identify individuals who personify desired behavior. Chapter 2 also introduces the reader to the idea of cultural hierarchies consisting of umbrella cultures and subcultures associated with each organizational element within the parent culture. In this respect, culture partakes of system theory ideas.

Chapter 3 elaborates the general ideas introduced in Chapter 2 and extends them operationally. The ideas of culture and climate are distinguished and explained in hierarchical terms. Organizational culture comes out of and is shaped by the larger community culture within which it operates. Full understanding of the culture of a specific organization is not possible except as we analyze it in relationship to the larger, umbrella cultures that surround it. They form the cultural nucleus for the individual members of the organization.

Chapter 3 also presents a comprehensive model of organizational culture that connects current organizational culture theory with more traditional social culture. This comprehensive model provides a convenient structure within which the many, often disparate, actions of both leaders and followers can be better understood. This chapter provides a solid base for later discussions of the component elements of culture, the development of trust, and the management of this system.

Chapter 4 suggests that the central task of leadership is to create these shared ideals and to make them work in bringing harmony out of disharmony, unity out of apparent chaos. To do this, leaders need to be expert in cultural change. This chapter introduces the idea of the leader as integrator, a largely ignored aspect in both the leadership and the culture literature. It also relates this integrator role to past organizational theory and to the emerging ideas of chaos theory.

Chaos theory suggests that variations in the minutest part of a system affects the whole because the part *is*, in reality, an extension of the whole. Applied to the leadership of culture, chaos theory reminds us that all parts constitute the whole. And, as the parts of our organizations change as more diverse people enter, leaders must be willing to expand their ideas and values to accept fully the reality of the actual culture, not just idealizations of it grounded in the past.

Applied to organizational leadership, the leader's task is to create a culture that integrates all individuals into a natural unity so individual actions can strengthen the outcome desires of the whole. Leadership is changing people and artifacts to find unity in apparent chaos. This idea is especially important as leaders begin to lead in cultures peopled by widely diverse individuals. Making these culturally diverse people a part of a harmonious whole is leadership.

# 2

# The Idea of Culture

## INTRODUCTION

An organization's culture becomes a prime definitional factor in placing that culture in relationship to other cultures and in predicting its success or quality vis-à-vis other cultures.

Culture study has a long history as a means of identifying and rating social groups. It has a short history as a means for defining and comparing organizational work units and their smaller subcultural systems, such as work teams. Similar cultural factors apply to work groups and social cultures. Local cultural feature differences are also common. And, obviously, the larger-scoped cultures constrain these different internal subunit cultures. For example, the dominant American culture helps define and constrain organizational work cultures. In the same way, the larger organization's culture defines and delimits subcultures within a given organization.

We can think of culture in hierarchical or systems terms in that a given culture may contain several subcultures. Each subculture, while similar to the parent culture can differ in some respects from each other and from the parent. The parent culture also may be a subculture of an even larger, more encompassing social culture.

This does not suggest that the subculture is an exact copy of the larger cultures in the hierarchy. Of course, similarities and relationships are present. But each cultural unit differs in specifics from any others in the chain. What we see, or what members experience, in one level may be reminiscent of another level's cultural features, but they also may differ significantly. Knowing the parameters of the larger culture helps in defining and analyzing the details of the subcultures making up the larger body. Thus, it is right to begin any culture discussion with analysis of the larger culture.

Analysis of organizational cultures in America must begin with an understanding of the larger national culture. This umbrella culture shapes and conditions the cultures in specific individual organizations. The cultural values, ideals, and artifacts that define American culture bleed into the definitions of the social, work, and governmental organizations making up our national society. They form a cultural base upon which these internal cultures are supported.

## THE PRESENT CHALLENGE TO AMERICAN CULTURE

Belonging is a fundamental human need. Human beings strive for community, but they also strive for independence. Now in America these two basic needs are in conflict. The quest for independence has led Americans to devalue family, community, and social commitment in the mistaken hope that it will liberate them. The record is clear, however, that the overfocus on independence has deprived us of the richness of community. It has devalued the mediating institutions in society—home, family, religion—that best foster personal development and autonomy (Hafen, 1993).

America is becoming rootless. Our culture is the culture of the crowd, not the community (Frederick, 1991). Though near, people do not feel close to each other. Each person (and group) is mostly concerned about his or her own exclusive interests. We can characterize our neighborhoods, local regions, states, indeed, the nation itself, as pluralistic and narrowly self-interested. Our cultural institutions are becoming largely single interest institutions. Our population is growing and density is increasing, but community is lacking.

Our civilization today is ill balanced. Our ethical, moral, and spiritual cultures lag so far behind our material culture in its development that we have no adequate control over the latter. This imbalance imperils us and our survival as a nation. We have overemphasized materialism and undervalued morality. We have honored independence and personal liberty and ignored the need for cooperative group action. We have eulogized wealth and ignored honesty and group integrity.

There is a growing concern that unless the culture is rebalanced to give weight to ethical and moral dimensions, we risk our very survival. Uncontrolled independence pits individual against individual and group against group. It has pulled America apart rather than strengthened it. It has challenged our traditional values of honesty, service, and concern for the group. It threatens to replace these community values with others more supportive of individual aggrandizement.

In the main, if we are to have ethical and moral balance, if we are to regain moral control in our culture, it will be our moral, religious leaders who will do it. A culture's moral leaders are the creators and the conservators of social ideals. Yet, our morals and our moral leaders have been, and remain, the target of concerted and comprehensive attack.

Today, analysts from every side challenge America's traditional morality as a force in contemporary culture. The natural result is that moral leadership is declining along with national morality. Science, education, and government can only do so much to help correct this lack in our moral, ethical, and spiritual development, and they have not made much progress to date.

Thoughtful Americans are becoming pessimistic about the future of our country. We have had many economic downturns. War has peppered our history. Internal strife is also a part of our background; crime and lawlessness are rife. Some see a lack of core values as guides for Americans as the source of our cultural problems. Perhaps a more accurate analysis would suggest that the problem is, rather, a failure to follow our traditional core values.

Two examples of the impact on our future of failure to adhere to traditional values illustrate the power of moral values in shaping culture. First, over the past several years, the courts have shown a pervasive hostility toward institutional religion as a legitimate moral force in public life. The justices seem to be imposing a religionless secularism on the rest of us by bowing to the intolerance of a tiny minority who insist on imposing their own secular preferences on all. This action and these results fly in the face of the overwhelming weight of experience on the side of religious pluralism, not secular monism.

Most will agree that a strong sense of the connection between American political governance and religion is part of our foundation as a nation. Analysis of recent cases suggest strongly that the courts have grounded ethical decision making in an autonomy completely separate and apart from God. Two examples illustrate this fact: George Washington wrote in his farewell address that religion and morality are vital supports to American political and social life; and Thomas Jefferson noted that we cannot secure the liberties of the nation apart from the strong conviction that these liberties are the gift of God.

These and many other examples can be adduced to make this obvious point about our national religious heritage. Yet, despite this historical connection, the courts have broken apart these two founding cultural systems. Isolating religion from social and cultural life jeopardizes our national persona and removes a vital and historic support.

The second example of moral breakdown is clear in the recent presidential election campaign. The campaign made clear the feelings of the cultural elites in this nation about family values. They largely ignored this central moral issue around which our nation and its prosperity depend. In pandering to special interests, the cultural elites have denigrated traditional nuclear family values. And, they have done this in the face of overwhelming evidence of the costs of alternative values.

The most pressing problems we face—crime, poverty, violence, low scholastic achievement, drugs, AIDS, and other health problems—are traceable to the changes in the priority given our core family values. The resultant behavior change has been to worsen, not improve, society and its members. The cultural elites ignore this basic loss of quality of life due to departure from traditional family values to the detriment of a generation of children and possible irreparable damage to our society. And they offer nothing to replace these values.

The personal cost of the denigration of family life is obvious. The social costs are staggering. Consider just these few descriptions of our current cultural status. America has a high percentage of low birth-weight babies. It boasts a lower standard of living for single parents and their children than for married family groups. The long-term probabilities of doing less well in school of children from single-parent families is real. It has been abundantly documented that children in these single-parent households are more likely to drop out of school, be unemployed or on welfare, be involved in crime, or end up dead or in prison. The root cause is a breakdown of core family values, and the solutions are also values (culture) based.

Some of our failures in interpersonal relations may stem from the fact that while our religious and ethical beliefs lie at the very center of our being—at the core of our cultural collectivity—they are being ignored, even denied us, in our institutional relationships. Official rhetoric gives place only to secular values. The lack of openness, candor, sharing, and trust around religious and ethical beliefs and feelings are signs of the basic challenge for leaders in American culture today.

Yet these ethical values are present, though unexpressed, in all of our interpersonal dealings. They affect our lives and shape our individual and collective behavior. That we cannot talk about them in our schools or explicitly base organizational action on them shrouds our leadership in ambiguity. The result is that secular values go unchallenged and the culture and all of its subordinate institutions suffer.

## THE CHALLENGE TO SOCIAL INSTITUTIONS

As we analyze our business and government institutions, we see the same fractionated situation. Many organizations—social groups, business corporations, and government agencies—lack community. They lack an integrating vision that coalesces a group of disparate people into work teams and functional unities. The results of this fragmentation of society and its work organizations are clear to even the most casual observer.

Our growth rate is high; our wage rate is low. We see dysfunction in even our most basic activities and institutions. The quality of education, law and order, quality of life, highways and transportation, community infrastructure, and so forth, in America are all in serious decline. Prisons are overcrowded; water and sewer distribution and collection systems are old and decaying; more and more Americans are without health insurance; and environmental pollution is increasing both in extent and severity.

One recent newspaper opinion editorial reported that over the past three decades—a period when so-called "freedom" was in full flower— our society has shown substantial regression. Since 1960, the record shows, there has been an over 550 percent increase in violent crimes in America. In that period, we recorded a 400 percent increase in illegitimate births and a quadrupling of divorce rates. Since 1960 there has been a 300 percent increase of children living in single-parent homes. Teenage suicide has risen 200 percent, and educational levels have decreased— 80 points on the precollege Scholastic Aptitude Test (Broder, 1993).

The net result of these facts is crisis. Our culture is deteriorating on all of the standard measures. Some say the solution must begin with a reversal of cultural values from those of the industrial era to a postindustrial society. Others (see Fairholm, 1991; Hart, 1988) suggest that we have only lost sight of the traditional values that provided the foundation for our formation as a nation (culture) and for its initial growth and maturation. They advocate a return to these founding values. At minimum we must prioritize American traditional values that foster a return to community values such as respect for life, freedom of action, unity, justice, and happiness.

## THE VALUES BASIS OF POSTINDUSTRIAL WORK CULTURES

Whether this listing of values is the magic list, or we need to develop another compilation more fully to meet the needs of this postindustrial information age, we must agree to accept *some* common values system. Change can only come if we create or re-create organizational and larger institutional systems that consciously intend to integrate members into a community based on shared values and commonly accepted behavior norms.

Past organizational and institutional systems that focused on control are fast becoming obsolete. We must form new relationship patterns that rely not on external control but on shared decision making, unified planning, and mutual trust. Thoughtful leaders are coming to see that we must create and then maintain organizational cultures and institutions that support the larger culture's dominant values and that gain their strength from those values.

The sense of objective experience is that shared cultures that work are those that include values and interrelationship technologies that empower people. Successful cultures are characterized by enough mutual trust and respect to let members be free to make their own choices—to become their best selves. Command and control systems and structures typical of past industrial age—business and government—bureaucracies seldom provide that trust or that freedom, except, perhaps, at the very top levels.

Such a postindustrial culture focusing on people-as-*customers* works. The defining characteristic of a customer is the power to make action choices about what to do, buy, or where and from whom he or she accepts services. It is characteristic of our evolving society today that most people have more than one choice about products they want or how they will receive services or from whom they will receive services or products.

We are coming to see the idea of customers as encompassing both internal and external stakeholders. Indeed, organizational employees are internal customers. More and more, the people making up our social organizations have or are stridently demanding this kind of independence or freedom. They are demanding to make their own choices about what they do, how they do it, and whether or not they will accept an order and obey it.

Shaping this evolving environment requires new leadership. Successful leaders will be those who can unite their followers around common values, a unifying vision, who employ methods that empower their followers, and who then trust them to behave in conformance to those values. We have seen the failure of past managerial models to cope with this new customer-orientation evolving in our organization memberships. What we see working in this new culture is leadership, not management.

Innovation is another characteristic of this postindustrial/modern culture. Traditional bureaucracies are typically reactionary. They do not anticipate problems and needs; they react to those raised by external customers. This reactive stance is no longer a viable strategy—if it ever was.

What succeeds today are proactive—not reactive—organizations and leaders. People are needed who can create and innovate to meet new customer demands and who *anticipate* customer needs. Close communication with internal and external customers is necessary if we are to be anticipatory, not reactionary. Traditional bureaucratic organizational and managerial forms are being replaced by open cultures and values-based leadership models.

Flexibility is also needed. Akin to innovation, an organization capable of anticipation and responsive to a variety of customer-stakeholders needs to develop operating systems and structures that can quickly respond. They also must meet specific and discrete needs of a growingly diverse customer pool, each of whom desires unique services and attention. These requirements argue against traditional tight managerial control. What we need today are trained, focused, and committed employees whom leaders can trust to respond appropriately in rapidly changing situations where top-level oversight is not desirable or, on occasion, even possible.

Such a new culture is one that focuses more on results than on process. Hard work by itself is not as important any more (perhaps it never was) as is making a positive impact on results. Hard work and a system focus are only inputs to the work and the process. They are not the results we seek by work effort. They are only valuable in situations where we work with vast numbers of repeatable products or services. As customer needs and wants change and differentiate, our organizations must become flexible and responsive. We cannot afford complex, staid, slow-to-change work systems that cannot easily respond to special, unique, constantly changing demands. We now define success increasingly as giving the customer unique service, rather than producing product at continuously lowered unit cost and forcing customers to take it.

Responding to the postindustrial culture asks us to reinvent our organizations (Naisbitt and Aburdene, 1985). This kind of response places demands on our organizations to eschew monopolistic tendencies for shifting market orientations. Market mechanisms such as competition in service delivery as well as product sales is becoming the norm. As the information explosion continues and accelerates, everyone concerned will have necessary information available to them. More than one option in receiving needed services or products are becoming available. This tendency can only increase as we find new, inexpensive ways to communicate information to empowered demanding customers.

## FUNCTION OF ORGANIZATIONAL CULTURE

Kalman, Saxton, and Serpa (1986) affirmed what we all know intuitively: organizational culture does exist. They say we can distinguish culture by three factors: direction, pervasiveness, and strength. Direction refers to the course of actions that culture is causing the organization to pursue. Pervasiveness refers to the impact of the cultural norms whether widespread or shared among only a part of the group. Cultural strength references the level of pressure that culture exerts on members.

These three aspects of culture impacts organizational performance either positively or negatively. When behavior is in the right direction, is widely shared, and puts strong pressure on members to conform, the cultural impact is positive. Cultural impact is negative when the opposite is true.

Barnard (1968) called our attention to the fact that organizations may have multiple cultures. Each organization has a formal, official culture. They also have various informal organizations. People—usually non-managers—create informal cultural groups to support their special needs and desires. Each of these informal organizations represent unique cultures or subcultures in addition to the official, formal one. Each culture has power to affect the life and behavior of its members.

Barnard noted two results of informal organizations and the tendency we see in organizations to display multiple cultures. First, each organizational culture settles on unique attitudes, understandings, customs, habits, and institutional forms. That is, informal organizations create values, methods, and attitudinal conditions that may affect those of the formal organization. Indeed, they may present a culture that is in opposition to the formal organization.

Second, Barnard also said that unless leaders take a proactive role in forming and maintaining understood cultural systems, they cannot expect their followers to follow. Cultural values bind people together in a unity far more effectively than do formal organizational charts, mission statements, or procedures manuals or other human artifacts. Culture deals mostly with the largely invisible elements of organization—with values, symbols, power, expectations, assumptions, and habitual behavior—than they do with tangible objects.

Barnard's work strongly suggests that the absence of known cultural norms results in alienation and anomie. Besides dealing with institutional anomie, organizational culture is a useful tool in shaping other factors in the organization to determine its nature and character, such as organizational action, effectiveness, service levels, compliance, member attitudes, leadership, and change.

## INTRINSIC AND EXTRINSIC ELEMENTS OF CULTURE IN ORGANIZATIONS

Our organizations are technical systems, but they are also social systems—systems of interacting human beings. That is, they are systems of programs, tasks, policies, *and* skilled people in interaction. Analysis of the organization from either system or human perspectives is incomplete. We must consider both in concert. That is what culture is and does.

The cluster of organizational elements we call culture has as much impact on our performance and effectiveness as do the formal structure and official work systems we often spend our time on to the exclusion of all else. These elements range from operating practices to relationships to values. Features of culture impact group members internally, at the values and beliefs level, and externally, at the working level. They, more than formal aspects of organization, determine the trust levels present in an organization.

Hertzberg (1966) helped us distinguish between intrinsic and extrinsic factors in the organization that impact our performance and happiness level. His work suggested that intrinsic factors of status, recognition, achievement, feelings, and interesting work account more for employee motivation and goal attainment activity than do external factors of working situation, fair regulations, and pay. These intrinsic factors build trust and cooperation more so than do the extrinsic factors of pay, security, and process.

From his research, Trist (1968) added a listing of job properties that relate to organizational culture and attainment of human needs within the organization. This list of intrinsic and extrinsic factors follows. It is similar to Hertzberg's synthesis.

| Extrinsic Factors | Intrinsic Factors |
|---|---|
| fair pay | variety, choice |
| job security | continuous learning |
| benefits | discretion, autonomy |
| health | recognition, support |
| due process | useful social contribution |
| | desirable future |

The intrinsic organizational factors shown here provide a more sure basis for developing trusting relationships than do the extrinsic factors. They provide a cultural foundation supportive of mutual trust, emotional security, commitment, and cooperation.

## CULTURAL ELEMENTS IN ORGANIZATIONS FACILITATING EFFECTIVE OPERATIONS

A comprehensive review of the literature lets us compile a list of organizational factors leaders need to consider when managing organizational culture in order to attain effective operation. If these factors aren't present, workers will fall short of meeting organizational goals. These factors deal with the impact of the organization's culture on the individual, on the structure of the organization, and on relationships.

### Individual Factors

1. Autonomy—individual freedom to choose how they do their jobs.
2. Degree of formal structure—are organizational functions loosely or tightly prescribed and defined?
3. Rewards systems—are rewards for performance positive, appropriate, and significant?
4. Heterogeneity—are members differentiated and polarized in their views, values, or needs?
5. Maturity—is the group experienced and able to take a good deal of responsibility for their own performance?

### Structural Factors

6. Concentration of authority—is authority for decision making centralized or decentralized?
7. Openness of communication—are messages accurately and easily transmitted throughout the organization?
8. Stratification—is the organization characterized by many rigid hierarchical layers?
9. Flexibility—are procedures easy to adapt and change?
10. Goal clarity.
11. Use of control data—are control reports used for training or punishment?
12. Task simplification—are tasks narrowly prescribed or openly flexible?

### Relationships Factors

13. Orientation to development and progressiveness—is support given for training, growth, and organizational change?
14. Consideration and support—the degree of warmth, support, and empathy received.
15. Risk taking—do employees feel safety and support to try new things?
16. Cohesiveness and morale—is there a feeling of belonging and loyalty?
17. Conflict—is there unresolved disagreement and hostility?
18. Hindrances—do workers feel they are burdened by routine duties and that the organization does not facilitate their work?
19. Union—are individuals meshing their energies and working together?

This listing, while comprehensive, is illustrative only. Other factors also may be present in an organization that shape and condition its culture.

Unfortunately, we cannot always make a direct link between cultural factors and effectiveness. It is safe to suggest that a positive, supportive culture is likely to contribute to a more effective organization. While anecdotal evidence supports this view, statistically convincing evidence is still sparse. Nevertheless, the logic of relating specific cultural factors to effective work is as clear as relating it solely to formal, structure, system, and strategy.

## OPERATING PRACTICES AS ELEMENTS OF CULTURE IN ORGANIZATIONS

We can define organizational cultural elements explicitly in operational terms. Culture refers to the deep-set beliefs members hold about the way the organization should be organized, the way authority should be exercised, and the way people should be rewarded. Culture also concerns the way members should be controlled and the way they should interrelate. Culture deals with formal structure: official interaction patterns as well as informal relationships. It shapes how much planning we should do and for how far ahead. It determines if workers will trust each other and their leaders or will require evidence of good faith to proceed. *trust*

Culture determines what combination of obedience and initiative is acceptable, when we work, and what customs of dress and grooming are proper. It dictates how we complete expense accounts, who gets what perquisites or other incentives. It prescribes whether individuals or committees control, and if that control is through results or rules. It prescribes sanctions systems and dictates their application.

Culture is visible sometimes (and partially) in buildings and equipment and branch offices. We see it in the kinds of people employed. It is obvious in the length and height of their career aspirations, their status in society, the degree of their mobility, and the level of their education. Operationally, culture is manifest in all of this and much more.

Cultural difference is obvious in the operating of a hospital and an auto factory, or of a bank and a city welfare department. It is also apparent between a government highway department and a private highway construction firm. Some operating dimensions of culture in our organizations, however, are not so obvious. Knowing something of these dimensions of culture prepares us to be effective in changing our organization's work systems if we need to.

Even a brief review of the literature reveals that there is no one universally best operationally effective culture. There is no one best way to develop a culture, no best values system to base worker evaluation programs, no universally helpful control mechanisms, no best way to budget, forecast, or plan. We make cultures and affect them by a variety of factors. Nevertheless, it can be argued, at least, that some of the ills of our organizations (and of our society) are explainable by culture and the match of individuals with their organizational culture.

## OPERATIONAL PROCESS AS ELEMENTS OF CULTURE IN ORGANIZATIONS

Some critical dimensions of organizational life have practical cultural implications. Among them we can identify the following as important.

- *Communications.* Organizations operate on information exchanges between people and work units. Communication is the nerve system of the organization. It is a complex operating system that can be blocked at many levels and in many forms. Barriers, interference, and blocking can come from systemic deficiencies but, more often, are the result of cultural differences in the sender or receiver. Communication problems sometimes result because honest people want to cooperate but simply do not understand each other. These cultural differences stem from personal environmental backgrounds or current organizational cultural limitations (e.g., structure, roles, reward systems, and so forth).

*Cooperation.* Chester Barnard identified attaining cooperation as a critical executive function. Fostering cooperation is one of the prime challenges leaders face in sociotechnical systems.

*Control.* Control is a prime goal of the formal structure. It involves rules, sanctions, and procedures. It is also an interpersonal process, involving individuals' needs and wishes for power to exert influence over others. It also involves feelings about others' control over us. Being controlled, however, is not a goal for most people. People resist control by others, especially overcontrol. The control mechanisms in place in a culture dictate how people will react to this managerial need.

*Conflict.* Conflict is a part of day-to-day life in organizations. It arises from several sources. It is seen in intractions that are intra- and interpersonal, as well as those that are intra- and interorganizational. Conflict is ignored in many traditional organizations or dealt with via rules. Seen as a factor in management, conflict ties in with ideas of esteem, rewards systems, and a host of motivations and values.

*Commitment.* Achieving follower commitment is a hallmark of excellent leadership and management. High levels of commitment are not easy to achieve and are even harder to maintain. Some elements of this task include clear, known goals, personal belief in the goals, and pride in their achievement. These are often present in new organizations but are replaced by rules and procedures as the organization matures. System may produce control but does not produce commitment. Commitment is a personal decision made by individual organizational members. Managing the culture is the only way to foster this kind of personal decision.

*Cohesiveness.* Related to commitment, cohesiveness connotes strong identification with the group or task, feelings of support from the relationship, and a desire to stay with the group and keep it together. Cohesiveness develops as people share common values, skills, or vision. Structure, system, and procedure alone do not build a sense of unity. In addition, members need to invest in and take ownership of the organization and its aims and purposes.

*Trust.* This is the most important and most intangible of the variables discussed so far. The central issue in trust is risk. The trust level determines to what extent people can be themselves—say what is on their mind, try out tentative ideas, express anger, and so forth. Organizations with low trust levels create "yes people" and other conformists who contribute little to moving the organization forward.

Developing trust requires clear statements from the leader about the values that the organization seeks to achieve. Trust in others demands that neither leader nor follower can exact retribution for speaking the truth. Rather, both need to encourage risk-taking behavior, even when it means disturbing sacred cows.

Trust and team development also go together. We need frank and open communications across organizational levels. And, finally, we should evaluate others based on long-term goal achievement rather than on image or some other standard. Trust building requires a long period of testing in which individuals take small risks and then wait and see the effects before deciding to trust more.

*Caring.* People differ in their need for close personal relations with others. Some are cool and distant; others warm and intimate. The culture of the organization helps define the acceptable level of intimacy in the organization, not the formal structure or operating systems.

These operating processes (and others) interact to form the social aspects of the organization. While the preceding have more obvious and direct impact on organizational culture and member performance, other factors are also present in any organizational culture and may change behavior and ultimate results. Among them, the following seem central:

1. Professionalism
2. Politics
3. Changing work values
4. Task design
5. Personal or professional biases
6. Task or system complexity
7. Training and development
8. Task assignments systems

Each of these factors are also in place in most organizations and can heavily influence how people respond to the requirements of the work system employed.

Employees come to their organizations with an implicit or explicit psychological contract. They know what they are willing to do to get what they want. This contract has to do with money and labor but also involves other factors, which includes assumptions and expectations we have about our relationships on the job, our status vis-à-vis others, the trust level, and so forth. These factors are a major cause of employee concern, frustration, and dissatisfaction but are often not discussed. The solution is to make these assumptions and expectations explicit, rather than implicit, and to negotiate openly these psychological factors, as well as the more common economic and task factors that define the work relationship.

## VALUES AS ELEMENTS OF CULTURE IN ORGANIZATIONS

We have defined organizational culture in terms of behavior norms (Homens, 1950), values (Deal and Kennedy, 1983; Peters and Waterman, 1982; Fairholm, 1991), philosophy (Hodgkinson, 1978; Ouchi, 1981; Fairholm, 1991), climate (Tagiuri and Litwin, 1968), and power (Fairholm, 1993). Most people's definition of organizational or corporate culture includes definitional elements such as shared values, beliefs, assumptions, patterns of relationships, and behaviors. Uttal (1983) explicitly defines culture as a system of shared values and beliefs that interacts with group members, organizational structures, and control systems to produce behavioral norms that aid feelings of cooperation, trust, and security.

Managing culture involves intrinsic, cognitive, inducement, and symbolic leadership activities. Intrinsic activities are those interpersonal relationships that aim to satisfy our personal, human needs. Cognitive activities involve us in providing knowledge and training to understand self and others. Inducement activities refer to those actions we take in our organized groupings that serve to reward or punish members for their appropriate or inappropriate performance. Finally, symbolic leadership describes leadership that uses symbols, ceremonies, and language to join group members into a unity. Each of these cultural activities imply a values basis for action.

Organizational culture can be thought of as a pattern of basic assumptions that have developed over time as a result of coping with external and internal problems in the environment (Schein, 1985). Seen in this way, the organization's culture is founded in core values and beliefs that have evolved in an organization over time (Nadler and Tushman, 1988). These core values are imbedded in generally known and understood statements about what is good or not good in and about an organization.

The core values define acceptable behavior as well as acceptable traits or characteristics. They become "if-then" belief systems: "if we behave in this way, then something good will result" or "if we value this idea, then we can expect acceptance from the group," and so forth. They constrain and direct member behavior in predictable ways.

Culture organizes values and focuses attention on what the leader thinks is important (Fairholm, 1991). Culture shaping and values shaping have become recognized as critical leadership functions. These tasks are essential to building the trust relationships upon which leadership depends. Leaders change the cultural surround by articulating a supporting values system to change followers. Indeed, values displacement is a hallmark of cultural leadership.

## SELECTING AN ORGANIZATIONAL CULTURE

The choice of organization within which one will make a career is also dependent on individual choice to harmonize one's work life with other like-minded people. Several factors influence the nature and character of an organization's culture and the formal structure related to it. These factors are part of that culture and are part of the data upon which we make cultural decisions.

At least the following factors have been key in determining the features of culture of a specific organization: age of the organization, its history of development, and the degree of centralization experienced over time. The ownership status of the organization—whether centralized in one person or defused—helps determine the nature of the culture, as well as the size of the organization.

Technology, or the nature of the work done, the organization's goals and objectives, the quality and quantity of values espoused communicate specific features of an organization's culture. So does the larger community environment, the economy, competition, geography, and social factors. These factors as well as the people making up the organization and providing its leadership help determine the original culture and shape it over time. They define a given culture's level of attractiveness to prospective new members.

Each organization, and its subparts, has a special culture supporting and defining it that individuals—also coming to the organization with their own cultural background—must adapt to. The degree of fit determines individual happiness and organizational success—that is, productivity and effectiveness.

We build organizations from a collection of groups, each with its own unique cultural characteristics. The key individual question we each ask about our organizations is do they meet our needs. If they do we will respond, if not we will be reluctant to trust it or commit to it fully.

The culture thus created responds to a unique set of common and continuing needs. Structural, technological, and environmental factors impact individual fit within a culture. Any of these can affect organizational relationships directly. The fact is that the nature of one's relationships with the organization impacts performance. High performers typically display a strong desire to keep membership, a willingness to exert high levels of effort, and a definite belief in and acceptance of the organization's values and goals. Commitment of this kind includes attitudes, perceptions, and understanding of the organization's place in the larger community, along with its missions and goals.

The vehicle by which we coordinate member activities and direct them toward organizational purposes is communication. The communications system facilitates coordination, motivation, emotional expression and information (Berlo, 1960). It impacts member attitudes and perceptions and their interpersonal interactions in the group.

Voluntary cooperative interaction is also a key to understanding organization and a critical part of culture. Cooperation is a measure of member attitudes toward cohesiveness, trust levels, and participation. Readiness to change is partly determined by cultural variables and impacts member willingness to change by affecting attitudes and perceptions about the utility of change.

We can also relate our study of culture to contingency theory. Culture can be thought of as one of the contingencies that impact managerial performance and success. Culture is also understandable from a group dynamics theory perspective. It describes the environment within which group dynamics takes place.

Systems theory also can aid in understanding the impact of culture on organizations and their members. It seeks to match people systems and technical and structural organization. In this connection, culture theory is the applied manifestation of a sociotechnical system, the idea first articulated by the Tavistock Institute to define the organization as an integrated system including both human and technical elements inextricably connected into one system.

## DEVELOPING ORGANIZATIONAL CULTURE

Explicit attention to the importance of culture management—culture formation, change, and maintenance—in leadership is new. The technologies of change are dependent on one's definition of what culture is and what it entails. The mechanisms for change depend on one's definition of culture. Changing culture is difficult. All of us naturally resist changing our basic value assumptions as individuals, as organizations, or as nations.

Organizational culture development involves creating heros, myths, and rituals that personalize and interpret core values (norms) for members (Nadler and Tushman, 1988). Primarily leaders form culture or change it. They institute values and lead by virtue of these values (Fairholm, 1991).

The literature suggests a variety of techniques. Key among them is the idea that leaders send clear signals about the kind of organization they want. They clearly articulate desired behavior and define and articulate group aims and goals, as well as model desired roles. Leaders send authentic and consistent messages that validate the desired culture. They create organizational designs that facilitates some cultural values at the expense of other values. They decide and act to communicate the organizational cultural message.

# 3

# Defining Culture

## INTRODUCTION

Interest in the ideas of culture and climate is a continuing thread in social literature. This interest, strong in the early years of this century, has gained renewed focus today. Kroeber and Kluckholm (1952) identified 164 definitions of culture used in the literature just in the first half of this century. Today, many more analysts and practitioners are using culture as the basis for clarifying our understanding of a variety of social, political, and procedural factors in our social institutions and work groups.

We can define culture as that character of commitment and order in a social organization that allows people to trust each other enough to work together. We generate commitment and order through the feelings and actions of the organization's founders and subsequent leaders in their interpersonal relationships with group members. These characteristics are also fostered through the whole of its beliefs, ideology, language, ritual, and myth systems. Leaders and followers create the assumptions, symbols, languages, beliefs, visions, ideologies, and myths present in the organization. And these features of culture let members understand each other, trust each other, and take personal ownership of the group's activities. Culture structures group member interactions as they live and work together.

## DEFINING SOCIAL CULTURE

Taylor (1877) defined culture in the first (chronologically) modern definition as "that complex whole that includes knowledge, belief, art, morals, law, custom, and any other capabilities and habits acquired by members of a society." More recently, Steers (1985) has added the idea of deeply held beliefs, or values, that affect subsequent behavior to common understanding of the idea of culture. Culture can be thought of as a metaphor for organization. It directs attention away from traditional structure, system, and technology features and toward elements such as values, symbols, and rituals.

The idea of culture is useful in a variety of intellectual pursuits, such as biology, human nature, and human groups. It is useful in understanding our human artifacts, human behavior, cognition, and our emotional connections to other people and things. Culture deals with whatever a group member needs to know or do to be successful in the group. It gives reality to the nonmaterial. Culture creates and transmits context and pattern in interpersonal relationships (Kroeber and Kluckholm, 1952).

## Origins

Culture is fundamental idea that is still in flux. It is, thus, defined variously by many people. The word derives from the idea of cultivation; it is an agricultural idea (Morgan, 1986). Normally, we think of culture as the pattern of development reflected in a social institution's system of knowledge, ideology, values, laws, and day-to-day ritual. It is an agricultural metaphor guiding attention to specific aspects or processes of routine social development and interaction. Culture defines the ways a group behaves similarly. It is also a means for comparing how groups of people differ in their routine ways of life.

Culture defines human beings and human beings define culture. Cultures—despite the metaphors we apply to them drawn from nature—are artificial. Culture is an artifact created by humans (Giamatti, 1989). Nature never made an organization's culture. Forests, oceans, deserts are beautiful parts of the organized environment that are born, die, and are reborn endlessly. They are, however, without moral sense or control.

We can explain at least some ills of our society and its organizations in cultural terms and the match of individual cultural heritage and organizational cultural artifacts. Culture more than structure may be the key to solving these problems and creating new organizations to cope with the issues a new century will surely pose.

## Modern Definitions

We can look at culture from two perspectives. First, culture is the overarching system of settled beliefs that define the person or institution initially and then give direction to daily life. Culture prescribes the general ways people relate to each other—whether in trusting or distrusting ways. This is a strategic, global perspective and proceeds from both internal and external guiding beliefs.

External guiding beliefs have to do with how one social institution and its people interrelates with the larger community on competition and collaboration levels. From this perspective, we can view culture in hierarchial terms of interconnected umbrella cultures, cultures, and subcultures. Cultures link social organizations and suborganizations through common values and accepted ways to behave toward each other and toward strangers.

Internal beliefs have to do with internal management, direction, and leadership of a particular organization. They form the base for mutual commitment among members. Application of guiding beliefs or values in the organization is best done through its vision statement. Davis (1984) believes that an organization can effectively deal with only three or four strategic guiding beliefs to support its vision. Articulation of more will require prioritization of some and diminution of others and cause member confusion and distrust.

The second perspective on culture is more tactical. It is about the daily routine of a given organization. Culture defines the accepted system of meanings (derived from guiding beliefs) that give direction to specific routine acts we perform daily. The culture provides the organizational/institutional surround within which group members can be free to trust each other because each shares commonly accepted values.

At this level, we see culture as a way to deal with rules and feelings that guide everyday action. That is, culture provides the basis for an orderly interaction between group members; it forms what Barker (1992) calls the group's paradigm. Cultural paradigms structure the group, not in formal, organizational ways, but at the deeper level of foundation values and causes for specific rules and regulations set up to order members' actions.

Social culture permeates our lives. It defines us, prescribes our belief systems, and conditions our behavior in the social groups that we join. It is a part of, and a way to define and analyze, all of our social contacts including family, social and work groups. Culture is as vital and controlling in our work lives as it is in the other dimensions of living.

## DEFINING ORGANIZATIONAL CULTURE

Anyone who has traveled in a foreign country will appreciate how values, beliefs, and cherished philosophies effect the way a society is organized. Do organizations have unique, definable, and malleable cultures as nations do? Can we define organizational cultures in the same kind of terms as we do social cultures? Do they differ in the same cultural ways nations differ? That is, do they differ in values, language, customs, dress, and so forth?

Of course, organizations are similar to countries in this regard. Understanding organizations requires that we consider their cultural dimensions along with other factors in their makeup. Anyone who has worked in a variety of organizations will have been struck by the differences in the atmosphere between work organizations, divisions, and work units. They differ in ways of doing business, in the depth of mutual trust exhibited, in the levels of energy required for success, in individual freedom, and in the kind of worker personality accepted and rewarded.

Organizations differ in cultural factors in many of the same ways as nations. They have differing values, norms, and beliefs reflected in differing structures and work systems. Events of the past and the immediate climate of the present, the technology of the work done, their aims, and the kind of people that work in them effect these cultures.

Organizations vary markedly in cultural terms. Some are fragmented; others are pluralistic systems. Some show unity; others are monolithic systems. Hampton, Summer, and Webber (1987) suggest that we include extrinsic, physical environmental factors such as resources, technology, written rules, customs, and common group practices in the definition of culture. Culture provides meaning, direction, focus. It is a social energy that moves our organizations into growth or decline; into survival or destruction.

Organizational culture is not so much the official system of goals announced by management as it is the whole range of shared models of social action containing both real and ideal, formal and informal elements. A variety of factors affect organizational culture. Among them are the goal context and the channel of communication used. The observed behavior of group members, official documents, and the verbal expression of the ideal situation also shape culture. Even humorous interpretations of the above help determine an organization's culture. These are contextual factors. Research characterizes these cultures by a strong reliance on only a few values.

The importance of culture in determining the leader's style is critical (Fiedler and Chamers, 1974). Culture provides the context of organized action. The cultural context conditions our actions, our beliefs, and widely held values. Many Americans might subscribe to the value, "thou shalt not kill," but few would argue that it applies on the battlefield culture or with a police officer in a shootout. Culture articulates commonly held values and applies them in the context of the organization and the work processes in which they are engaged.

Organizational culture refers to the deep-set beliefs about the way that we should structure any organization, community, or nation, and the way we exercise authority, reward, control, and interrelate people. Culture consists of a set of cognitive reference points that form a framework within which organization members can interpret meaning to their own behavior.

For our purposes, we can define culture as the shared and enduring pattern of values, beliefs, and assumptions that allows people to attribute meaning to an otherwise meaningless flow of events. This definition summarizes much of the literature. Sathe (1983) defines organizational culture as shared important understandings. Culture for Steers (1985) is the perceived properties found in work situations that result largely from actions taken consciously or unconsciously by an organization that affect subsequent member behavior.

Organizational culture also consists of the pattern of basic assumptions about which organization or group members agree. It includes the history of experience, the values held. It concerns who members trust and to what degree, and the way the group solves problems. And, it is about what the group considers a problem in the first place. Culture defines how a particular group has adapted to its environment. Culture is real, if often assumed, and implicit rather than explicit. It defines the nature and character of the organization. Leaders must consider culture as they practice their craft within the group.

Organizational culture includes both historical precedent and present experience. It defines current expectations and expectations for the future. It organizes the values that condition behavior. Without general agreement on acceptable behavior, and the value context within which we will operate, the organization members are free to follow divergent paths. No coherent, cooperative action is possible where common agreement—at least implicitly—in a common culture is missing.

Parenthetically, this fact is the best argument to counter the present popular interest in multiculturalism in organizations. Of course, we ought to accept the divergent views, skills, and thought processes that members may bring into the group. But acceptance of difference in our employees does not mean we must accept their divergent standards, customs, and values if these values work against cohesion and commonly accepted values, mores, and standards of vision-directed conduct.

An organization is a unity precisely because members share some specific common values to the exclusion of others. Leaders must tie the divergent views of an increasingly differentiated work force together in a strong set of cultural values that define that group and give it coherence and form. Homogeneous groups can be led to achieve vision aims; heterogeneous groups cannot.

## CLIMATE AND CULTURE

Organizational climate is also a part of culture; organizational climate is a subset of the larger social culture (Morgan, 1986). Originally, climate focused more on details of group practices. It is a time-sequenced, shorter-term perspective of the overall culture that is a little more changeable (Stewart and Garson, 1983). Recently, culture and climate have taken on a similarity of meaning in the literature. Nevertheless, climate still has reference most often to the more current, immediate state of affairs, and references specific objects.

Climate refers to a group member's perceptions about the organizational environment. It includes issues of individual autonomy, the degree of structure imposed on the position, the reward orientation present in the organization, the level of consideration, warmth, and support present, and the expected interpersonal trust.

Climate takes the "temperature" of the organization at a given point in time. It is a measure of whether people's expectations are being met, not of what the expectations are. It is transitory, tactical, and manageable, whereas the overall culture is longer term and strategic. Climate may indicate the employees are negative, but they do not question the existing instructions. Climate accepts the context as given. Culture *is* the context. Climate measures the fit between the prevailing culture and the individual values of the employees. If group members have adopted the culture's values, the climate is good; if not, it is bad. Climate is a function of how individuals perceive the organization *today*.

Culture is more inclusive and refers more to the general underlying values, historical (customary) context, and philosophy as well as the immediate climate concerns. When we think of the idea of culture, we think of it as an intrinsic network of shared trust about meanings and values. Culture depicts the members cognitive thoughts and ideas as well as their feelings about whether something is good or bad, likeable or unlikeable, desirable or undesirable (Hampton, Summer, and Webber, 1989).

Organizational climate is the perceived properties or characteristics found in the work environment that result largely from actions taken by the organization that affect subsequent behavior (Steers, 1985). Operationally, climate consists of several dimensions. Some are task structure, degree of decision centralization, levels of interpersonal trust, modes of communication and feedback, problem-solving processes, and problem resolution systems.

## ORGANIZATIONAL CULTURAL HIERARCHIES

It is convenient to think of organizations as collections of subcultures. Each unit has a culture as well as being a subsystem of the overall organizational culture. Culture is an invisible quality, a certain style, a character, a way of doing work. Culture may be stronger than the dictates of any one person or any formal system. To understand the soul of the organization requires that we inquire into the underground world of organizational culture (Kalman, 1984).

Organizations and their component units appear to develop cultures that incorporate the values and practices of their leaders (Peters and Waterman, 1982). These leader-set cultures provide meaning, direction, and mobilization. They provide a social energy that moves the organization into either productive action or destruction. Culture creation and maintenance become another tool leaders can use to lead their organization to desired results.

## CULTURAL LEADERSHIP IN ORGANIZATIONS

Evidence suggests that leaders engage in shaping culture based on the organization's vision and the requirements for success implied by that vision. Recent research documents that leaders are coming to support the idea that culture management flourishes in American organizations. Leaders are proactively engaged in creating cultures that unify followers around a common vision of what the organization is and can become.

Elements of culture shape life experiences, historical tradition, class, position, and political circumstances. These are all powerful forces that resist directed change (Reynolds, 1986). Culture is at the symbolic level of existence, and leaders are reaching into cultural values and symbols to help shape and guide their organizations.

## IMPACT OF LARGER CULTURE ON ORGANIZATIONAL LIFE

Culture is implicit in much of what we do in organizations. We do not, however, always recognize the cultural parts of our experience. In the United States, for example, we take for granted a whole set of cultural conditions that permit the effective and efficient functioning of our complex organizations. These conditions include, among others, a high level of literacy, relationships built on authority structures, and an emphasis on achievement as a prime basis for judging people rather than inherent characteristics.

These factors explain a good deal about our society and its organizations. If leaders take these factors for granted, they miss the opportunity to change our society in ways that can help us attain our desired goals. By looking at one example, we can get some idea of the pervasiveness and power of cultural factors on our lives.

Americans key their organizational life to implicit ideas about time. We precisely time our organizational life. We work by the clock, regulating our day—lunch breaks, meetings, and so forth. The documents we use are time-date stamped. We make and keep appointments and measure productivity in time terms.

This one cultural factor—along with many, many others—does much to regularize our organizational life and ease personal and institutional goal accomplishment. Understood well, time, and other cultural perceptions like it, can help us lead successfully.

But, do we really understand time? Time is one of the common "mysteries" of life. The statement attributed to St. Augustine on time summarizes much about organizational culture and its component factors and values: Everyone knows what time is until someone asks us to define it. While we run our complex organizations by the clock, not all of our employees or our customers perceive time in exactly the same way. One or two simple examples may suffice to illustrate the problem our organizational perception of time might give us.

Many of our business and governmental service organizations (for example, welfare agencies or personal service businesses such as barber shops) run on a schedule that may be convenient to employees, but quite often are inconvenient to their customers. School classrooms are crowded in the fall and winter and empty for one-third of the year.

On another level, rural citizens have a flexible time perception, based more on nature's clock and the rising and falling of the sun. Latin Americans (and some Mediterranean cultures) culturally have a much less precise time orientation. They are less committed to precise scheduling of their life. Industrial engineers sometimes sacrifice sensible work procedures to introduce cumbersome artifices so they can calculate productivity on individual items and jobs in terms of units of time. One important measure of organizational status relates to whether or not one must punch a time-clock.

We improve our understanding of cultural differences in individual relationships as we relate them to differences in perceptions of time. They can help us better manage our programs and people. The idea of time as an element of culture opens some intriguing prospects for leaders as they think about the cultural impacts and ambience within which our organizations operate and our effectiveness and that of our workers.

What we say about time we also can say about many, many other factors of our culture, such as authority, competition, respect for life, freedom, justice, teamwork, and trust.

## UNDERSTANDING ORGANIZATIONAL CULTURE

Several recent works have raised our conscienceness about organizational culture. Peters and Waterman (1982) began the recent resurgence of culture study. Schein (1985) suggests that changing the culture of an organization is essential if a leader is to function effectively. Barnard

(1968) said that we pay too little attention to the relationship between formal and informal organizations.

One idea is unmistakable; the study of culture is complex. Over the years, many writers have studied this social phenomenon from a wide variety of perspectives (Ott, 1989). Each author has added to the definition of this social artifact. The result is that the literature reflects multiple definitions and definitional elements describing culture. They add to the complexity instead of reducing it. This semantic confusion has carried over into more recent studies of organizational culture making simple, concise definition difficult. Much of the early work in culture in organizational settings equates informal organization with culture (Nadler and Tushman, 1988). More recently, experts see culture as a facet of any organization, whether formal or informal.

Wallach's (1983) typology of organizational culture includes several aspects, each of which place organizational culture squarely within the realm of organizations. For him, organizational culture includes:

*Bureaucratic dimensions*—hierarchical, procedural, and structural aspects of the culture

*Innovative dimensions*—level or freedom of creativity, results-oriented, challenging work environments

*Supportive dimensions*—exhibits teamwork and a people-oriented, friendly, encouraging, trusting work environment

These, and a rapidly growing body of other studies are beginning to focus on organizational culture as another perspective from which to view the organization and as another mechanism leaders can manipulate to attain personal and organizational goals.

## MODELS OF ORGANIZATIONAL CULTURE

As noted culture involves a set of values, beliefs, and norms (i.e., expected behaviors) that group members hold in common. Hult and Walcott (1990) include the idea of "shared ideology" by members of the society. They see culture as similar to human personality. To Tosi, Rizzo, and Carroll (1986) culture is the repeatable patterns of thinking, feeling, and reacting acquired and transmitted by members of a group, organization, or society. We communicate cultural features mainly by symbols, constituting the distinctive achievements of the organization. The essential core of culture consists of traditional ideas and especially their attached values.

Schein (1985) identified three levels of organizational culture: artifacts, values, and basic assumptions. For Schein basic cultural assumptions form a pattern guiding member actions. Each social group invents, discovers, or develops certain definable assumptions as it deals with the task of adapting to external problems. Other assumptions concern internal integration. Together these assumptions form the core of a group's culture and define adaptations that work well enough to be considered valid and, therefore, taught to new members. Others have identified the idea of values as a basic unit of culture (Ott, 1989).

Reynolds (1986) examined 14 aspects of culture from the perspective of type of industry, position within the firm, and comparison of excellent firms with other groups. He concluded that employees in differing organizations perceive their cultures as different.

Kalman, Saxton, and Serpa (1986) define culture as the shared philosophies, ideologies, values, assumptions, beliefs, expectations, attitudes, and norms that knit a community together. Culture defines a group's agreements on how to approach decisions and problems.

## Recent Organizational Culture Studies

As we have mentioned previously, every organization has a culture, which explains why organizations respond differently to the same stimuli. Schein (1985) suggests that the rise of Japan in management circles has focused attention on questions of national and international culture formation and management. He says the study of culture illuminates leadership as a separate discipline. Culture is forcing an interdisciplinary focus on the study of organizations. Since it is pervasive in the group, leaders need to manage it to accomplish their ends.

Culture change involves values and behavior, the two main elements of leader involvement with followers, hence, culture cannot be incongruent with leader vision, or the leader risks failure. Traditionally, managers attempt to change structure and procedure and function. The record suggests that this narrow focus does not always work. Leaders, on the other hand, undertake change at the more basic, cultural level. There is growing evidence that this approach is more successful (Fairholm, 1991).

Peters and Waterman (1982) suggest that culture management reduces the need for policy manuals, procedures, and organization charts. If this proves out over time, the impact on traditional managerial skills and practices will be revolutionary. Focusing as it does on values, culture management may substitute for direct, close supervision.

## A Comprehensive Culture Model

The work of a few social scientists adds to our understanding of the idea of culture and its application to work situations. Following Sathe's (1983) analysis, we can separate the study of culture into three principal schools: the cultural adaptationist, the ideational, and the functionalist.

The cultural adaptationist school comes out of anthropology. Theorists base this model on what is directly observable about members of a community—patterns of behavior, speech, use of material objects, and so forth. This is the simplest and most common approach for describing culture, especially among nations or other social groups. The focus here is on cultural *behavior*.

The ideational school looks at what is shared in the minds of members of a community. Here the focus is on cultural *beliefs*. An important aspect of this school is the interpretive perspective that views culture as a system of shared meanings. Ideationalists see culture as the implicit meaning of the organization or its parts. Assuming this theoretical orientation, managing culture is a difficult task because different people in the organization may focus on different aspects of the idea when they talk about culture. We need to consider both behavior and beliefs in managing organizational culture.

The functionalist school comes out of the ideational school and views culture as a system of shared ideas, knowledge, and beliefs. Functionalists see culture as a characteristic of the organizational entity. This school describes culture as an organizational variable. That is, culture is something the organization *has*.

From an organizational cultural perspective, the most useful model is the ideational model. It provides important insights in understanding culture, its formation, composition, and its management.

For ideationalists cultural beliefs are both descriptive and valuative. Thinking of organizational culture descriptively, we can describe culture as the composite of the assumptions we have about the world and how it works. From a valuative perspective, it is an amalgam of the core values we hold about the world. Values are also assumptions but implicitly contain an "ought" element in them. We determine cultural beliefs not just by the content of the beliefs, but by how they relate to one another as well—by the ordering of our cultural beliefs.

A convenient analysis model for understanding details of culture is to think of it in terms of thickness, extent of sharing, and clarity of ordering of those beliefs. The more shared beliefs a culture has the thicker it is. Cultural beliefs may be relatively widely shared within the social grouping and may be ranked or prioritized in a clear way or may be ambiguously ordered. These three measures help us compare different cultural belief systems and rate weakness or strengths in a given organizational culture.

The thicker, more widely shared, and more clearly ordered cultural beliefs systems are stronger and have a more personal and profound influence on cultural behavior than do other sets of beliefs. The stronger the beliefs the more efficient the culture is. That is, the simpler it is for the leader to affect desired communication and to coordinate group effort.

Still following Sathe (1983), we can analyze culture from the standpoint of acceptance of those belief systems by group members. Culture members can either accept cultural beliefs or assimilate them or both. Acceptance implies that the person behaves as desired because he or she complies with organizationally imposed (external) beliefs. Assimilation implies that the member considers these beliefs to be his or her own, that is, has internalized them (Kalman, 1984).

Assimilated cultural beliefs operate most often outside the realm of awareness of the member. Members take them for granted and are often not conscious of these belief systems. Assimilated cultural beliefs have a more enduring influence on member's organizational life than those of people who have merely accepted the organization's belief system. Assimilated cultural beliefs have both a subtle and a persistent influence on organizational behavior.

At times, leaders need to change behavior; at other times, they need to change beliefs. Sometimes behavior change alone is sufficient to gain needed compliance and support. At other times, we need to alter beliefs to get necessary compliance. Changing beliefs is more difficult. Leaders need to be aware of the nature of acceptance or assimilation of organizational values among their workers. The greater the assimilation of cultural belief, the greater will be the commitment of members to organizational values and systems of work and relationship. The greater the nonconformity to cultural beliefs on the part of workers, the greater will be the need for imagination, determination, and marshaling of personal and organizational resources for the manager to be effective.

Getting others to assimilate the organization's values and beliefs is difficult and rare. The process includes communication of new beliefs to workers, helping workers make a personal connection with the leader, and gently persuading workers to adopt the new beliefs without relying on financial or other extrinsic forms of motivation.

# 4

# Leadership: A Cultural Change Technology

## INTRODUCTION

People coming to work in our organizations desire independence. They sometimes resent the constraints imposed on them by the formal organization. This tension between the individual and the organization has always been with us. On the one hand, the organization member needs self-expression. On the other, the organization exists only as it can control and coordinate the energies and activities of its members.

The task of leadership is to make this tension a creative tension to accommodate both sets of needs, even magnify them. The key to a solution is in integrating the various individual needs into a cultural unity that can address and meet both group and individual core needs. Unfortunately, past (and too many present) managerial systems either ignored this tension or treated it as an organizational evil. Leaders install most supervisory systems to try to shut off at least the overt manifestations of worker discontent.

Indeed, our present organization theories flow out of past ideas about the individual-in-the-group and how to deal with him or her. Past theoretical (even philosophical) models raise issues associated with the actuality of this tension. They catalogue it and describe ways to control it. These past models proposed various techniques to resolve this tension, such as organizational dominance over the individual or motivating the individual to do the organization's work by material inducements. Past models also advocate appealing to enlightened self-interest by letting employees control part of their work lives. And, some past models endorse the exercise of organizational authority to dominate individual self-interest that might refocus worker energies away from organizational needs-accomplishment.

These past theories are helpful in understanding the foundation of interpersonal relationship on the job. They are, however, incomplete and unsatisfying and do not help us fully understand organizational behavior. They omit the power of human beings as factors in the controlling organizational activity dynamics. These models see management as controlling organizational structure, not as also controlling the organization's human environment, its culture. And they fail to see the leadership task of creating the conditions within the organization where we can meld human and organizational needs.

The result of overreliance on these models is that we lose a lot of individual freedom and group cohesion, creativity, and growth. The challenge of leadership today is to integrate, not further subdivide people. We need leaders in all of our organizations who are both accepted and trusted by members because they have gone beyond localized self-interest to a collective self-interest (Bennis, 1989). Attaining this state of affairs is the task of the next decades.

## A BRIEF HISTORY OF SELF-GROUP INTEGRATION

Solving this problem asks leaders and followers to find common values and a joint vision that both can accept and around which both can bend their best efforts. It is not, as some today suggest, a passive task of mere acceptance of difference; it is a proactive task of unifying growingly diverse communities and organizations.

The task of integration of disparate individual and organizational values and vision has a long tenure in the history of ideas. It has been a recurring theme in the intellectual history of this country for at least 200 years and has occupied the attention of social philosophers and organizational leaders for at least that period of time as well. Foundation ideas that may be helpful to us in the coming century have their origin in the previous two. They are worth revisiting.

### Early Ideas

Early concern with integrating people with system centered on the dialectic between the individual's needs to exert self-control and society's need to organize and control human activity (Luke, 1975). Following Luke's argument, there is an inherent tension between individuals' needs to express their individuality, to exert self-control, and to be recognized for their special contributions to the group and organization needs for uniformity. Self-expression must, say the thinkers of the past, be mitigated by the needs the organization has to attain control and to regularize task activities.

The social philosophers proposed various models of integration to reduce this inherent tension. For example, Rousseau proposed a corporate community idea to satisfy his sense that the individual worker needed independence. Rousseau advocated lodging overall control over the society with the community, not just with a few leaders. The effect, he said, would be to release the individual from personal dependencies on individual leaders. It is easier and less tension producing, said Rousseau, for individuals to subordinate themselves to the group than to individual leaders.

On the other hand, Claude Saint-Simon saw people as motivated more by material needs than personal stress. He proposed that organizations should direct worker energies away from dominating each other and more toward dominating the larger society, the environmental surround. The method he proposed was to control structure rationally. Development of a logical, rational organizational culture would allow workers to become more rational and, therefore, more predictable (controllable) in their behavior. As a result, both workers, the organization, and larger society would prosper.

Other writers added the principle of self-interest to the mix. Self-interest was, for Charles Fourier, the integrating and controlling force in organizations. Self-interest, he said, will enable group members to assign themselves to tasks that maximize their self-interest and to change these tasks periodically as self-interest dictates. Organizations should be structured on the principle of individual self-interest. Organizations that reflect this reality will not stifle individuality even if at the sacrifice of some productivity.

For Emile Durkheim self-interest was present in our social and work organizations, but negatively charged. Durkheim saw a world where the individual was dominated by a debilitating self-interest that the larger society must contain. He looked to power and authority as the integrating force in organizations. Institutional authority should be "imposed" on the individual to control self-interest. He also suggested subordinating individual conscience to the group conscience.

Both the ideas of personal tension with the organization and a rational motivational basis geared to individual material desires have survived to the present as parts of the current interest in the culture-creation dynamic. So, too, has the idea of personal self-interest survived. These historical antecedents of modern cultural theory agreed that tension is present. They disagreed on the nature of this tension between the individual and the organization. They assumed in common the need to control people or they and their organization would suffer, and they agreed that membership in an organization requires a choice between self-direction and organizational needs for collective action. They concluded that an organization or a society founded on rules or principles was more desirable than one governed by individuals.

## ⚹ Modern Iterations ⚹

These and similar ideas have dominated our work, social, and governmental organizations for most of the last century. They have been imbedded in our organizational and management theories and have been played out in our organizational designs. They have implicitly proscribed organizational decisions for two centuries. They form the foundation of the Scientific Management movement and the structural forms and formats flowing from that philosophy of management. They also dominate current management theory.

More contemporary researchers have proposed other factors that have also had a major impact on our organizational experiences. This research challenged, in some cases, and, in others, added new conclusions to those of the earlier social philosophers' ideas about inherent tension, self-interest, and authoritative control. The net effect, most often, has been to adjust, not replace, traditional theory.

Research in the twentieth century did, of course, add new insight into the relationships implicit in working in group contexts. The famous Hawthorne experiments by Elton Mayo, Fritz Roethlisberger, and William Dickson found that both the quality and quantity of leader attention given to worker needs and interests are important in determining organizational productivity. This research gave legitimacy to the individual's need for self-determination and satisfaction of personal (self-interest) needs. The sense of the Hawthorne experiments was that individual need satisfaction was possible while also meeting organizational requirements.

Small group research by Kurt Lewin and his colleagues described and delineated the relationship between a group's interpersonal structure and individual behavior. Their work began a barrage of research by people who have become the pioneers of management and organizational thought. Such management theory pioneers as Douglas McGregor, Chris Argyrus, Robert Blake and Jane Mounton, Rensis Lickert, Warren Bennis, and a host of others trace their intellectual foundations to Lewin's work.

These applied social scientists found that conscious manipulation of the interpersonal relationships systems in organizations can affect individual and group behavior. By the same token, they added weight to the conclusion that alteration of the organizational environment (cultural features) is as influential in controlling individual behavior as anything in the worker's personal psychological make-up. In addition, they found that cultural features are or can be equally powerful forces in shaping worker behavior as are the details of structure and system imposed by managers.

These researchers concluded that understanding the nature of the human worker is at least as important as understanding organizational structural principles in accomplishing organizational goals. They added to the work of the older social philosophers new ideas such as (1) self-control, (2) the interaction of structural features and behavior, (3) the importance of the work done, and (4) the nature of the informal versus the formal organization.

They found that individual competence, motivation, and organizational productivity were more a function of the fit between task requirements and worker needs than of just structure and system. They concluded that the more we engage the individual worker with organizational leaders in problem solving, the more we can produce commitment, trust, and loyalty. And, they concluded that leadership is a critical force in helping workers make the fit between personal self-interest and organizational self-interest.

Organizations reward a manager for getting others to meet organizational goals. They reward leaders for getting individual workers to unite in common cause to accomplish what can be seen as a mutually beneficial enterprise. Leaders get workers to prize openness, mutuality of interest, trust, and collaborative effort. The leadership task is to create a culture or change it to attain these features.

## THE PROCESS OF CULTURE CHANGE

Cultural change is a continuous process. It engages leaders in activities to create and then maintain the desired cultural milieu. A culture set, however, is not static. Culture responds and reacts to changes in the larger community as well as internal changes within the culture. Culture leadership considers periodic changes in the elements of the culture due to changes in the overarching community. It involves leaders in culture setting, strategic planning, standard or norm setting, values setting, and innovation to establish and then foster cultural features conducive to their desired goals.

Schein (1985) suggests correlation of mechanisms of culture change with the various growth stages of the organization. Some methods work better at certain levels of organizational development. At beginning or birth stages, the culture change technologies include natural evolution, self-guided evolution, and managed evolution through outsiders. Organizational midlife requires culture change technologies such as planned change and organizational development, strategic planning, technology education (e.g., electronic office technologies, computerization, telecommunications), or change via scandal or explosion of myths and incrementalism. At organizational maturity, change is accomplished typically through coercive persuasion or reorganization.

Culture change is typically a long-term problem. Unfortunately, many leaders have short tenures. Especially in large, old organizations, the problem of entrenched cultural assumptions is severe, making change cumbersome and slow. Efficiency is a longstanding value in many organizations. Changing this value or adding others of equal or similar priority is difficult. Culture change is a costly task, requiring many resources—time, money, people, structure.

The key to making cultural change is to understand the existing culture. Making needed change may involve the leader in finding and then encouraging organization members who oppose the existing culture. They may be asked to propose ideas for a better one. The leader may need to find the best subculture in the organization and hold it out as an example from which others can learn. Co-workers may need help finding new ways to accomplish their tasks that is consistent with the leader's desired new cultural values.

Culture creation is a long-term process not easily susceptible to miracles. For example, we cannot count on the leader's vision alone to work. It may take five or ten years for significant change in the culture to take place. The process is to do all we can, to live the culture wanted, to model desired cultural values and behavior, and trust co-workers to see the utility for them in making needed individual changes.

## LEADERSHIP: THE TECHNOLOGY OF CULTURE LEADERSHIP

The present result of this continuing ferment of philosophical ideas is that our ideas about leadership are changing. Leadership is no longer seen to be another name for so-called good management. Now few would argue that leadership is not a separate set of ideas, philosophical principles, and techniques.

Most observers agree that leadership is guided by different values and measures success against these values, not only in managerial terms of efficiency and effectiveness. It is a task of securing trust and cooperation where people do not have to give their trust or cooperation. It is a social phenomenon. It is present in both small and large-scale organizations. And it is identifiable as partaking of the same "stuff" in either venue.

Nor is leadership the equivalent of mere office holding. We find organizational leaders at any level in the organization, not just at the highest levels. Leadership is a function of the individual leader and a group of volunteer followers; it is not merely a structured and controlled role relationship formally imposed by the system. Leadership need not be present in an organization for activity to happen. Management can and consistently does produce desired output results. But, organizational achievement is not the sole result sought by leaders, as it is with managers. Organizational survival and, importantly, organizational and individual worker growth and maturation guide leadership action as well as effective goal accomplishment.

## LEADERSHIP AND CULTURE

Leadership grows out of the historical character of the particular organization led. It is a function of the habits of interrelationship developed in a given organization. It develops its special character out of the dynamics of the interaction between followers and between a follower and the task assigned. Leadership facilitates joint activity by accommodating difference and *redirecting* it to joint action. Leadership is possible in situations where people trust each other enough to be open and honest about their needs and the tension between those needs and organizational needs.

Seen in this way, leadership and culture are intertwined. One requires the other. Much of the discussion on the creation or initialization of an organization's culture deals with the efforts of the founder in creating the initial work ambiance and fostering it. The first leader of any new enterprise creates a work culture along with the work process and product. The founder's idea for a new work unit begins the process. It is enlarged, if successful, by the addition of a founding group of co-leaders who are integrated around the founder's central idea. As the founding group acts in concert with the budding cultural values and assumptions, they, in effect, create the organization. As others are brought into the new organization, these initial assumptions become the basis for a formal culture that perpetuates itself.

Thus, the leader creates and is constrained by the culture created. It allows the leader to establish the values basis for joint action. The culture created defines success and appropriate behavior. It provides the parameters for adding new people to the organization and their acculturation. It also sets the pattern for mutual interaction and interrelationships. Leaders interact with the culture to determine what they should pay attention to, how they should react to member behavior, and what is to be communicated (taught) to followers. They are living models of the organization they project to others.

Both the first or founding leader and subsequent leaders embody the institutional purpose, and they create that purpose out of present and future need and experience (Selznick, 1957). They preach it to others and behave personally according to it. They attain follower support because the purposes they articulate come to mean as much to followers as they do to the leader. Leadership is, therefore, a values displacement activity (Fairholm, 1991). It is a task of creating united teams—teams unified by common purpose and common values that leader and led both can use to measure institutional and individual progress toward that common purpose.

## LEADERSHIP: HEAD AND HEART

We can define any organization (as done in the previous section on self-group integration) as a psychological structure that selects and molds some cultural values and not others. Leaders create their own culture from the larger, umbrella cultures they and their followers represent. That is, they create unique psychological structures (i.e., cultures), not just technical systems conducive to joint action.

The distinction is that psychostructures focus on how to attain a "fit" between the individual and the system. Technical organizational systems focus on the work system and force (via management) workers to accommodate. To lead psychological structures, we need leaders who contribute both their heads and their hearts to their leadership. We need leaders who bring to their job the best intellectual, theoretical, and practical skills, knowledge, and ability available. They also must bring to their job their emotional selves.

In his book, *The Gamesman,* Maccoby (1976) elaborates on this dual capacity of leadership. His chapter "The Head and the Heart" make the case that leadership is a task of both intellect and character. Maccoby found that leader capacities to take the initiative, display self-confidence, or be creative are important. He also found that the people he surveyed felt their leaders needed to reflect the values of independence, loyalty, trust, and honesty as well. Organizations need both sets of capacities for effective leadership. Leaders appeal to followers on the basis of idea and emotion.

Some may say the qualities of the head and heart are opposites—that acting from the emotional self is soft. Rather, the demonstration of emotional integrity and emotional strength determines not only compassion and generosity, but the quality of one's knowledge and the will to cooperative action. It becomes a prime basis for interactive trust. Unlike the head, the heart is not neutral or objective about knowledge. It values facts differentially, based on their utility, but also on their coherence to established values and principles of conduct. The heart adds conscience to concept.

Followers as well as leaders have these kinds of heart thoughts. And, these heart thoughts guide our behavior more surely than rule or even law. When both are congruent, leadership can take place; that is, others will follow our lead. In their absence, external control is necessary to ensure compliance of organization members. Indeed, the proliferation of managerial control systems to constrain and delimit worker behavior is a result of our ignoring the emotional, ideological, and values levels of interpersonal relationships. We can manage from rules alone, but we cannot lead from that narrow foundation.

The exercise of the heart, Maccoby suggests, is that of experiencing, of thinking critically, of willing, and of acting in concert with this experience to overcome narrow self-interest. And, it is vicariously sharing similar experiences our followers have. Only in this way can we understand followers enough so we can propose plans and actions they trust enough to follow. This kind of leadership eliminates follower dependency. It substitutes shared independence (interdependence) conditioned only by mutual understanding and acceptance of common goals and values both use to measure individual and group results of action.

The individual's sense of identity, integrity, and self-determination is lost when leaders treat them as an object, to be used in given work situations or for some tasks and not others. Rather, leadership sees followers as resources to attain mutual goals but also as human beings to support, encourage, and comfort. Leaders see followers as friends—people who share common goals of personal integrity, trust, and realism.

Leadership is a humane, interactive process of mutuality. It is founded, sustained, and grows in an environment of mutual trust and encouragement. It is present in stable, slow moving organizations as well as in those characterized by rapid growth, change, even chaotic fluctuations in normalcy. The world is moving more fully into a cycle of rapid change where history no longer is a useful guide to present action. Leadership that uses intellect and heart is critically in demand in this environment.

## LEADERSHIP IN CHAOS

An interesting idea on the current intellectual agenda is chaos theory. The idea of leading in situations of extreme turbulence and chaos (see specifically Wheatley, 1992), is new and holds promise of providing new insights on the task of leading culturally diverse groups. The sense of social chaos is becoming a common experience in our personal and professional lives. More and more, personal, community, and world events seem to be out of control. More and more people are defining their personal world as one of unconnected formlessness, of chaos.

Many of our social institutions are fragmented and apparently rudderless. Our work situations are diverse and getting more so. While the idea of diversity flies in the face of past and present principles of management and leadership, people are saying that diversity is good, a value to be honored merely because of difference.

There are voices abroad saying this situation is natural, even desirable. They say uncontrolled diversity allows for more freedom. They argue it is a normal aspect of nature to move away from predictability and that our organizations should move this way too. Diversity, says the current conventional wisdom, leads to a desirable variety and to innovation and creativity.

Chaos theory tells us that even minute variations on the cultural surround can have explosive results in nature. It does not suggest that total randomness is either the fact or the desired goal in nature or any other place. Rather, chaos theory proposes that these dramatic results are, in fact, predictable, if previously ignored. They reflect an essential and unified wholeness, but a wholeness at a much lower level of specificity than heretofore considered.

This theory is another, perhaps more dramatic, way to describe a basic unity in nature and in nature's creations and artifacts. Chaos theory is a more exact way of describing an essential wholeness in systems. While subsystems do shift and change, they change around an essential wholeness that resists incremental diversity. The universe is not, as some suggest, random but planned and predictable. The task is to understand nature's core unity—a unity that still has largely escaped human understanding.

Applied to leadership, chaos theory suggests that the natural state of organizations is a fundamental unity even given surface variety. The key contribution of chaos theory to leadership may be the idea that minute parts of a system effect the whole. What we used to call parts of a whole are in some real ways equivalent to the whole. Our attempts to describe the organization by analysis of its component parts may miss the mark unless we see the whole reflected in the parts.

No longer can leaders ignore small anomalies in our organizational or other systems. Leaders must accept variation from the norm as part of the whole and ways found to deal with them in holistic terms. To deal with parts individually will produce chaos, since each part is a unit of the whole and affects the whole.

Wheatley (1992) took from recent research in chaos theory ideas that might help us explain leadership action, goals, and methods. Rather than accepting the common definition of chaos as a state of total unpredictability, we can find in chaos theory more validation of integrity and interrelatedness of the part—even minute, seemingly irrelevant parts. As we move away from viewing organization as a complex of parts and deal with it as a unity, then problems met in leadership can make more sense and solutions become obvious.

Where formerly we ignored ideas of individual (or unit) difference in skills, ideology, or values, now we cannot omit them from the mathematics of leadership. They must become part of a formula for organizational success. The cultural surround, too, is as important in understanding the organization as are the component systems, structure, and operating strategies employed. Thus, the leader's expectations are as important in shaping organizational action and success as are official orders, policy statements, or procedures manuals.

As leaders come to understand these formerly ignored details of the organizational situation, the so-called cultural features, they can understand more fully why people act the way they do and can determine directions for change. As they learn to trust the power of principles and values to change co-worker's behavior, they add another powerful tool to aid in accomplishing organizational goals. Organizations, like biological ecosystems, maintain stability precisely as they come to understand and learn that we must rationalize change at local levels in relationship to the unity of the whole system.

Wheatley's work brings us back to the pioneer's ideas that governing principles, a vitalizing vision, and a few uniting values are powerful. They—with structure and control systems—shape individual and group behavior. If leaders communicate on these formerly ignored levels of group interaction, they will succeed in creating, adapting, and maintaining organizational vitality because in so doing they pay attention to the wholeness, the unity, the cohesiveness of the organization.

Unified at the values level, all people in the organization will do their best to produce results implicit in these values. As leaders overcome the historical tendency to either ignore these factors, or fear them, they realize that random difference, united by shared values, may actually help produce desired results. They need no longer fear randomness and autonomy, since acceptance of shared values and customs by all organization members allows them to respond in ways that eventually contribute to the overall wholeness that defines this organization as opposed to all others.

By understanding the ideas of chaos theory, leaders can teach core values to followers and then let group members act independently, knowing they are, or can be made to be, congruent on the essential levels of cooperative action. They need not overcontrol variation. They can, in fact, revel in it and reap the benefits of more creativity, more innovation, and more overall energy expended on needed tasks. This result is inevitable as a collectivity of individuals expend their best efforts on tasks all agree with.

For too long we have confused control with order. Of course, we can attain order via tight control, but it is at great cost and in the face of sometimes fierce resistance. Order also can result from shared vision and values and the softer, subtle processes that are constantly at work to create, mature, and enhance the central organism.

## SUMMARY

Chaos theory tells us that organisms and organizations maintain stability because of all of their parts, even those often less visible than outward form and function. As we find the organization's core unity, we can maximize the use of different peoples, systems, and methods. All that we need is for leaders to focus on unifying values and principles as the glue holding the organization together and let individuals be free to operate within that central unity.

# PART III

# SHAPING ORGANIZATIONAL CULTURE

Changing culture requires that the leader ascertain completely the group's values and observable behavior. To do this, leaders need to delve into the underlying assumptions that actually determine how group members see, think, and feel and why they trust themselves to the leadership of others.

Leaders involve the people being changed in the process. Indeed, they are the focus of change. Leaders also try to recognize and support people in the group who are trying to change others (Havelock, 1973). Argyrus (1973) said that the more we make the people involved aware of the change, the more it can occur with minimum dysfunction because people *are* the organization, not the artifacts we create to ease their work effort.

An effective change agent needs to facilitate all possible types of change interventions. These might include developing a supportive organization and training of participants in new knowledge, information, skills, and values. Change agent leaders also might use consultation and reinforcement, monitoring the change process and using external communications—public relations and public information. An effective change facilitator is a trailblazer (Havelock, 1973).

Whitley (1989) identified ten skills change leaders typically use. Leaders are opportunity-oriented, future-oriented strategists, and trend spotters. They are idea-oriented, intuitive, and extraordinarily persistent. Change leaders are also unprejudiced, resourceful, feedback-oriented, and superior team builders.

Change requires a compatible culture. Possible methods for creating such a climate includes institutionalizing work processes for collecting innovative ideas, actively seeking idea-generating mechanisms, protecting risk takers, and fostering innovation. Deal and Kennedy (1983) offered possible cultural norms that help the change process. They suggested that leaders can ease change in an organizational culture characterized by collegiality, openness, high expectations, appreciation, caring, and recognition, humor, participation, and protection of important matters. An especially important element in a change culture is the level of trust, confidence, and support received. A culture characterized by high trust levels helps members change and all else.

The demands on leaders to create a values-based culture does not end the task, nor are well-planned strategic programs enough. Leaders need to manage the culture once it is established. Managing the culture involves the leader in setting up and maintaining specific standards, articulating and enforcing organizational values, and prescribing acceptable behaviors within the organization. Maintaining a culture once set is a team-building activity. It involves leaders in continuous effort to ensure that they interrelate organizational group members in ways that let them want to work together cooperatively.

As noted, clearly articulated core values (Selznick, 1957) in effect are a system of shared meanings. These shared meanings shape interactions and attitudes (Blake and Mouton, 1981) to form a pattern of basic assumptions (Schein, 1985). Together, they are the foundation of shaping and maintaining a culture. Articulation of strategies that extend these values into the future activity of the organization are also critical.

Leaders use mechanisms such as symbols, rituals, or enactments of shared reality (Morgan, 1986) or a system of informal rules that define the way people do work and that regulate the magnetism between opposing forces (Deal and Kennedy, 1983). Physical arrangements (Schein, 1985) that define culture spatially and help shape its character are also common tools, with myths and symbols (such as language).

The energy, enthusiasm, values, and actions necessary to create an organization also act to shape its cultural "personality" (Kalman, 1984). The organization's culture forms quickly based on the requirements for success. These requirements include its mission, environmental setting, and its operating values, such as efficiency, quality, service, hard work, trust, and loyalty. Culture impacts the environment and the environment impacts the leader's style and capacity to lead.

Perhaps equally critical are the actions of the organization's key leaders. The leader's aims are critical in forming the new organization and its new culture. The core values and behavior provide the skeleton of culture. They model organization member actions. They prescribe culture. They form the raw material for tradition and rituals that define the organization and distinguish it from all others.

Critical incidents stemming from leader actions also shape the evolving organization's culture. Critical incidents often evolve into stories that describe and place organizational values into a work context. Such incidents might be, for example, the firing of someone that clearly showed core values, or it may be a reprimand that operationalizes those values. Other examples of how the leader deals with conflicts, or what the organization really thinks about quality service, or conflicts with supervisors that define superior-subordinate relationships can shape and/or alter an organization's cultural foundations.

The chapters in Part III deal with details of leader actions and requirements in shaping culture to meet their individual needs for group action.

Culture is a composite of ritual, ceremony, stories, special language, and accepted actions and events. Our understanding of culture presupposes understanding these components and their interrelationship and their impact on member performance.

Chapter 5 places the leader's need to shape culture in the context of several major organizational systems. The intent in this chapter is to define culture leadership as a function of the values, strategic, communications, and office politics systems present in any organization. It relates cultural leadership to these ideas and those of the sanctioned actions the organization expects of its members. It ties cultural leadership to the measures of effectiveness of that action used, the attitudes engendered in members by cultural artifacts, the service goals established, how leaders manage change, and how one exercises leadership. The attempt here is to show the relationship of these traditional ideas about organizations to new ideas about cultural leadership.

Chapter 6 discusses culture from another perspective, that of its major components. It introduces the belief systems undergirding culture. This analysis adds another insight to our understanding of organizational culture by focusing on the artifacts leaders create to operationalize cultural values. The overall focus of chapter 6 is on how and by what means leaders create meaning within the organization.

# 5

# Shaping Culture

## INTRODUCTION

Changing culture is the hard part of change management. Change, according to dictionary definitions, is making or becoming different. Havelock (1973) defined change as an alternation or disturbance of the existing situation. Kanter (1983) defined change in innovation terms. Garfield (1987) agreed. He said change throws off our equilibrium.

Organizations develop cultures that incorporate the values and practices of their leaders. Culture evolves through the accumulation of actions and events the members of an organization experience. Leaders—especially the organization's founders—play a key role in this evolutionary process. They, more than any other actor, are critical in structuring experiences within the group that point toward desired results.

Leaders also emphasize some experiences over others and, in this way, further focus the acculturation process. Creating an organizational culture involves the leader in several important implementation tasks. Among them are setting the values base for mutual interaction and thinking strategically about the organization and its future. It is also systematically shaping a desired culture within which members can trust and expect others to trust them.

## VALUES

The values, or settled beliefs, that group members share act to support member interactions respecting accepted levels of trust, the right level of commitment, and the strength of that commitment. Setting values is the first and most crucial cultural implementation leadership task. It includes leader action to adopt a formal set of basic beliefs to inculcate desired founding and other values in stakeholders. This sometimes includes use of symbols to explain, re-enforce, and interpret desired values. The values thus set become the basis for organizational standards that guide later individual and group interaction.

An organization's core values are a kind of leaven that permeates the organization and provides the definitive measures of group success. They also are a kind of boundary fence defining acceptable individual and group actions. Core values determine how we treat people, whom we trust, and what actions are acceptable or unacceptable. They determine what excellence is, what results we seek, and how we rate these results.

*Values def.*

While leaders shape values, they are made manifest in the organization's culture though attitudes fostered and rites, rituals, myths, strategies, and goals assumed. Leadership is a culture-shaping, value-infusing activity. Selznick (1957) saw the leadership task as infusing the organization with value, and the values that work are those that value the person in the organization and the individual client, as well as excellence in service delivery. These values foster mutual interactive trust and aid in stabilization of the culture system.

*goals.*

Values establish the foundation for more specific operational and interpersonal work standards needed by the group. Operating standards setting tasks involve formally adopting specific performance standards aimed at creating a particular organizational climate. The precise standards adopted set the parameters for group action. They are, in effect, social paradigms guiding group member actions and choices. They go a long way in determining the nature and character of the culture and the level of success members experience in the group.

Several forces are shaping cultural leadership today. All have values components. The work force is changing. It is becoming older, more educated, populated by more minorities and women. The work ethic is also changing. We are moving away from the traditional Protestant work ethic with its strong hard-work-yields-results orientation that guided our parents. Now the tendency is toward what some call a bureaucratic ethic characterized by conforming and getting along.

*American Rights— True.*

As Americans, we are becoming more wanting. The concept of entitlement is at work in our organizations. Entitlement means that workers and clients see their relationship with an organization in terms of their *rights* to its benefits more clearly than did former generations. As the general society assumes this value as a priority, organizations follow.

These and many other forces, such as life experiences, past tradition, socioeconomic class, and political circumstances of the members of any organization, are all strong cultural forces that direct change (Reynolds,

1986). They are equally strong in resisting change and preserving a desired former culture. Culture is at the symbolic level of existence. Organizational culture is the whole range of shared models of social action, containing both real and ideal elements accepted by members and enforced by organizational systems.

We learn and internalize our values and our standards from society. Our values change as a result of changes in our interaction with the larger society. When someone challenges a settled belief in practice, the choice is whether to change the circumstances or change the value. Pressure to change values occurs when we feel dissatisfaction with current values as applied in social context.

As noted, sometimes a culture becomes maladaptive, a situation where the implicit culture and formal policy differ. One way to turn around a maladaptive organization is to determine the implicit culture (as opposed to the formal one) and correct it. These culture gaps divide energy and commitment. They allow multiple goals or methods of goal attainment to develop. They blur commitment and reduce trust levels. Our organizations today need leadership in these situations to counter this cultural values pluralism and to give needed attention to cultural maintenance tasks.

## STRATEGIC PLANNING

Strategic planning is a popular technology today. Many organizations are undertaking strategic planning projects as a way to focus and concentrate their resources on what their leaders see as horizon issues and programs. The key elements in strategic planning are cultural. The success of these programs depends on the work done to develop and operationalize a vision statement that incorporates core values that pay attention to what the leaders feel to be critical to success. The effort is to concentrate group member energies on one set of values and programs as opposed to all others. Strategic planning is actually a focusing and a reduction of interest, not a broadening and generalizing of interest as the name might imply.

Strategic plans define the range of acceptable member behavior and operationalize a vision and a self-definition of what an organization wants to be in the future. They may help form that vision initially, as well as guide implementation activities later. Strategic plans help form the cultural base for group member action.

The purpose of strategic planning is to integrate the actions of organizational units and enable the headquarter units to capitalize on its synergies. It lets individuals and subgroups better understand their various roles and relationships and who and what to trust. Strategies are the sources of cohesiveness in the organization (Eadie, 1983) and can be articulated at several levels: global, functional program areas, and detailed administrative implementation. They support directed organizational action (or hamper such efforts) at each level.

Leaders now are coming to feel that they are strategic thinkers and can do the strategic plan development their organizations need. The quantitative, formula-mathematics approaches to strategic planning developed in the 1960s are out of favor. They did not produce excellence. Rather, they too often focused on market share growth and underemphasized needed aspects of relationships such as innovation and leadership.

The trend now is for operating managers to plan strategically. They may use outside facilitators, but strategic planning is no longer a third party activity. The challenge in strategic planning is to turn leaders into strategic thinkers. The technology provides leaders a language of strategy to use in doing it themselves. This is a culture maintenance technology asking leaders to become expert in shaping culture to focus organizational effort on team principles and commitment-building techniques.

Planning strategically is a cultural implementation tactic, involving formally undertaken programs to identify and rank long-range, strategic issues and programs. Often, strategic issues include those dealing with creativity and innovation. Fostering innovation and change involves leaders in organizing and managing formal programs to encourage creativity and entrepreneurship in setting up or implementing service programs. The key to success in strategic planning is not so much the details of the plan developed as it is in the interpersonal system of trust relationships implied by the strategic programs adopted.

## COMMUNICATION

Communicating understanding is dependent on both the sender and the receiver sharing certain essential cultural parameters, such as common language, common experiences, and common values. That is, successful communications depend on the sender and receiver understanding the cultural context of the communication situation. The sociocultural experiences of the sender and receiver must be congruent for communications to be successful, that is, for someone to predict desired change. Culture helps us create a situation in which empathy between the partners in the communication exchange is possible.

One problem in communicating for understanding is that we are forced to mask our true intent because we cannot fully trust our listeners. We are reluctant to expose our true feelings and to show our true selves, even to our closest professional associates. Whether this is universally true or not, it is true that our communications with each other are not always simple even when we intend them to be.

Communicating requires openness. For instance, if we were helping someone in making a change, we would need to be candid. In these situations, we also may need to face the other person with reality, doing so in an atmosphere of trust so he or she might accept the proffered help. In only this way can our communications flow be reciprocal.

*trust.*

The process of cultural change through communications asks leaders to develop special communications skills. DeCormier (1991) and Cavalari and DeCormier (1988) suggest some special leadership communications skills (called microskills) that ease cultural change programs. Leaders facilitate changes to protect important extant cultural features. They do this by *acknowledging* followers' comments with polite and friendly responses that do not commit them to the followers' proposals for change. They can parry unhelpful follower questions by responding with questions of their own, thus *reversing* the direction of change. Other microskills include attitudinal advocacy and countering attitudinal advocacy by supporting or arguing against specific follower comments about a given feature of organizational culture.

We are all captives of our culture. Hall (1976) says that people try to read another's true intention by interpreting multiple aspects of the relationship, such as who they are, what they do, as well as what they say. The problem is that each culture sets up specific action chains for all social conventions (e.g., sex, marriage, corporate mergers, shaking hands, buying a loaf of bread). An action chain is a ritualistic series of behaviors that all members of a culture typically follow—like the steps in a dance; a kind of dance with a goal. Only through shared culture can we expect participants to understand either the dance (ritualistic behavior) or the goal. And, only by sharing culture can group members learn to trust another to behave predictably.

Knowing the cultural context of a receiver can aid in attaining needed understanding. When we do not know the cultural context—or misinterpret a feature of the other person's culture—we risk misunderstanding that person's action chains. Distrust results because we do not follow our cultural pattern. We misread others because we cannot decipher the steps in their action chain (dance).

Hall has elaborated on this idea at a national level. Each national culture, and each organizational culture or subculture, is characterized by a unique cultural chain. As we introduce more cultural minorities into our workplaces, we can expect the cultural differences they bring with them to challenge our efforts to integrate these divergent cultural contexts into our organizations. Nevertheless, until we do integrate new people into our organizational cultures and induce them to accept our common core values, we cannot expect to attain a trusting, cooperative relationship.

Some of Hall's examples may illustrate the nature and extent of the challenge to cultural creation in a situation of diversity. For example, in China when faced with a troublesome situation, the Chinese may ignore it. For them to acknowledge a situation imposes the duty to deal with it, and if the indicated action is serious, they may deny its existence until they have selected a proper course of action. Americans, on the other hand, often begin immediately to acknowledge the problem and act while they are planning how to solve it. We misread the Chinese because we cannot follow their cultural action chain and, instead, substitute our own. Americans repeat this behavior many times for each culturally different member of our organization.

Context and communication are inextricably interconnected. In some cultures, messages are explicit. That is, the words carry most of the information. In other cultures, such as China or Japan, or the Arab countries, the verbal part of a communication contains less information. More information is in the context of the situation. The American complaint that the Japanese never get to the point is a reflection of our misreading this context dimension of our communications with them. The Japanese would not dream of spelling the whole thought out. To do so is to diminish the status of the receiver. It would be like doing their thinking for them.

Much of contextual communication is unconscious. We pick up contextual understanding from the cradle. We learn what to notice and what to ignore, how to divide time and space, how to walk and talk and use our bodies. Cultural context tells us how to behave as men and women, how to relate to other people, how to handle responsibility. It lets us understand whether or not we see experience as a whole idea or fragmented. Context gives meaning to these and a bewildering complex of other actions, behaviors, and ideas. These assumptions are subconscious. Often we are not aware of them at the conscious level though they structure our behavior and our communications.

Hall divided national cultures (and, perhaps we can divide organizational cultures) into high and low context classifications. Examples of low context cultures, according to Hall, include Germany, Switzerland, Scandinavia, and the United States. Similarly, high context cultures include the French, English, Italian, Spanish, Greek, and Arab nations.

In general, high context cultures require less of the legal paperwork we think essential in America. In high context cultures, a person's word is his or her bond. In these cultures, one does not need a paper to enforce behavior. In high context cultures, we give a job to the person who will do the best work and whom we can control.

In contrast, in low context cultures we try to make the specifications precise so the incumbent finds it hard to do a bad job. This is typical of America today. In the past—and in the West—America was high context. "The Buck Stops Here" sign on President Harry Truman's desk was a high context sign—from his old-America value system.

One complication of low context culture is the fragmentation of experience. The plethora of experts exemplifies this feature of America. The prenuptial agreement is another example. High context cultures suffer from slowness to move or change, rigid class structures, and family structures that overcontrol (by our standards).

Context affects our communications on all levels: actions, relationships with space, time, color, and so forth. The problem with Americans is that we train people to deal with wholes (ideas, situations, things) in terms of their disparate parts, not as unities. We fail to realize that nothing is independent of anything else. Yet, we are prone to deal with parts. We do not easily make integrating connections; we do not attempt to synthesize, or pull things together in a situation in which there is uncertainty or "descensus" about choices (Pfeffer, 1981). As we move into multicultural organizational contexts, leaders will have to change and widen their zone of acceptance and accept values and behaviors that are now alien to them, but will become common in the organization in the twenty-first century.

## OFFICE POLITICS

Office politics, like regular politics, is the art of who gets what, when, and how (Lasswell and Kaplin, 1950). While some denigrate the practice of office politics, it nevertheless is part of organizational life (Fairholm, 1993). It is the basis for much of the interpersonal interactivity we engage in on the job. Office politics define the emotional infrastructure of the organization. It operationalizes trust, commitment, and security issues for the members of the organization and determines their strength.

The practice of office politics includes much of the regular and routine interchange among people in group relationships. It is how we get what we want in the group. People in power positions differ from the rest in their capacity to impose their personal defenses on to organizational life. This is the art of politics. The adjustments we might have to make to get our way are sometimes major obstacles to some. It is the character of the culture that determines precisely the nature of these adjustments in our relationships with others. Culture prescribes the kind of office politics we engage in as it does most other interpersonal connections we make.

These adjustments and obstacles stop some from engaging in office politics, or at least from saying they do—all engage in this practice. These adjustments sometimes involve bending the rules, an exchange of favors, and offers of rewards for cooperation. Some see these as wrong and morally abhorrent. Office politics means this to some, but it need not descend into violation of one's moral standards. Indeed, it most often does not.

Possible areas of office political action include at least four generic situations: (1) colleague versus colleague, (2) superior versus subordinate, (3) union versus management, and (4) line versus staff. Organizational power politics is present in each of these relationship situations. They are especially apropos in choice situations in which leaders and followers engage. They determine the level of trust and acceptance we offer to others.

Research has identified at least four decision-making models of the organization: rational, bureaucratic, decision process, and political. The political model is as active a perspective in organizations as any of the others. This mode of decision making works with the other three. We can describe it in terms of goals, power methods used, rules, information requirements, beliefs about action-consequence relationships, and ideology. These refer to elements of organizational politics and by extension to organizational culture. And, so too do the others.

The only way we can avoid office politics is by maintaining slack resources, that is, allow a situation where we have a surplus of needed resources. There is no need for conflict in these kinds of situations. Similarly, we do not need office politics in situations where there is a homogeneity of goals and beliefs, where members share one ideology, or when the decision made is less important or not important to the membership. In most other circumstances, organizational power politics is routine (Fairholm, 1993).

Given the above, we can determine the prevalence of political power action within organizations in large part by factors of culture—shared or diverse distribution of resources, information, power, goals, or methods. Culture sets the parameters of political (and other) action in the groups within which we engage. In large part, culture defines the appropriate tactics of power (Fairholm, 1993) and constrains their use.

## ORGANIZATIONAL ACTION

Culture acts as a form of social energy to move members to act (Ott, 1989). Culture is also a means of interpreting organizational action. It guides members in how to act and think, who to trust, and what to hate or revere. It lets members know what to value and how to feel about certain actions or events. Indeed, culture defines and maintains organizational borders. It serves a gate-keeper function in that it prescribes and prohibits certain behaviors and attitudes while encouraging others. It may effect organizational performance directly or indirectly (Ott, 1989). And, it negates the need for detailed procedure manuals.

The total of member actions taken together defines an organization's culture. Culture interprets member actions and defines the level of trust and respect members ought to have for each other and sanctions member behavior against cultural norms.


## EFFECTIVENESS LEVELS

Among the many ideas implicit in the study of effectiveness and efficiency is the idea that organizational culture, or climate, impacts individual and group effectiveness. One can analyze effectiveness from several levels: individual, group, department, community, or nation. Each of these foci are cultural domains that leaders must consider in leading our modern organizations.

Schein (1985) says culture helps explain organizational effectiveness in that it constrains organizational strategy. Odom, Boxx, and Dunn (1990) suggest that it affects employee satisfaction and commitment, work group cohesion, strategy implementation, and organizational performance. They found bureaucratic organizations to be more procedure bound and less innovative and supportive.

Innovative and supportive cultures influence employee trust action, commitment, satisfaction, and cohesion more so than do system and structural features. The culture determines, in large part, the level of mutual trust, commitment, satisfaction, and cohesion of the group members (Steers, 1985). These factors are essential aids to the flexibility and adaptability essential in today's world.


## ATTITUDES

Culture also deals with attitudes, feelings, and member emotions, as well as the physical facilities of the organization. It provides and defines the emotional ambience (total surround) within which group members work. The local culture helps or inhibits what people do, why they do it, and the level of excellence attained. Culture is a part of the organizational ideology (the body of doctrine, myth, or symbols of a social group or movement) and, therefore, helps shape member ideas about what is right, good, and true.

Culture sets the values base for the group. Values are the standards people agree on about how to measure and rate individual and group performance. Values define acceptable actions, appropriate levels of interactive trust, and the quality of the services or products produced. Cultural values permeate the workplace and constrain individual and team perceptions of what is proper and what is not.

## SERVICE GOALS

Organizational culture in our public, private, and not-for-profit sectors share similar features. Organizational culture is based on an ideology of service coming from the values implicit and explicit in the founding documents that define our nation and its institutions. Culture is also conditioned by agency mission and environment, but the culture is a primary determinant of group goals. It provides the standards of conduct, defines the levels of excellence expected, and otherwise constrains and prescribes acceptable performance toward understood and mutually agreeable final products.

## SOCIETAL LEADERSHIP

Ehrenhalt (1991) developed an interesting and evocative idea about why political leadership in America is declining. Some of his ideas also apply to business and third-sector leaders. He said America is going through a change process from leadership to openness. Ehrenhalt sees a major shift in the character, values, and purposes—the culture—of our political leadership today. He says everybody sees everybody else as an equal. Even the leadership does not believe in leadership, quo leadership, any more.

His thesis is that bright, ambitious people have replaced the part timers in key policy positions in our social organizations. These professionals have made politics and holding public office their prime profession. Political office for them is not a means to accomplish a social or political party's philosophical agenda. It is the object of their work.

According to Ehrenhalt, today's political officeholder comes to office without party allegiance and without a platform beyond that necessary to get elected. Public office is seen as a profession, therefore, being out of office is failure. As a result of this perspective, voting against the interests of vocal constituents amounts to a form of professional suicide. These officeholders try to please everyone; consequently, they develop no base to support them in times of trouble. Often, they form only temporary alliances to deal with immediate concerns, issues, or problems. Today's political leaders will not follow others. Their attitude is why take the trouble to get elected and then defer to someone else. With this kind of attitude, nothing gets done and the system slides into irrelevance.

Ehrenhalt's thesis is unsettling; unfortunately, it describes much of our current political leadership. This culture of the immediate and of the utilitarian is shaping our political leaders. Whether or not it is also descriptive of many of our institutional and organizational leaders is unproven, but the tendency to this direction is present.

## CHANGE

Conventional wisdom teaches that to change our social institutions we must change our structures and/or our common practices. If we alter the system, then people will change to conform. First, change the system, or the culture, and people will follow. This method is common in all sectors of society, business, government, and politics. People assume that introduction of new programs, new parties in office, automation, and so forth, will affect a change in the quality of life, standard of living, productivity, or satisfaction.

The common assumption is that the only way to make change is if leaders exercise control over their subordinates. We assume that changing the organizational environment will result in changing people's behavior. So we impose change and then supervise those under us, control them, and direct them to do what the new, altered system requires of them.

The facts, however, suggest otherwise. Thoughtful analysis of the major changes in our personal, organizational, and social life highlights another, more effective change strategy at play in cultural change. To change the culture we must first change the individual. The many changes by individual group members produce change in our collective circumstances as an organization, a community, a nation, a world.

Culture changes as people change their values, beliefs, assumptions, and expectations. It is not laws, rules, or management that change society. It is the result of many individuals who choose to accept a new value, a new behavior, a new attitude that changes us.

The only lasting change is when individuals independently change themselves. The challenge of leadership is to foster this change and to direct it through articulation of and then maintenance of common core values acceptable and internalized by group members.

## SUMMARY

Culture provides the meaning, direction, and social energy that moves the organization into productive action, mediocrity, or destruction. A culture may be functional at first, but in time, it can become independent of its initial purpose. Uncontrolled, it may become distinct from the formal strategy, reward systems, and structure of the organization and from the workers and leaders. In these situations, the culture is dysfunctional. It leads members to conflict, rather than to cooperation; to distrust, rather than trust; and to work against, rather than to build teams.

Sometimes the culture becomes a counterpoint to the formal top management policy and structure. When it does, we waste energy as workers devote time to both sets of values, ideologies, and socioemotional activities. The impact of a group culture on its members is powerful and when opposite to the formal articulated strategy can become a stumbling block.

# 6

# Components of Culture

## INTRODUCTION

Peters and Waterman (1982) identified culture as the basis for the excellence of many of the business organizations they studied. Their findings concluded that strong, cohesive cultures produce desired organizational results. Their eight-element model for understanding culture defines an organizational environment characterized by shared values and beliefs, heros and heroines, rituals and ceremonies, and cultural priests and priestesses—that is, storytellers, gossips, and spies. These are all aspects of cultural theory, not of organizational theory. They based their book—like culture itself—on a symbolic frame of reference in dealing with internal (co-workers) and external (customers) clients.

When talking about culture, we are really talking about reality construction. Culture helps member perception and understanding of particular events, actions, objects, utterances, or situations in distinctive ways, but ways acceptable by the group. Culture creation—that is, reality construction—involves generating rules and systems of enforcing rule compliance. It is a task of creating social norms and customs. Enforcement of social norms is a major part of culture management. Effective enforcement determines success in reality construction and assurance that leaders can communicate desired meanings.

Leaders use several mechanisms to manage meaning in the organization. These mechanisms, or systems of relationships, bind group members into a unity, making it distinct from all others. They communicate the system of meanings via symbols. Selznick (1957) talks of the embodiment of values (a form of symbolism) in an organizational structure through statements of mission, programs of activity, selective recruitment, and socialization. Clark (1972) defines values-specific stories (another symbolic mode) as a system of collective understanding of unique accomplishment in a formally established group.

Culture is the point of contact where philosophy comes into contact with organization (Davis, 1984). As such, culture is concerned with ethics, the set of moral judgments, standards, and philosophy that help define the organization (Davis, 1984). Ethics are the moral code that legitimizes the organization and its actions to members and to the larger culture within which it operates. A group's ethics are the yardstick by which employees and all other stakeholders can judge leadership.

Obviously, there is a link between culture and leadership. Successful leaders connect the minds of their followers with the prevailing culture. They conform their style to the current cultural surround. In the minds of their followers, at least, leaders have integrated their values with group values, their goals with group goals, their ideology with group ideological underpinnings.

Different leadership styles hinge on a question of organizational meanings. Authoritarian cultures induce the leader to use telling techniques to communicate with followers. Democratic cultures focus the leader on selling techniques. In either case, they are enforcing a particular organizational meaning on the group members. Davis (1984) suggested that the guiding beliefs that define the central culture of the organization are, and should be, set by the leader/CEO. Culture and strategy making based on cultural values are a top-down affair. Those not directly involved, including others in the leader's top executive team, play a more important role in effecting the vision rather than in creating it.

## CULTURAL BELIEF SYSTEMS

Analysis of the idea of culture asks the individual to become familiar with a variety of ideas that aid in infusing meaning in activities and in communicating that meaning to group members (Pettigrew, 1979). As shown in Table 6.1, culture is an amalgam of a family of concepts. The leader needs to be familiar with these various concepts making up the idea of culture. They are the building blocks of organizational culture and the tools leaders use in its management. These belief systems, and their equivalents, act primarily as points of reference in thinking about and making sense of the organization and its work contexts. The remainder of this chapter discusses these belief system technologies.

**Table 6.1**
**The Shared Basis of Cultural Belief Systems**

| | |
|---|---|
| ASSUMPTIONS and EXPECTATIONS | CEREMONIES, RITES, and RITUALS |
| CULTS | CUSTOMS |
| HEROS | HUMOR |
| IDEOLOGY | LANGUAGE and JARGON |
| METAPHORS and MYTHS | PHYSICAL ARTIFACTS |
| PLAY | RELATIONSHIPS |
| STORIES | SYMBOLS |
| VALUES | VISION |

Among these tools are symbolization, use of language; shaping ideology and belief systems; creating ritualistic behavior patterns; and creating, setting, and enforcing performance expectations. Slogans, symbols, stories, myths, ceremonies, rituals, and other patterns of cultural behavior also are clues to the existence of underlying meanings. They provide the context within which we communicate these meanings and structure them into organizational member action and thought. Pettigrew (1979) confirms these illustrations and reminds us that organizational culture also includes language, stories, and myths (Ulrich, 1984).

Organizational members root their understanding of organization in these processes. They operationalize the culture's system of shared meaning. The organizational structure and systems of rules, policies, and procedures operationalize these processes. They are also applied operationally in goal statements, mission statements, job descriptions, and standard operating procedures.

## Assumptions and Expectations

The organization will stand or fall on what leaders do and on followers that follow (Kelley, 1989). We can define leadership as a process of communication of expectations from the leader to followers. Leaders' expectations of followers convey the leader's intentions toward them. The trust of the leader's expectations can be toward higher commitment to organizational goals or to loyalty to the leader as an individual, or to anything else. The leader's expectations direct follower effort, trust, and commitment.

Everyone expects followers to know how to follow. Unfortunately not all do. Without knowing what to expect, followers cannot understand their roles; indeed, they cannot know what to do. It is faulty thinking to expect followers automatically to know what to do. We base this idea on the thought that leaders are more important than followers; anyone can be a follower. All followers need to do is to follow orders. The conventional wisdom is that followers are reactive and draw their energy, talent, and aims from the leader.

Leadership is, in part, setting expectations to guide followers to right actions. Expectations and assumptions set by the leader become part of the organizational culture and define acceptable behavior. This is a leader culture-shaping tool. Too many guidebooks for leaders ignore this truth. Nevertheless, assumptions and expectations about follower actions are present, if often implicit in group action.

Assumptions are the biases about the organization, its people, and its tasks that are present in any social organization. Expectations are similar to assumptions. They are the expression of our wishes, hopes, desires, and anticipations as they concern the organization and the roles of all members in it. Assumptions and expectations drive much of our group behavior. Leaders consciously work to create assumptions and expectation constructs to induce followers to behave in desired ways. In doing this they engage in shaping their cultural surround.

Expectations are mind sets that leaders consider proper or necessary. An expectation is what the leader desires from and feels followers own them. The leader's role is to persuade followers to want, to desire, to expect, and ultimately to demand what the leader wanted in the first place (Burns, 1978). Follower behavior occurs after and is a result of the communication of an expectation. The expectation process is a part of the stimulus-response formula. That is, expectations are stimuli that elicit follower responses.

Expectations are part of most any success we see in management by objectives systems. We often couch our expectations on the job in formats such as job descriptions and performance evaluation criteria systems. Management by Objectives (MBOs) systems are, in essence, nothing more than formalized, ritualized expectations systems. They define explicit, measurable expectations in the form of work tasks expected of employees. Both the formal MBO and less formal procedure-based systems have in common precise, quantifiable expectations as the basis for leader-follower relationships.

This form of expectation is in contrast with the often imprecise, unwritten, difficult-to-quantify expectations about values, attitudes, and philosophy that are also imparted daily by managers to employees everywhere. They represent technical matters of day-to-day management. Nevertheless, it is in the values expectations that real follower development takes place.

The leadership of a system of assumptions and expectations is fully within the context of culture maintenance. Leaders make full use of (often imprecise) assumptions and expectations as a means to inspire and stretch followers. Expectations are a kind of self-fulfilling prophesy or Pygmalion effect (Batten, 1989). People usually rise to meet the expectations that others have of them. By raising expectation levels, leaders can increase follower efforts.

Leaders use several kinds of expectations. Lee (1991) suggested that followers help leaders create the vision because the leaders expect it. The vision is a form of what leaders expect from their followers. Kouzes (1989) suggested that leaders expect that followers will come to a relationship characterized by honesty, competence, trustworthiness, and effectiveness. Lundin and Lancaster (1990) added versatility, responsibility, and integrity. And Kelley (1989) maintained that we should expect enthusiasm, intelligence, self-reliance, humility, and pursuit of the organization's goals.

Communicating expectations is the leader's job. Batten (1989) said tough-minded leadership is nothing more than the setting of expectations—he called it Management by Expectations, or MBEs. Leaders set expectations based on follower strengths. They should strive to set expectations that inspire commitment to a cause greater than self.

Manz and Sims (1991) identified strategies that leaders adopt to get followers to lead themselves. Leaders, they say, set up expectations of the following:

1. Valuing self-leaders
2. By modeling self-leadership
3. Encouraging self-set goals
4. Creating positive thought patterns
5. Using rewards and constructive reprimand to create self-leadership
6. Promoting self-leadership via teamwork
7. Encouraging a self-leadership culture

These leader actions are examples of setting expectations and assumptions to guide follower behavior. As leaders integrate them into the normal patterns of organizational action and decisions, they become a part of that organization's culture. Setting expectations and assumptions like those above is a basic and crucial technology at the leader's disposal to prepare followers for desired action.

Gardner (1990) referred to expectations as the trade secrets of leaders and teachers. They set expectations by creating challenging job standards, communicating respect for follower abilities, delegating important tasks frequently, and by directing and guiding while allowing freedom for the follower.

### Ceremonies, Rites, and Rituals

Ceremonies are celebrations of an organization's cultural values and basic assumptions. They are events that display the culture and honor it and are experiences usually remembered by members (Ott, 1989). Rituals are consciously elaborate, dramatic, planned sets of activities that combine various forms of cultural expression. They often have both practical and symbolic results. Rites define a kind of ritual. The uses of rites in culture creation and management are similar to that of rituals and serve largely the same purposes in this discussion.

Ceremonies serve a wide variety of purposes, including the following:

1. Maintain uniformity
2. Initiate new members
3. Provide a sense of social involvement
4. Convey symbolic messages
5. Provide connections and order
6. Bridge between order and chaos
7. Provide hope

An organization's ceremonies communicate meaning from one individual to another and from one organization to another and to its environment.

Often ceremonies are staged at more or less fixed intervals. They have explicit purposes—for example, a political party convention to elect a president. They also often involve stylized, or ritualistic, behavior.

Rituals are customs or repeated sets of actions (as opposed to events) that take on specific and powerful symbolic meaning within an organization. They are standardized, detailed clusters of techniques and behaviors that manage anxieties but do not always produce intended technical, practical results They set up boundaries and relationships between people—for example, customers and representatives, managers and employees, unions and management. Rituals may include two-hour lunches, evaluation and reward processes, staff meeting attendance rosters, parking spaces, farewell parties, work schedules, and much more.

Rituals communicate the shared values of the organization and revive common feelings that bind members together. Rites and rituals have many characteristics in common. Some writers define both simply as repetitive sequences of action conveying implicit meaning to the actors in the ritual. Bocock (1972) defined them as the symbolic use of bodily movement and gesture in a social situation to express and articulate meaning. For example, social amenities are rituals.

Rituals include set ways we do something(s) in the organization. For example, coordination is often a ritualistic set behavior for clearing actions with specified powerful others (Fairholm, 1993). Decision making is another system of set (ritualistic) behaviors by specific individuals that assure leaders that decisions arrived at are trustworthy. Staff meetings also are often ritualistic.

It is through ritual that organizational relationships become stylized, conventionalized, and prescribed. Rituals create order, clarity, and predictability in dealing with complex or ambiguous problems that leaders cannot control in other ways. The functions of ritual include socialization and stabilization of the culture, reduction of anxieties and ambiguity, and conveyance of messages to external constituencies. Other examples of organizational rituals include the following:

Performance appraisal—does not produce new data for decision making

Regular meetings—often produce few results except platforms for speeches

Management training programs—produce little visible improvement but do socialize the participant into the management culture

Tests and interviews—produce doubtful data, but communicate specialness to those hired

Retirement dinners

Welcoming speeches to new employees

Rituals are mediums of culture creation. Their central purpose is in the message they contain, not what they do. It is what the ritual means symbolically (Beattie, 1966). What rituals say is that these are the central (or peripheral) values that specify dominant or marginal people and/or the important or less important goals and actions of an organization.

Rituals are specific to culture. What works in one organizational culture may not work in another. They need to be attuned to values the people desire—to desirable myths. Given this situation, they can release creativity and create meaning. They also can stifle creativity and counter the introduction of new knowledge. Deal and Kennedy (1983) reminded us that organizations with strong cultures create rites and rituals of behavior in organizational life to influence the way we do something. They also can specify what the organization will not or does not do. Rituals confirm and interpret values and operationalizes them.

Some people react negatively to prescribing rituals in detail. They claim they are authoritarian. The reverse also can be true and is more likely. Rituals, like laws and rules, are liberating, since they define a set of agreed-upon ground rules for behavior.

Rituals are most often unwritten rules of personal communication. They take a lot of organizational time. They let people know where they stand in the group, and they reinforce individual identity and relationships. Rituals signal to the outside world just how strong and valuable the culture is.

### Cults

Cults are closed-off, self-contained social entities that demand one's total agreement. Cults ask members to affirm their membership is some overt ways, for example by asking members to displace all other rules and laws for the prevailing social system culture. The cult aspect of culture further separates members from other available cultures. This feature of organizational culture has a binding effect on members. It bonds them in specific, if sometimes dysfunctional, ways.

Cults within our larger organizations can represent dysfunctional enclaves within which individuals can find support for aberrant organizational actions. These cult subcultures can become major problems for parent-organization leaders. They can become opposing power centers challenging formal leadership; on the other hand, they can be a positive part of organizational life, if they function to provide focal points for innovation. Cults can help leaders by pointing out new directions or in focusing organizationally beneficial energies toward specific problem-solving tasks.

### Customs and Conventions

A custom is a habit in which sufficient members agree. A custom can appear as a convention but it is actually a lesser act—the result of passive acceptance rather than the imposition of active design. A convention is not a custom but is active, volitional. A custom is more passive.

Both customs and conventions are supported by explicit values. Conventions are made by common consent. It is a social agreement we all make to act "as if." Culture is, as Thoreau said, making the earth say beans instead of grass.

Culture, then, is a social pattern we have chosen to make conventional because we prefer this pattern over whatever the raw world proffers. And conventions are usually accepted by members of the culture so the agreement is widely operative.

### Heros

Heros are people who personify organizational values and epitomize the strength(s) of the organization. Cultural leaders use heros, or stories about heros, to motivate others. Heros can be founding fathers of the organization, present or past top executives, or common workers. In any case, heros reflect shared values in their behavior (Deal and Kennedy, 1983; Ott, 1989).

## Humor

Humor showcases cultural values, in that it helps determine hierarchical relationships of domination and submission. It has an "as if" function also. Humor lets us assume something stands for something else in the situation. It can mute strong emotions or reinforce them. Humor integrates otherwise disparate groups; humor can express skepticism. It can contribute to desired goals of flexibility and adaptability. Who uses humor and who cannot, who can make light of whom, what humor is about, all show the status of the user of humor.

Humor socializes; it conveys membership. It can help sustain and establish solidarity. It is a face-saving tool, and it is a way to show arbitrariness in a situation. Humor is a little used, but powerful tool leaders can use to gain control over a situation or group, to socialize new members, and to gain or retain desired results.

## Ideology

Ideology is a set of beliefs about the social world and how it operates. They are beliefs, moral principles, and values that provide the basis for an organization. An organization's ideology contains statements about the rightness of certain social arrangements and what action members should undertake in the light of these statements. It mobilizes consciousness and action by connecting social burdens with general ethical principles (Pettigrew, 1979).

A strong ideology serves to define relationships with outsiders and proscribes relationships with group members. It unifies, motivates, and commits members and is the map guiding their behavior in task activity, decision making, and in interpersonal relationships.

## Language and Jargon

Organizations often take special words as their own, give them particularized meanings, and imbue them with unique connotations. Jargon is a particularized form of this type of usage to convey special meanings to members of the group. This special language serves as a kind of verbal shorthand to let members communicate easier and more completely. It also can take on an exclusionary character. Failure to understand the organizational jargon quickly identifies strangers and isolates them.

### Metaphors and Myths

Metaphors are things that stand for something else. They play an "as if" function, simplifying complex, ambiguous issues. They make the strange familiar.

Myths are extended metaphors—expressive forms of language that communicate symbolic meaning beyond the obvious content of the words (Ott, 1989). A myth is like a story or legend in its content and purpose, often explaining the origins or transformation of something. Myths also communicate unquestioned belief about the practical benefits of certain techniques and behaviors that may not be supported by facts.

All organizations have myths (Clark, 1972). Myths play a crucial role in the continuous process of establishing and maintaining what is legitimate and what is unacceptable in the organization (Cohan, 1969). Myths provide explanations, reconcile contradictions, and resolve dilemmas (Cohan, 1969). They are often thought of in negative terms—it's only a myth. Myths can be resistant to change and prevent organizational adaptation; however, they may also communicate significant truths. Shared myths make it easier to develop internal cohesion and direction.

Myths are unique to the organization. They relate to specific past events or historical people. It would be difficult to provide specific examples of organizational myths, since the reader would need context-specific background information or experience to interpret precise meanings and implications. There are, however, a few general organizational myths that have helped shape our theory and practice. For example, the myth of managerial infallibility suggests that whatever the manager says or does is right. Similarly, there is the myth of the primacy of organizational health. This myth suggests that organizational health and survival is the primary goal, value, and measure of one's action. In actuality, both of these ideas are only partially true all of the time, and not always true. Yet they shape our ideas about the organization and its leaders and condition what group members do, say, and even what they think.

Myths or metaphors are not subject to proofs like theories. Myths arise to protect people from uncertainty. We can think of metaphors and myths as weapons used by people and groups to justify public and private stances and affirm wavering power positions. Myths impart values, justify extant positions, and reconcile differences.

People use myths to explain and express ideas and to maintain solidarity and cohesion, to legitimize their position on an issue, and to communicate unconscious wishes and conflicts. Myths and metaphors are also used on occasion to mediate contradictions and to provide narrative to anchor the present in the past or to bridge past and present.

Myths and metaphors serve two purposes. First, they are used to blind others to new ideas, information, or opportunities. Second, they allow us to ignore reality (e.g., the myth of planned change, the myth of the expert, or the myth of the one best way). Many people believe their organizational myths even in the face of concrete contrary evidence. Often they are necessary to ensure meaning, solidarity, stability, or certainty.

Myths arrange themes that in reality are unacceptable or bipolar into holistic units. They remove matter from the current agenda and place it in the realm of the mystical or traditional. Myths forestall social crisis by providing explanations for causes, meanings, and results that otherwise might be inexplicable.

### Physical Artifacts

Artifacts are the material objects that surround people physically and provide them with immediate sensory stimuli. They carry out culturally expressive activities. Artifacts include buildings, logos, office layout, and furnishings. Artifacts are symbols that convey to members what is important to management and what makes an organization different from others.

While a definite part of culture, artifacts may have less impact on member behavior than more mental elements of the culture (Schein, 1985). The technical, artistic, and physical environment created by human beings have a role in conditioning human behavior. They reflect the values of culture members, and in some degree, they rank those values. They contribute to the definition of a given culture and are instrumental in communicating that culture to others over time and space.

### Play

Play is what people do when they are not working. Play can connote aggression, competition, and struggle; it can convey either work or leisure. We can engage in any activity playfully (Batten, 1989). He says play lets us treat goals as hypotheses, treat intuition as real, or hypocrisy as transition. Play treats memory as an enemy and experience as a theory.

### Relationships

Culture defines the intra- and interorganizational relationship patterns of its people and other stakeholders. It prescribes who talks to whom, who listens to whom, and even what is said. Culture formalizes interpersonal interactivity in more powerful, if more subtle, ways than formal authority patterns.

### Stories

One important way to think of culture is understanding an organization as a complex of the possible meanings people ascribe to organizational events (Taylor and Novelli, 1991). Stories help a newcomer to an organization find out what meaning members give to particular events. They are symbolic of some quality of the organization, such as its effectiveness, its values, or its creativity. Organizational stories are narratives based on true events but often combining truth and fiction.

Stories about people or organizational events enliven the dimensions of organizational cultural. They are symbolic of some quality of the organization, such as its effectiveness, its values, or its creativity. Stories are "evidence" of some unique quality that epitomizes an organization.

Most organizational stories contain one or more of at least three general themes: (1) the value of equality, (2) how the organization helps employees and gives them security, and (3) how people cope with internal or external obstacles and still maintain control.

Stories actually convey information, morals, values, and myths vividly. When present in an organization, they describe events in easily remembered ways. They summarize key ideas and detail and present a clear, simple message to both insiders and outsiders. They focus on problems of morale, socialization, and legitimacy and reflect and reinforce faith and belief in the program. They can also obscure failure of bad programs. Regardless of focus, stories codify collective meaning.

There are several kinds of stories potentially present in any organization's culture. Sagas and legends are types of stories with a historical twist that describes unique group or leader accomplishments. Group members hand down narratives of some wonderful event based in history but sometimes embellished by fictional events. Sagas and legends are collections of stories about the organization's history that provide useful information about current organizational culture and behavior. Critical incidents sometimes develop into organizational legends or folklore. Folklore dramatizes what an organization really wants, how it defines itself, and how members can progress or stay out of trouble. Stories are unwritten rules of the organizational game.

Scenarios are another form of story that provide direction for action in uncharted and seemingly uncharitable terrain. Scenarios are a kind of future story about the organization's potential. Organizational fairy tales comfort, reassure, and offer general directions and hope for the future. They externalize inner conflicts and tensions and fulfill a wishful dream. They also entertain or give security. Organizational fairy tales are a form of propaganda in that they convey data to both insiders and outsiders.

A good story must have several qualities. It must be told broadly. The audience intended must know the story and know that others know it also. This helps the story be repeated, commented upon, and magnified symbolically. It must be vivid, be about a person or people, and have a strong sense of time and place. It should be told in vivid language—dramatized. It must inspire by teaching—provide enough information to define the whole and provide a suggestion of how one should act in view of the story. It must claim uniqueness—imply that the organization is a unique place to work.

Stories help us understand how the organizational members decide, assign resources, and cooperate in shared value terms and are consistent with their shared vision of the future. They substitute for leadership in some real ways. An event is changed into an organizational story if it meets the above criteria, does not contradict other messages stakeholders are receiving, and is continually retold—usually in oral form. A story can play a role in shaping organization culture. If the leader originates some of the organizational stories, he or she is shaping the culture.

### Symbols

Symbols are any object, art, event, quality, or relation that serves as a vehicle for conveying meaning, usually representing something else. They also can be objects, acts, or linguistic formations that stand for any of several meanings, evoke emotions, and impel people to action (Cohan, 1974). Symbols in organizational culture include facility architecture, office arrangements, the organization's name, subunit titles, and its attitudes toward outsiders. How we place chairs in our meetings can have symbolic meaning. All of the physical environmental features within which we do work can carry symbolic meaning and is a part of organizational culture. Who gets invited to meetings has symbolic meaning, as well as the order of the agenda, its content, and the items left off.

People create symbols to cope with uncertainty, confusion, and chaos. Symbols are helpful to counter uncertainty and give it structure, even if the structure is not fully accurate with reality. Deal (1986) suggests that symbolism gives leaders the ability to be out of control comfortably. It lets leaders accept surprise occasionally, but surprise within the parameters of mutual symbols of what is acceptable and appropriate.

One perspective from which to analyze and understand organizational behavior is by the symbols used (Bolman and Deal, 1987). We can analyze organizations by reference to structure, people, or the symbols they use. The symbolic frame of reference differs from the other more traditional, rational foundations. It is a political process. It focuses on meanings of events, not necessarily on their causes or system. It counterposes a set of concepts that cope with the complexity and ambiguity of organizational life and mediates the meaning of organizational events and activities.

Rational structural and human resource models of organization work in routine times. They are not so useful when dealing with complex, ambiguous, and uncertain situations. In these kinds of situations, symbolization can be an effective means of gaining insight into organizational operations. The symbolic frame of reference is proper when the organization's goals are unclear, technology is uncertain or changing, and when it is in the midst of change. These factors are present in some degree in all organizations. The symbolic reference frame centers on concepts of meaning, belief, and trust.

We can understand something of how communication works as we analyze the symbols we use (Berlo, 1960). When we think of an event or something concrete, the brain deals with it symbolically. We think by reasoning with these abstract ideas or objects rather than by trial and error. The brain uses words as symbols of concrete events. The marvel of the brain respecting information processing is its ability to deal with symbols. Symbolization is the ability of the brain to represent an experience when the stimulus itself is absent.

A symbol is anything in our minds that stand for something else: words, diagrams, drawings, and events (e.g., the return of the robins symbolizes spring). A sign is also a symbol to people. Indeed, one aspect of a definition of culture is that culture is a system of signs signifying specific objects, ideas, and ideologies. A sign is a symbol of a physical object or event whose function is to represent some other thing or event.

Language is such a sign. Language is a common symbol and as such is an aspect of culture. It can typify and stabilize experience and integrate disparate experiences into a meaningful whole (Berger, 1966). Language embodies implicit exhortations and social evaluations as well as communicates simple meanings.

Every organization has its icons, or its symbols, in the form of ideas, words, objects, processes, and relationships that its leaders use to represent aspects of the organization's culture, values, or future vision. These symbols define the character of the organization more than do organization charts or policy statements or procedure manuals. In large part, leadership is the use of cultural symbols, legends, and traditions.

Leaders are symbol users. According to Bennis (1982), leadership is effective when leaders place symbolic value on their intentions. By using symbols, the leader engages the heart as well as the head and the hand of followers. There is little specific guidance for the leader in most leadership texts on using symbols. Anecdotal evidence suggests that most leaders make conscious use of symbols to help them attain their goals (Fairholm, 1991). President Clinton's bus ride from Charlottesville to Washington on his inaugural did little to advance critical national program improvements directly. It did not create jobs, solve our health care crisis, or reduce the national debt. As a symbol of the values of the new administration, it symbolized an executive branch focus on traditional values and approaches. The use of symbol is an area for additional attention as leaders attempt to improve their leadership behaviors.

Symbols focus attention in emotional, sometimes dramatic, ways. By the same token, whatever a leader concentrates on can become a symbol of that individual's leadership style. Surely symbols communicate priority. Use of one or a few key symbols lets coworkers become aware of these leader obsessions. Once followers understand the symbolic message, the organization can operate in desired ways without close supervision or management.

The words leaders use and promulgate throughout the organization, that is, the jargon characteristic of a given organization, is symbolic. Referring to customers as associates or to supervisors as colleagues, symbolizes a value focus about those served. This symbolic language can be a strong force in the organization to either stabilize or change present behavior. The symbolism in this kind of language use is obvious and effective in changing people's perception of themselves and their role in the organization.

Important words are not as potent as actions in rewarding some kinds of behavior and not others. For example, a leader's promotion record is an effective and accurate symbol of what he or she thinks is important. Promotions signal what behavior we value most. Who a leader promotes communicates the leader's true interest and is the most accurate measure of what kind of follower behavior he or she values.

Similarly, how leaders organize space is symbolic. It communicates in concrete terms the values held by the leader. The de facto policy implicit in the allocation of an organization's resources also can be symbols of larger, more basic values held by that organization's leaders. Who gets company cars, window offices, or which functional work units get the larger share of budget says much about what people and what functions leaders value most and who they trust. Who leaders talk to, eat with, avoid, and emulate helps followers know what they value.

### Values

Values define both expectation and actual experience (Schein, 1985). A culture's ideology, moral code, and ethics are grounded in the core values espoused by the group. They characterize human experience and give meaning to that experience. For these reasons, Ott (1989) ranked the group's values system as an important dimension in defining and differentiating cultures.

### Vision

Vision dramatizes the stated purposes of the organization, but more important, it represents the system of beliefs and language that give the organization texture and coherence. In this sense, it is also a cultural symbol. Vision implies an almost sacred quality of the organization. It uses distinctive language to define roles, activities, challenges, and purposes. It creates patterns of meanings and consciousness defined as the organizational culture.

Vision raises the consciousness level of the organization's people. The vision statement is simple, symbolic, and ambiguous but appeals to the emotions of the reader. It is a potent mechanism for directing and influencing others.

## SUMMARY

Culturally the organization is a complex, value-laden entity that shapes member behavior in a wide variety of ways. Features of organizational culture like those identified in this chapter besides defining culture, combine to constrain member behavior. These cultural components are perhaps more powerful in shaping member values and actions than more traditional organizational features such as structure, system, and procedures. Leadership must include leader efforts to manage these cultural components.

# PART IV

# THE LEADERSHIP OF TRUST

As seen in the discussion in Parts I, II, and III, organizational culture and the leadership of culture are important to understanding organizational dynamics. Cultural leadership engages leaders in more than system, structure, and strategy formation. It involves them also in shaping the social, emotional, and spiritual dimensions of interpersonal work relationships. These aspects of organizational life may be far more significant than heretofore thought. And, importantly, they may be far more susceptible to orchestration by leaders to the mutual benefit of leader, follower, and organizational goal attainment.

The discussion thus far has described critical leader activities and responsibilities in shaping the culture to the special needs of an organization, its work goals, and its personal and institutional vision. Part IV directs attention to a special aspect of culture formation: creating a culture that is supportive of interactive trust among leaders and organizational stakeholders. The element of trust in a culture is critical to leader success in attaining both personal and organizational ends. No collaborative work can be done over time without some measure of interpersonal trust. It is a necessary and essential element of any culture.

Trust is central to leadership in organizations because followers are people who *choose* to follow leaders. They are not forced to do so. The trust of followers allows leaders to lead. Low trust cultures reduce the willingness of members to follow. Therefore, these low trust cultures necessitate use of control mechanisms to secure member compliance. That is, low trust cultures force us to manage, not lead.

Direct treatment of the element of trust in organizational life is rare in the organizational behavioral literature. Trust has not been given much specific attention by either the theoretical or practicing professionals. Material that is available focuses on the trustworthiness of the individual leader. There is little on how trust is created and used and less on how to create trusting cultures.

The purpose of Part IV is to facilitate understanding and application of the ideas of trust building to the critical tasks of culture creation and leadership. It summarizes and extends recent renewed attention to the idea of trust in organizational life. The current literature suggests that a given cultural situation defines and delimits the nature and extent of member trust. Unfortunately, neither the present theories of culture and trust clearly define trust as an element in the cultural surround. Nor does it provide us with guidance in increasing trust or directing available levels of trust to the leader's personal and group goals.

Yet trust is central in understanding the pull of culture on individual actions. Organizational culture establishes a paradigm that provides an assured basis for action. The cultures we create allow us to behave with varying levels of assurance that certain actions or events will produce known results. The cultures leaders create produce a trust situation in which we can trust certain actions to produce certain results. It also prescribes our willingness to trust. One culture may allow us to trust others more or less than another, but without the constraints imposed by the cultural features noted in Parts II and III, we could not exercise trust at all.

Culture affects willingness to trust, and willingness to trust helps define culture. This little homily may be obvious as stated, but there is little in the theory of culture that helps us define and place in context the element of trust in culture formation and maintenance. The chapters in Part IV define and place the idea of trust in context. They relate it to the general definitional and contextual material provided in the previous chapters.

Trust is the glue holding the organization and its programs and people together. It is the prime mechanism for group cohesion. Indeed, no organization can take place without interpersonal trust, and no organizational leader can ignore the powerful element of trust as he or she creates and manages his or her organization's culture and induces stakeholders to behave in needed ways.

Leaders build trust, or tear it down, by the cumulative actions they take and the words they speak—by the culture they create for themselves and their organization's members. They come to trust others based on the developing record of authenticated reality built up in their interactions with followers. The cumulative effect of a given culture is to define a specific level and quality of interpersonal trust between stakeholders.

Trust is a risk relationship, but a necessary one. When we trust another person it places us at some risk of loss of control. The risk is always present in trusting others or in relying on given systems or policies or procedures or specific structural forms that they will not behave as expected. In essence when we trust another person, event, or thing, we agree to rely on the authenticity of that person, event, or thing.

In theory, we do not need to trust in situations of absolute knowledge of the truth of a given person, action, or event. In these cases, there is no risk, we *know*. Such absolute knowledge, however, is rarely present in most organizations. Leaders rarely can rely on this level of mutual understanding of the reality of a situation; hence, the need for cultures that support a high degree of trust.

We define trust in chapter 8 as reliance on the integrity, or authenticity, of other people. It is a logical, thoughtful hope in their reality, their authenticity, their truth. Trust becomes both an expectation and a personal obligation to be authentic, trustworthy, and reliable, which is provable by ensuing experience. Seen in this light, trust is one of the values supporting a given culture that helps define how and in what degree members value others.

Trust places obligation on both the truster and the person in whom we place our trust. It is the foundation of success in any interpersonal relationship. While organizational theory assumes, but largely ignores the idea of trust, nevertheless, it is integral to that set of interpersonal relationships.

Trust implies proactivity. When we trust another we act toward that person with assurance, even when we do not have all needed or desired information about them. With trust we can function in an otherwise unknown, ambiguous, even risky, situation. With trust we can take control of a situation or circumstance. Without trust the individual has no power in relationships, no control over other people not actually in sight. Trust is central to cultural ideas of empowerment, expectation, and predictability.

Success in our social or organizational life is based on trust in someone or something however intangible and ambiguous it or they may be. Without at least some assurance that the unknown information, actions, events are real, trust is extremely risky. That kind of trust is, in fact, not trust at all, but foolhardiness. The fact is that all life (that is, personal as well as institutional life) is always more or less unknown. Trust represents our best guess—and hope—that things are in truth as they appear to be.

Trust is transforming. It is a process of change. Having trust in a person or something (we believe to be true) impels (empowers) us to change. It lets us act out of that trust. Properly placed trust empowers us, misplaced trust spells defeat.

Trusting others is not simple or fast. It takes time fully to trust a person or group. It is an incremental process. Each successful attempt is immediately reinforcing the trust. Successive positive experiences with another cumulate until we come fully to trust that person. Negative trust experiences produces the opposite result.

Trust and trustworthiness are closely related. The less trusting a person is, the less others trust that person. And the reverse is also true; the more we trust, the more others trust us. Trust is a learned capacity and the best teacher is example. The bottom line appears to be: If you want someone to trust you, you have to tell them the truth, act on that truth consistently, and then patiently wait for the relationship to mature. A practical, operationally useful description of trust in formal and informal interpersonal situations is explained and related to the overarching concept of cultural leadership.

Chapter 7 begins the discussion by defining the role of trust in theory and in operations. Sections of chapter 7 relate the act of trusting to the several cultural determinants critical to success as a leader. It connects the trust relationship to features of the situation coming out of the leader's prior efforts to manage the culture. This chapter provides an awareness of elements of the trust culture and the critical role leaders play in forming trust cultures.

Chapter 8 defines and places trust in proper perspective. Trust is a universal idea. We all know intuitively what it is to trust and be trusted. But defining it operationally is difficult because the idea of trust permeates all that we do and are.

Trust is a unifying and coalescing idea. Without it, the idea of joint, cooperative action would be unthinkable, let alone practical. Chapter 8 relates the idea of trust to culture creation and leadership in concrete ways. Since trust and truth are interrelated concepts, the essential truth we come to believe about another person or thing is the basis of our trust. Trust becomes more powerful than charisma, blind faith, or the threat of punishment or the promise of reward. Trust in the essential truth about another person or thing, not a leap of blind faith, impels us to action. The sense of chapter 8 is that organizations with high trust levels are more competent and more unified than other organizations. This unity eases leadership and vision accomplishment.

Chapter 9 explores the process of developing and using trust in organizations. It describes the process of trusting and identifies some salient characteristics of a trust culture. It describes some personal behaviors conducive to building trust and suggests details of the interpersonal process of trust building. This chapter provides a working list of trust tools leaders and followers can use to encourage trust and build a cultural environment supportive of high trust levels.

Some level of trust is essential, and present, in any cultural grouping. The exact level and nature of the trust relationship, however, varies with the organization. Chapter 10 identifies and briefly discusses a variety of factors in the culture that may limit trust.

Among the potential problems leaders face in creating and maintaining a trust culture are those dealing with the emotions of followers. Feelings of apathy and alienation in the larger society sometimes seeps into the organization's culture and causes similar emotions among the workers there. Personal self-interest may hamper development of a fully trusting culture. In addition, the personal and institutional risk of loss or failure to meet necessary goals may constrain full trust.

Sections in chapter 10 also deal with issues of trust as a factor in communication, in using authority, and in turning around an organization with an institutional history of distrust. Past events have a powerful affect on our willingness to trust. Past overreliance on office politics or leader inconsistency in trusting followers or other erratic leader behavior affects present trust levels and are hard to change. In these situations, an enduring trust relationship may be hard to create.

The general decay of moral values, the fear others will see us as gullible, and the fact that building trust takes a lot of time also works against development of a trust culture. The lack of effective accountability mechanisms is also cited as a reason for lack of trust in some organizations.

# 7

# Leadership and Trust

## INTRODUCTION

We build our lives on trust relationships. The cultures we are members of—organizational, social, political—define its quality and extent. Our actions apply it in everything we do or say. We trust others to obey basic traffic rules. We trust stores to honor our credit cards. We trust maintenance people to repair our household appliances. Indeed, all aspects of the working relationship—our organizational work cultures—are based on trust of others.

Much of American culture today is fragmented and conflict ridden. Leadership in this kind of environment requires adherence to ethical principles that highlight trust (Maccoby, 1981). Sadly, people appear to have lost confidence in their leaders and in the programs they lead. We see this confidence gap today in business, in government agencies, in education, and even in our churches, especially the televangelists.

This general distrust of our social leaders and institutions points to a cultural breakdown. We have lost the sense of community that former trust cultures provided. Now people are together as individuals, not as a community. Many of our organizations, even our families, lack the cohesion that mutual trust provides. One result is that many people suffer from isolation, anomie, and anxiety. Unless workers trust not only leaders' motives, but also their ability to lead, they will not follow (Hitt, 1988).

Lipset and Schneider (1987) suggest that this distrust of leadership is endemic. Our national character—shaped by our national culture—tends toward distrust of leaders. Americans generally are suspicious of the

*distrust*

motives of those in authority. Especially today, we distrust the political, social, and economic leaders and their operating systems to deal effectively with our complex and multidifferentiated society. Our basic, almost intuitive, distrust of our leaders has made leadership more difficult and maybe even impossible. As noted, the problem is not a lack of leaders, but a lack of trusting environments within which leadership is possible and without which it is impossible.

## LEADERSHIP AND TRUST

The thrust of leadership today is toward seeing the leader as a developer, not a controller, of followers (Fairholm, 1991). The leadership task is developmental and integrative. The challenge is to mold followers into a unified, balanced whole capable of sustained cooperative action. We can view this task as physical, that is, structural, or we can see it in the psychological or social contracts leaders and followers make.

In the past, reliance on structural form or work flow processes have improved efficiency. This focus alone largely ignores the sociopsychological dimensions of organizational life. This is the cultural dimension. It is in this dimension of group interrelationships that we can find the solution to many contemporary problems.

An always present, but often overlooked, factor in our group and organizational relationships is trust. Unless followers feel confidence in the leader's fairness and trustworthiness, they will not continue to follow (Vanfleet and Yukl, 1989). Leadership technologies can only operate when trust among members in relationship is high. Trust can significantly alter individual and organizational effectiveness (Golembiewski, 1983). It is trust more than power or hierarchy that really makes an organization function effectively (Barnes, 1981).

Trust is a critical definitional element in defining modern leadership or cultures that sustain effective leadership. Indeed, it is a key ingredient in all human interaction. Daily living requires us to trust those around us. Organizations also require members to trust each other in order to function, let alone attain excellence.

Trust is prerequisite to any attempt by the leader to transform or change his or her organization's culture (Sashkin, 1986). Vision setting and dissemination depends on trust in the leader. Carrying out vision-based programs requires trust. Trust is the salient factor in determining effectiveness in many relationships (Zand, 1972). Trust makes interpersonal acceptance and openness of expression easy. Mistrust evokes interpersonal rejection and arouses defensive behavior. Trusting behavior increases one's vulnerability to another in ways and in circumstances in which the risk is greater than the potential outcome to the trusting person.

Trust is a conscious realization of one's dependence on another person. It is a central factor in understanding culture's impact on group members. Leaders need to be aware of the existence and the potential significance of trust in established cultural beliefs and norms systems. They should learn to identify and alter those cultural norms that act to limit trust. Once shaped,. cultural values and norms provide the base against which we can measure changes in organizational activities and assess potential changes to determine the level of interactive trust. Trust can help us lessen conflicts and avoid potential conflicts before dysfunctional behavior takes place.

Rogers (1964) said the quality of trust is the most significant interpersonal element in determining effectiveness. He said that the basic nature of people who function freely in interpersonal relationships is constructive and trustworthy. We can measure this interpersonal quality by the congruence of the communications so both are genuine and open. Rogers also suggested that helping relationships are a function of the empathy of the participants and the positive regard each has for the other. These factors relate directly to trust. They are also key to understanding a given culture.

Rogers defined a two-way trust relationship as simply expressing trust in others and receiving trust from others. One without the other aborts the trust relationship. This suggests that leaders can generate a climate of trust when they can trust first. This task is difficult because many leaders and followers see the relationship as that of a parent-child, where trust is only given upward. On the other hand, Culbert (1970) said leaders need to develop trust before they begin problem solving or other significant activity.

Gibb (1964a) listed trust (acceptance of the communication of others) as the most important of four common concerns in interrelationships (the other three are data flow, goal formation, and control). To Gibb, trust and acceptance of self as a leader must precede acceptance and trust of others.

Kostenbaum (1991) presented a diamond theory of leadership composed of four points: vision, ethical behavior, reliability, and courage. These factors provide a culture within which both leader and follower can commit to each other. The combination of these four characteristics lead to trust, the critical element in leadership theory and practice. Where trust is present, leadership can take place. Where it is missing, we lose the ability to lead. A well-known example is the Nixon White House.

## IMPACT OF TRUST ON THE INDIVIDUAL

A critical factor in culture management and in a leader's attempt to change values and attitudes is the quality of the trust relationship present and accepted by members. How the individual relates to others is critical to organizational success in whatever functional or task area, and the key element in these relationships is trust.

If followers consider their leaders trustworthy, they will probably have faith in their orders, instructions, values, and visions. If the necessary trust is lacking, leaders will find it difficult to have their ideas accepted. This is true regardless of the intrinsic utility of those ideas.

Recently, the level of trust in the leaders of our public institutions has deteriorated (Shaver, 1980). We criticize most of our traditional leaders—doctors, politicians, teachers, the police, even the clergy. We show more trust in institutions than in leaders in America, and even that focus of trust is deteriorating. While we criticize our leaders, we continue to show trust in our immediate associates—the people we deal with daily. The implication is that social cohesion is breaking down. The decline of traditional social institutions, such as the family and church, increase the reliance we have on the workplace to fulfill needs once met in these other institutions (Britton and Stallings, 1986).

Shaver (1980) attributed this lack of trust to unrealistic expectations about our leaders and the unwillingness of leaders to stand behind controversial public issues. Shaver's work suggests that the higher the level of education the more trusting one is. It also suggests that white Americans are more trusting of their colleagues than Afro-Americans. To turn around this general slide, our organization's leaders need to nurture cultures that emphasize trust relationships based on shared values visibly used. The value of mutual trust is key here.

## CRISIS OF TRUST

Despite this need there is a low level of trust in our social institutional cultures (Beck and Hillmar, 1989). Barnes (1981) suggested that the failure of many of our organizations and managers is a result of the tendency to think in either/or terms. He says it is a natural tendency to assume that important issues fall into conflicting camps. Also, we have grown accustomed to the thinking that hard facts are better than soft ideas and speculation, and we assume that the world in general is unsafe—that we have to distrust the universe around us. These three ideas drive our organizations and help shape contemporary cultures. Unfortunately, these ideas do not produce trust, which is the prime human relationships system that holds an organization together. This situation creates a crisis of culture.

Our recent national history is a history of real or perceived crises of trust. Former president Jimmy Carter identified a crisis of confidence in America that permeated all social institutions. As president, Ronald Reagan referred to a pervasive cynicism in America about its place in the world and the competence of its leaders. Both former president George Bush and President Bill Clinton based their presidential campaigns on a pervasive need to change and renew the institutions of government and society.

We can list many examples of recent events that have served to stress the crisis of trust in America. The following list, while by no means inclusive, is illustrative:

Watergate

Vietnam War

Iran hostage crisis

Savings and loan crisis

Tragic Challenger space shuttle mission

Civil rights

Iran-Contra

Corruption in government/business

Decline in American industrial productivity

Notwithstanding this litany of crises, trust is still at the heart of our organizational/institutional success. Barnes (1981) said that we determine organizational satisfaction more by the level of trust present than other factors. With trust, the immediate environment is more important than either our background or our perceptions. It sets the expectations and sanctions right behavior.

## ELEMENTS OF THE TRUST RELATIONSHIP

Developing a trust culture is critical to the success of the leader. Defining trust is, however, difficult. Even casual observation suggests that the elements of trust are many and varied, and precise analyses are scarce. Table 7.1 illustrates the key elements in a trust relationship and, therefore, of the definition of trust. Each of these factors are explained in this section. Indeed, there is only a small amount of research literature on the theoretical and operational element of developing intimate trust relationships with another person. We know even less about the intricacies of development and maintenance of a trust culture. It is encouraging, however, to note that more people are beginning to recognize the need to understand trust as an element of culture. The research cited in this book is illustrative of a spate of research findings that are beginning to become available. They draw on older, largely, ignored findings and recent syntheses, as well as add to the overall body of knowledge.

The following ideas, drawn from experiential as well as literature

**Table 7.1**
**Elements of a Trust Relationship**

| | |
|---|---|
| ACCEPTANCE | OF SELF AND OTHERS |
| | OF GROUPMADE DECISIONS |
| | OF GROUP AIMS |
| | OF INTRA- AND INTERPERSONAL CONTROL |
| | OF THE NEED TO PARTICIPATE IN GROUP ACTION |
| | OF DIFFERENCE IN OTHERS |
| ASSUMPTIONS | ISSUES FALL INTO TWO OPPOSING CAMPS EXEMPLIFIED BY: EITHER-OR THINKING, HARD DATA DRIVES OUR SOFT, AND THE WORLD IS UNSAFE OR SAFE |
| AUTHENTIC CARING | PERSONAL INTEREST |
| | OPENNESS TO OTHERS |
| | WILLINGNESS TO RISK CLOSE RELATIONSHIPS |
| | WILLINGNESS TO SERVE OTHERS |
| ETHICS | PEER RELATIONSHIPS |
| | ORGANIZATIONAL PRACTICES |
| | FISCAL POLICY |
| | THE MORAL VALUES OF THE LARGER SOCIETY |
| LEADERSHIP | PREDICTABILITY |
| | CONSISTENCY |
| | COOPERATION |
| | SERVICE ORIENTATION |
| INDIVIDUAL CHARACTER | EXPECT TRUST |
| | EXPECT HONESTY IN OTHERS |
| | EXPECT SPONTANEOUS BEHAVIOR IN OTHERS |
| | EXPECT OPENNESS (NOT DEFENSIVENESS) |
| PREDICTABILITY | CONSISTENCY OF ACTION |
| | CONFIDENCE |
| | ACTIONS ARE BASED ON TRUTH |

sources, may help codify this emerging dimension of organizational life and leadership. It is interesting to note the close congruence of these trust elements and the main features of culture defined in Parts II and III. Culture and trust appear to be comparable in definition and result.

## Acceptance

We do not have to pay back trust given freely, unconditionally (Lagenspetz, 1992). As mentioned before, Gibb (1964a) identified four dimensions of trust: acceptance, data flow, goal formation, and control. Acceptance is the center piece of his model. Acceptance has to do with the formation of trust and acceptance of self and of others. Acceptance of self reduces fear of personal failure and of the negative actions of others. It also produces a consequent growth of confidence.

Gibb's other dimensions relate to acceptance also. Data flow deals with the flow of feeling and perceptual data through the person and through the group. This concern finds its expression in acceptance of decisions made. Goal formation concerns the continuous assessment of intrinsic motivations in the person or the group and integration of individual motives into actions to support group aims. Control has to do with inter- and intrapersonal control or regulatory mechanisms that facilitate cooperative and coordinated effort among individuals in the group. These four dimensions are continuingly recurring themes or processes in groups.

Rosen and Jerdee (1977) surveyed 148 business students. They determined that willingness to accept and participate in group task accomplishment is a function of the trust levels of subordinates. Subordinate job level and minority status are key determinants of the level of trust displayed in organizations. Low-level employees and minorities are statistically less willing to trust management and therefore accept unconditionally the need to participate freely in joint endeavors. Higher level workers and those not in the minority are more willing to accept group goals and expend energy to participate.

## Assumptions

According to Barnes (1981), people behave according to their assumptions of how the world works. For him, important issues naturally fall into two opposing camps exemplified by either/or thinking: (1) hard data and facts are better than soft ideas or speculation, and (2) the world in general is an unsafe-safe place. Acting on our assumptions in these areas pull us away from full trust in another's actions, words, or statements. When we act outside the parameters of these assumptions we can increase the level of trust in our organizations. When others see our initial behavior as predictable and caring, they can develop positive assumptions about the interactivity. These positive assumptions about the future are the basis of hope that accompanies trust.

### Authentic Caring

Trust creates a perception among followers that their leaders authentically care for them (Gibb, 1978b). Trusting followers come to see their leaders as open, personally interested, and worthy of their trust. While openness is a risk relationship, a leader's willingness to be open enhances his or her inherent trustworthiness. Fairholm (1991) said trust protects and enhances the dignity of followers. Caring leader behavior communicates the leader's willingness to serve the needs of followers. As this value becomes a part of the organizational ethos, the culture changes and becomes more open to interpersonal trust.

### Ethical Considerations

We base our trust in others on mutual confidence and in our relationships with them. We can connect several issues with mutual confidence on the job. One issue has to do with the presumed linkage between ethical conduct and trust within the organization. We distribute ethical codes and standards on the assumption that they improve trust performance within an organization. Some observers contend that ethical codes also improve an organization's external image.

A variety of cultural forces shape a leader's ethical values and in turn are shaped by the leader's values. Among these forces are peer relations, traditional organizational practices, financial policy, the general social morality of the surrounding community, and organizational policy. How do we (or can we) hold individuals responsible on an ethical level given these disparate causes and sources of ethical values? The answer lies partly, at least, in the overarching cultural values present in the organization.

The idea of ethics is imbedded in the ideas of culture, custom, and character (Sims, 1992). Ethical behavior is that behavior group members accept as right and good. In an organization, it is sometimes institutionalized in a document codifying the organization's values and norms. It is also reflected in the institutional structures, interpersonal relationships, and sanction systems. Most often, and most influential, an organization's ethical foundation is a function of the values implicitly revealed in its leadership cadre's actions, decisions, and comments.

Our organizations will take on new character in the coming years as new technology, the push for high quality, a growingly diverse work force, and extension into international markets permeate the workplace.

Each of these changes will place pressure on existing ethical systems and induce change. Ethical leadership in the coming years will be a function of accommodating these new features of organization with a leader's values and those of the followers. This task will involve leaders and followers in working together at the values level, not just at the working level of organizational interactivity.

While the reality of ethical change is clear to the careful observer, the potential for success in ethical leadership in an increasingly different organizational cultural setting is not as clear. As an organization's culture changes, it risks ethical change as well. The task for leaders is to ensure that the values foundation keeps pace. New people with differing ethical standards are coming into the work force. The leadership challenge is to build a new ethics that is founded in the past and is responsive to the future.

Acceptance of every value introduced into the culture by new workers is a formula for failure. There are too many cultures that condone favoritism, bribery, subjugation of the sexes or of the old (or very young), and so forth, to let us accept a new person's values as we accept the new person into our organization. Ethical leadership is a task of setting and enforcing one ethical standard as opposed to all others, some of which may be also good. In this regard, leadership in ethics is the same as cultural leadership. Both ask the leader to articulate a clear, compelling, and useful set of values to guide individual action in the group.

## Leadership

Earning trust is a function of leader-follower interaction. Several factors have been noted by a variety of writers that condition the process of developing trust. Among them the following appear to be key:

1. Predictable leader actions and behavior builds trust (Bennis and Nanus, 1985).
2. Consistent and persistent open communication is essential in the trust-development process.
3. Cooperation is another key to developing trust (Sinatar, 1988).
4. A gentle manner is important and congruent actions, in which word and deed convey the same message, are essential (Sinatar, 1988).
5. A record of service to followers is critical in defining the leader's trust relationship with followers (Greenleaf, 1977).

## Individual Character

We can also view trust as a characteristic of the individual (Klimoski and Karol, 1976). For Klimoski and Karol, trust in others is a way of life for some individuals. They view trust as an expectancy held by an individual that he or she can rely upon the word, promise, or statement of another person. In Klimoski and Karol's model, trusting is a hallmark of a healthy organization.

The level of trust present in a group situation affects the degree of defensiveness present in a group (Gibb, 1961). Meadow, Parnes, and Reese (1959) suggested that a trust culture also affects the degree of problem solving effectiveness of the group. For them, a group member who does not trust others will distort, conceal, or disguise feelings or opinions that he or she believes will increase his or her exposure in the group. They also correlate high trust levels with honesty. High trust levels are critical in situations where spontaneous behavior or frankness is desired.

### Predictability

Predictability is also a building block of trust. Erratic and or irregular behavior limits trust relationships. People appear to trust others only as they can confidently predict what the other person will do in a given situation. Trust and predictability also imply truth. We trust when we are confident that the relationship will produce a true result, giving us what we expect.

### DEVELOPING TRUST

Developing trust is difficult. Haney (1973) said that to trust is to take a chance on the other person. Trust is a risk relationship that increases the truster's vulnerability (Zand, 1972). His work, including a survey of 4,200 supervisors, suggests that high trust relationships stimulate higher performance. Haney revived Rogers's (1964) assertion that we can causally link trust to increased originality and emotional stability.

Trust and distrust is cyclical. The more one trusts, the more trusting the relationship. Alternatively, the more one distrusts others, the more distrust is present. Breaking this cycle is difficult, although two ways are apparent. First, a follower strives to gain a leader's trust. This requires maturity, strength, and perseverance on the part of the follower. Second, leaders give their trust, which also takes strength.

People cannot demand trust of another. It must be earned and developed, which takes time. While leaders can ask others for their trust, they cannot enforce that demand simply because they have the authority to hire and fire. Trust is a gift given freely by others because it is based on their confidence, respect, and admiration for another.

Trust is a range of observable behaviors and a cognitive state that encompasses predictability (Rossiter and Pearch, 1975). Trust behavior is that which shows a willingness to be vulnerable to another. The cognitive trust state is reflected in an attitude of faith or confidence in another person. This faith is such that we believe another person will behave in ways that will not produce negative results for us. Faith is also an unquestioned belief in and reliance on someone or something. We foster faith by open, nondefensive communications. Confidence implies trust based on good reasons, evidence, or experience.

Trust is a condition in which we are willing to share our intimate feelings. It is contingent on several situational contingencies: (1) the trusted person's behavior affects the results of the trust in nontrivial ways; (2) individuals can predict with some accuracy a given behavior or result from a trusted person's actions; and (3) trust is possible when the trusting person can do more than trust, that is, he or she can increase or decrease vulnerability to the other.

Trustworthiness also flows from self-trust: confidence in our own ability, integrity, and ethical fidelity. Self-trust results from several characteristics, including knowledge, responsibility, and faith. Knowledge refers to the stored truth we gain from learning and experience. Responsibility defines an individual's acceptance of accountability for self, work, and other actions. Faith is confidence in the correctness and appropriateness of our course of action and our abilities to attain desired goals. Self-trust produces trust by others. It helps ensure loyalty, cooperation, efficiency, and satisfaction.

## SUMMARY

Our willingness to change depends largely on the trust levels present in our relationships with others in a group (or groups) in which we find ourselves. Feelings of trust develop initially by the way in which two people interact. These feelings become established only after a series of incidents that prove the intrinsic level of trust in the relationship.

Established cultural values also influence the development of feelings of trust. However, it is only though direct interaction that we can develop a deep conviction in others of our basic trustworthiness.

# 8

# Importance of Trust in Organizational Life

## INTRODUCTION AND DEFINITION

Trust is a social expectation. It has to do with our perception of the integrity, justice, caring, and competence of someone or something that is subsequently verified by experience with that person. Trust is a condition of the situation as much as it is of human relationship. The organizational situation also encourages or discourages trust. The expectations and assumptions members hold about how much risk they can (or should) accept in working with others in situations where full knowledge is not present also shapes relationships.

We trust others when they, or the environment, lead us to believe that what they say they will do will eventually come to pass. We can define trust, then, as confidence in the authenticity of the words or actions of a person, or similar qualities or attributes of an organizational symbol, ritual, or something. Defined this way, trust becomes a central element in culture formation and leadership.

To trust another person or thing means that we have confidence that person or thing will prove to be real and that what we see or hope for in or about that person or thing is the truth about them. Trust is a hope in reality based on characteristics and behavior of a person and the situational context. Thus, trust is, or can be, a logical, thoughtful hope or expectation. It need not be blind.

To be useful and sustaining over time, people must base their trust on at least some creditable evidence in an assumed reality of or about a person or thing. This kind of definition of trust, effective trust, conforms to experience. Most dictionaries support this conception of trust. They suggest that trust is a firm belief in the honesty and reliability of some person or something. Trust, as a word and as an idea, connotes feelings of security, confidence, self-reliance, intimacy, and integrity in the absence of hard proof. To be trustworthy is to be a dependable, deserving of confidence, reliable person; one who is faithful, believable, or who others see as having a firm belief in honesty and justice.

Barber (1983) said that trust has to do with the expectations people have about another person or thing. Most of us expect that others will persist and fulfill our perceptions of the natural and social moral order. As Zand (1972) suggested, most Americans define trust as a behavior that conveys useful information, permits shared influence, encourages self-control, and avoids abuse of other's vulnerability. According to Zand, trust also involves the idea of competence. We expect that those we trust, especially our leaders, will be competent to perform in their roles. Most people assume technical competence in our leaders.

Trust follows our acceptance of an assumed truth about another person or thing. Our trust continues and is sustained and enlarged only as future experiences confirm that early perception to be, in fact, correct. That is, trust builds as experience proves the essential truth of our initial perceptions. Trust diminishes by the reverse; as people or things are proved to be less than or different from our initial perceptions, we withdraw out trust.

In essence, trust can only be given; it cannot be commanded. Trusting people are willing volunteers. Trust is an interactive, interdependent process of taking a risk to trust, gaining experience, and then enlarging or diminishing trust as that experience proves our initial perception truthful or not. The key to continued trust relationships is the willingness of people to follow based on their experience with others in the relationship. It is a voluntary, noncompulsory relationship.

## DIMENSIONS OF THE TRUST RELATIONSHIP

From an organizational cultural perspective, to trust our leaders means we expect them to assume a stewardship relationship toward those who follow them. We expect our leaders to work for their followers and to assume this obligation as a primary responsibility. Trusting relationships are characterized in definable ways. For example:

> Trust is a generalized expectancy that we can rely on the word, the promise, the verbal or written statement of another person (Rotter, 1980). It is a particular expectation about the likely behavior of another person (Gambetta, 1988).

> When we trust another we assign trustworthiness to that person (Dasgupta, 1988). Trust involves subtlety, intimacy, and intuition. To trust is to express

confidence in or reliance on some quality or attribute of a person or thing, or the truth of a statement. Trust generates feelings that by trusting we can meet our expectations. It is an expression of our faith in the integrity or strength of the potential behavior of another person (Batten, 1989). This kind of relationship cannot be coerced; it must be earned.

Economically, trust implies a confidence in the ability and intention of someone to deliver agreed goods or services without present payment. It is a means of getting people to realize they matter as individuals (Britton and Stallings, 1986). It is a human passion and a modality of human actions. It is a more or less consciously chosen policy for handling the freedom of other people (Dunn, 1988).

Thus we can trust another person or an idea or a system if they or it are characterized by these qualities. Real trust, however, is confidence in the *reality*, the truth, about a person or thing. Mistrust, or misplaced trust, is when we place our trust in something or someone based on inaccurate or untrue foundations.

Trust is the confident expectation about someone or something. It is a hope in their reality. That is, our hope that they are as we perceive them (or it) to be. It can be, and often is, however, a logical, thoughtful, considered hope. Most often we base our trust on at least some creditable evidence of the reality—the truth of the person or thing in which we place our trust.

Trust may be the first principle of human interaction. It is the foundation of success in interpersonal relationships. Trust lets us act *as if*. Trust lets us act as if information is true without solid evidence, or any evidence at all. Trust lets us act as if the people we work with are competent—before they prove to be or not be competent. Trust lets us act as if a future event or a distant place or a past event are real, actual, and sure.

We can identify several dimension or attributes of trust that help define and delimit this basic, foundation of human interactivity. First, trust is both an expectation and a personal debt to be authentic, trustworthy, and reliable. In law, trust is a fiduciary relationship in which one person, the trustee, holds responsibility for the benefit of another in a stewardship capacity.

Second, trust places obligation on both the truster and the person in whom we place our trust. It is constraining to both. Third, trust is also seen as a principle of action. Because we trust someone or something we act with assurance, even when all the information is not available. Without trust, we are constrained not to act. Finally, trust is a principle of power. It allows the trusting person to function in an otherwise ambiguous and risky situation.

Trust is a governing part of all human exchange. It allows organizations to form and sustains them. Without trust, an individual has no dependable power in relationships. Trust allows us to expect others will do what is asked of them in the absence of direct supervision.

## Trust and Truth

As noted, the foundation of trust is truth. The information we use on which to base our trusting behaviors must eventually prove accurate if we are to expect success now and in the future. The people we trust to do their job professionally must, in fact, perform competently or we withdraw our association and our trust. The future we rely on must come to pass or our plans (and the planning process) are meaningless. Unless the past is prologue to today—and tomorrow—we do not trust today's actions and events. Our leap of faith to trust another must pay off in reality or we lose interest in and sever our association.

To trust in untruth is costly. It results in failure, dysfunction, and inaction. Success in our social/organizational life is and must be based on something however intangible and ambiguous. Blind trust, that is, trust without at least some assurance that the unknown information, actions, or events are real, is extremely risky. That kind of trust is, in fact, not trust, but foolhardiness. Nor is it an example of trust when we act out of absolute knowledge about the information, person, or event. The fact is that social life—community as well as institutional life—is always more or less unknown. Trust represents our best guess, our hope that events and situations are as they purport to be. It gives us the assurance we need to act today in expectation of a desirable tomorrow.

Trust is a part of the process of change. Having trust in a person or thing, if seen as true, empowers us to change. Trust, therefore, is a principle of action. It focuses and intensifies our confidence in the other person or thing enough to let us act appropriately out of that trust.

Trust and an eventually proven reality are inseparable. Properly placed trust empowers us. Misplaced trust spells defeat. Trust is effective only as we use it in terms of an ultimate reality—a reality that eventually will be proven in practice. We must exercise trust, if it is to be effective in aiding the trusting person to act, in terms of the reality trusted in. This means that to trust we must have some evidence, some clue, an assumption, at least, about what the real truth is. Only then can the trust be potentially effective. Failing this preassessment of the final reality, the risk of trusting is too great to let us take action.

All of us are continually engaged in trusting relationships. Farmers plant seed without total assurance that a harvest will result. We marry without really knowing the full truth about our partner. We delegate work to subordinates, or accept our leader's guidance without knowing their full importance or relevance to our personal concerns or responsibilities. We exercise faith in a Supreme Being without visual or tactile contact. Yet, we engage in these relationships and countless others daily, trusting that the person or thing trusted will prove to be true.

### Trust in Organizational Life

Organized human life is a connected series of trust relationships. It is the glue that holds the organization, the organizational culture, and its programs and structured relationships together. Leaders build trust, or tear it down, by the cumulative actions they take and the words they speak, and they trust others based on the developing record of authenticated reality built up in their interactions with followers.

Trust involves a risk. We need not need to trust in situations of absolute knowledge of the truth of a given person, action, or event. However, such absolute knowledge is rarely, if ever, present in our organizations. It takes faith, hope, and trust to lead or to be an "engaged" and effective follower.

Trust in reality yields results. Trusting an engineer to be competent lets us reap the results of a well-designed bridge. Trusting a co-worker to perform an assigned task within acceptable error rate levels lets the leader spend time on different tasks. Trusting that the forecast statistics accurately reflect reality allows us to make decisions respecting our present actions to change the future. In the same fashion, trust in an incompetent engineer, co-workers, or item of information produces error, incompetence, failure, or an alternate future, one in which we are unprepared to be successful.

To give our trust, we must first have some knowledge of the truth about a person or situation. Trust given then lets us gather additional data that we can analyze to determine the truth therein to further build trust or to diminish it. Trust is, therefore, increased by the acquisition of more and more true knowledge. We diminish it by the same process; acquisition of information that belies our initial concept of the truth that formed the basis of our initial trust. We increase (or diminish) trust by this process of incremental development of accurate, truthful information.

Knowledge gained through the process of developing trust is powerful because it is true. The process of trust is a process of empowerment. It involves allowing the trusting person to act with increasing assurance that what he or she wants to take place will take place. This kind of confidence cannot be thwarted. It ensures personal and organizational success. An organization built and developed on high trust levels can expect more desired results than one built on trust in false assumptions. Indeed, it is hard to imagine organizations or leaders who cannot attain their visions if they move toward them with a trust based on truth.

Learning to trust is not a simple process. While we can extend trust of another person or organizational entity immediately, it takes time fully to trust that person or group. Developing trust is an incremental process. A sincere effort to be trusting begins the process and nurtures it until we attain complete trust in another person or thing. Each successful foray into trusting another immediately reinforces the trust relationship. Successive positive trust experiences with another cumulate until we come to trust fully in one or more dimensions of our relationship.

We are all continually faced with the problem of whom to trust. While a variety of factors are present in the relationship that may bear on trust levels, experience suggests that three factors are critical: truthfulness, patience, and altruism. People who display these qualities are trusted more than others.

Trust and trustworthiness are closely related. The less trusting a person is, the less we trust that person. The reverse is also true: The more we trust, the more others trust us. Trust is a learned capacity and the best teacher is example. The bottom line appears to be that if we want to be trusted, we have to tell the truth, act on that truth consistently, and then patiently wait for the relationship to mature.

## IMPORTANCE OF TRUST IN ORGANIZATIONAL LIFE

A culture characterized by trust provides the contextual environment within which positive interaction can take place and the work of an organization can be accomplished. According to Batten (1989), success as a leader depends on the ability to establish a solid base of loyal, creative, inspired, trusted, capable, and knowledgeable stakeholders. For Peters and Waterman (1982), trust was an essential and critical part of the atmosphere of the excellent companies they surveyed. A culture that includes a trust atmosphere allows the leader to empower followers by building mutually compatible relationships rather than coercive ones. Trust relationships are central to instilling in followers a sense of personal capacity that is the essence of empowerment, and a part of a trust culture includes building ownership relationships.

The following sections elaborate on the element of trust in organizational life and define some of the factors that help people willingly give their trust to leaders or others.

### Values

Trust is key to the task of creating a corporate culture built on the values of respect and candor and is critical in values leadership (Fairholm, 1991). Indeed, part of the definition of leadership is that leaders command the respect, trust, and loyalty of their followers (Fiedler and

Chamers, 1974). Trusting relationships are necessary for organization to take place (Culbert and McDonough, 1985). It is vital to the one-on-one relationship. In net effect, trust is a critical value helping to guide both organizational and individual performance.

## Productivity

Trust is a key to productivity (Britton and Stallings, 1986) and to organizational effectiveness (Harvey, 1983). The key element of a trust culture in this connection is that effectiveness is based on the willingness of participants to rely on another person for some or all of their individual success. A culture of trust lets members relate to each other in this way.

American culture encourages individual competition as the basis of achievement. This, however, is the antitheses of a trust situation that requires mutuality in relationships. Competition creates a culture of individualism, not one of trust relationships (Deming, 1986). In the absence of a trust culture, workers expend energy in protecting themselves, as well as producing needed goods and services.

Zand (1972) proposed a conception of trust and productivity, suggesting that trusting (or distrusting) behavior is an inner mindset that is a function of information, influence, and control. For Zand, trusting behavior consisted of actions that increase one's vulnerability to others where the possible penalty for a failed trust relationship is greater than the chance of reward for a successful relationship. In the context of organizational productivity, trust becomes a conscious regulation of one's dependence on another that will vary with the task, the situation, and the other person to produce maximum output.

A distrusting person (or an organizational culture that lacks trust) distorts or withholds information from others in ways that lessen the utility of that information with regards to timeliness, comprehensiveness, or accuracy. Distrusting people resist or deflect others' attempts at influence by not receiving suggestions of goals, methods of reaching goals, or definitions of criteria for evaluating progress. They will resist attempts to control their behavior when coordination is necessary. Distrusting people will try to limit their vulnerability and in so doing limit the level and degree of cooperation and resultant productivity.

On the other hand, trusting people will increase their vulnerability to others whose behavior they cannot control in the interests of organizational success. Trusting people disclose more accurate and relevant information and accept more influence from others in goals selection, choice of methods, and evaluation criteria. They accept more interdependency with others and impose less procedure to control others tightly. Trusting people show greater confidence that others will do what

they say they will do and show greater commitment to do what is agreed
to.

### Individual Performance  & *high trust*

Klimoski and Karol (1976) found that people in high-trust groups per-
formed better than those in low-trust groups. They showed improvement
on a variety of measures including the following:

1. Willingness to share intimate information
2. Freedom to express themselves
3. Willingness to confide in others
4. Trust in others
5. Discomfort in the group
6. Openness in discussion
7. Willingness to work with the same group again
8. Self-receptiveness

Savage (1982) suggested that we can increase personal productivity by
raising the level of trust in our organizations and among managers and
employees. Scott's (1980) review of available literature concluded that
theoretical statements as well as empirical research show the positive
relationship between trust and management by objectives programs.
Trust is a positive force from which we may derive more individual
employee participation and cooperation.

Research has shown that interpersonal trust is a powerful influence on
personal worker behavior (Rotter, 1980). For example, a trusting, supportive relationship must be part of an effective MBO system. It affects
the willingness of people to commit themselves personally to mutual
goals. Employee trust in management helps determine how successful
the process will be.

### Problem Solving

Zand (1972) found trust to have a significant impact on managerial
problem-solving effectiveness. His research suggested that high trusting
leaders/followers will exchange useful information, ideas, and feelings
more readily. They find it easier to clarify goals and problems and to
search for multiple alternatives to solve problems. A trust culture allows
others to have influence on decisions, not just managers and supervisors.
An environment of trust results in workers who are more satisfied with

their efforts and that of others, who are more motivated to work, who see themselves more as a team, and who are more bonded to the group.

On the other hand, an environment without trust results in workers who demonstrate resistance to others' attempts to use power, and their behavior is characterized by more concealment and distortion of information to produce facts of little real use. Also, they show minimal dependence on others' views or suggestions for reaching mutual goals or using specific methods.

### Key to Meaning and Context

Trust is the key to understand meaning in organizations (Culbert and McDonough, 1985). Individuals assign meaning to people, ideas, words, or events according to their perception of reality, not just by objective reality. Assigning meaning is a subjective, not objective, activity. Communicating subjective data requires trust relationships. It asks the trusting person to be willing to accept the proffered information.

Trust takes the form of an interaction between two or more people geared to the bilateral transmission of information and understanding. It is an interpersonal relationship that conveys needed information, permits mutuality of influence, encourages self-control, and avoids abuse of the vulnerability of others. Each of these actions and behaviors helps convey understanding. They contribute to organizational productivity and individual effectiveness.

### Organizational Health

We define organizational health in part by the trust factor. Unhealthy organizations display lack of trust and are institutions where the energy expenditure is low, there is conflict, change is viewed with suspicion and alarm, management is top-down, and people feel locked into their jobs.

Healthy organizations, on the other hand, exhibit an alternate character. They demonstrate certain basic precepts that aid in moving an organization to a more trusting situation:

1. Managers empower employees with information
2. Managers endow employees with power, authority, and responsibility
3. Managers encourage the creativity, intelligence, willingness, and drive of employees
4. Managers recognize the value of conflict
5. Managers reward productivity of employees with fair incentives

## Team Development

Klimoski and Karol (1976) contend that high levels of trust are a necessary condition for organizational effectiveness as well as long-term development of individuals and organizations. They say that the trust dynamics operate in groups and on individual members to affect positive group output. Their experiments confirm that high trust levels increase willingness to share information. It widens the scope of freedom of expression, willingness to confide, and communication openness. Consequently, high trust in the team increases member willingness to work again with the same group members.

The hallmark of organizational effort is goal accomplishment. Organizations reach their goals through the collective work of all organizational members. The literature describes teamwork in terms such as alignment, common goals, mutual interaction, common language and symbols, joint problem solving, and shared decision making. Kozlowski and Doherty (1989) call attention to the need for close interdependence in attaining excellent organizational performance. This can only happen where trust is present and active.

Collaborative, shared group action is the mark of team leadership. Integrating leader behavior, values, and norms with those of individual group members results in improved trust, cooperation, and performance. A framework for this kind of integration comes out of the work of Kozlowski and Doherty (1989). They proposed a theory of integration using multiple dyad linkage theory and culture theory. They proposed that leadership includes a process of integrating culture and norms in ways that allows members to perceive themselves as part of the "in-group," as trusted colleagues. This research implies that a trust relationship serves to supersede team structure and task limitations.

## Commitment

Commitment is a foundation attribute of trustworthiness. People trust those whom they honestly believe to be committed to the common purpose. Everyone knows committed people and can tell the difference between them and those on the fringe of the organization. A scientific definition of commitment is difficult to make, and a precise measure of someone's level of commitment is hard to prove. Nevertheless, commitment is a personal attitude or value that excites us to do whatever needs to be done because we see the need.

More than mere identification of intent, commitment is *doing*. The attitude of commitment flows out of our beliefs and values and is part of our definition of who we are. The values that shape our personal and social-institutional life and around which we commit our lives are matters many find hard to speak about. While we can recite some traditional shibboleths, their application in our life is less sure (Alfano, 1985). But, when we find someone committed to values we also espouse, we trust them almost implicitly.

De Tocqueville (1956) noted that American habits are still more powerful in describing our individual and group self and behavior than the physical dimensions of our communities, our natural resources, or our formal institutions. While we still pay lip service to the ancient rhetoric of American democracy, we are changing from these old habits of the heart to others. We are learning to commit to other values or to redefine or reprioritize old values.

History would lead us to believe that our ancestors connected self and community values in ways that made being true to self synonymous to being true to the community. We see some vestiges of this ideal organizationally in the Japanese philosophy of leadership. Today in America, we find it easy to commit separately to each level: to individual self-interest and to a community interest. It is harder to commit to both simultaneously. We compartmentalize our commitment, and those seeking to trust us can become confused as they see us behave differently in these two contexts. Trusting others in this situation is harder than when both adhere to common values of full allegiance to the common cause.

The solution is to refocus the idea that the sum of individual benefits equals the community benefit. This mindset has led to a national focus on single-issue politics. On an organizational level, the stress between individual and organizational level, the stress between individual and organizational values and goals is great. It has contributed to the decline in patriotism and a deterioration of trust in our social systems and our organizational and greater community leaders.

We need to move away from a competition of single-interests to a true community interest (Alfano, 1985). Alfano suggested that World War II was an example of a major issue around which most, if not all, Americans could and did rally their support. Other committing events in our past might include the unionism of the late nineteenth and early twentieth centuries, the civil rights movement in the 1960s and 1970s, and the 1990 Gulf War. The need today is for another idea or issue to galvanize Americans into a greater commitment to community than to individual self-interest.

Commitment is a decision of the heart and mind to follow one course of action rather than another. It asks us to select and then to act on that selection and not others, which may have many positive qualities as well. Commitment is a matter of what we pay attention to and use as the basis for action rather than randomly following ideas and actions that may appear tantalizing when considered alone. Commitment is focusing on one set of cultural values to the exclusion of any other value set. It is a decision process that selects one course of action, one attitude of mind, one set of values, one culture to the exclusion of all others.

Commitment is both limiting and liberating. The decision to commit to one course of action forecloses other possible decisions to guide our lives in limiting our allegiance to one course of action, idea, or attitude. It allows us to govern our actions via known and understood values and models and thus frees us to be our best self within this accepted construct. Dedication to one value system defines us and prescribes our actions in all of our life situations. When we commit to one partner, other possible partners are out of bounds. When we commit to one value system we cannot honestly measure our progress in terms of another system of values.

Oliver Wendell Holmes said that we should be anxiously engaged in the actions of our times at the peril of being adjudged not to have lived at all. Commitment to life is part of the irreducible formula for living. Not to commit places us on the fringe of life. Commitment defines us, gives us focus, and identity. To remain "free" and uncommitted denies us definition. We do not know who we are, nor does anyone else. Being on the fringe forecloses significant action to affect our lives or our social groups.

Only committed people play controlling roles in our organizations. Most organizations have some members on the fringe. They are secondary actors in the overall scheme of things. The fringers among us want the freedom and protection and prosperity potential in the organization. They are not, however, willing to do the work necessary to ensure that prosperity for themselves and others. We reserve the benefits of membership for the committed.

We each need something at the core of our life to which we can devote our whole heart. It must permeate all phases of our activity. All that we do must relate directly, be influenced by, and be subservient to our central value set.

## Leadership

Jones, James, and Bruni's (1975) work confirmed the hypothesis that people who identify with their work and their leaders place greater emphasis on leader effectiveness. These ideas are central to a trust culture. They found a direct correlation between confidence and trust in leaders and behaviors such as support, goal emphasis, successful interaction, work facilitation, upward interaction, and leadership effectiveness.

In addition, Harvey (1983) suggested that a leader has three tasks when developing a trust culture: (1) to encourage people to agree to work in ways that allows them to make a strong contribution to the organization and to themselves, (2) to recognize success, and (3) to give encouragement after failure. To accomplish these three tasks, a leader needs to enjoy the trust of followers. Part of the essence of the Japanese success in these areas is the willingness of their leaders to trust followers and vice versa.

## MEASURING TRUST

In the past, people have measured trust by many things. Among the simplest is observation of trusting behavior exhibited in the relationship. While subjective, this means of measurement is, nevertheless, useful in assessing the relative levels of trust among organizational units and between members. Other methods used have been self-reporting instruments and questionnaires probing details of an individual's feelings of trust toward significant, but unspecified, others (i.e., parents, teachers, the press, politicians). These measures of trust are also subjective but often informative.

## SUMMARY

According to Britton and Stallings (1986), trust strengthens competence and enhances self-confidence. A trust culture increases productivity and reduces negative energy spent on protecting self. It reduces fear and increases happiness, encourages interdependence, and allows co-workers to rely on each other more fully, reducing the risk associated with openness. Trusting cultures enhance creativity and facilitates introduction of new ideas. They support common values and reduce the risk of expressing deeply held values.

People are energized and motivated when leaders place trust in them (Fairholm, 1991). Trusting others places them under obligation to us (Dasgupta, 1988). Trusting relationships get people through rough times (Culbert and McDonough, 1985). The trust culture can make relationships useful sounding boards. It is a situation that helps to reduce stress, let off steam, and reduce misunderstanding. And, importantly, it can lessen the expenditure of the misplaced energy many workers expend to cover their rear.

# 9

# The Process of Developing Trust

## INTRODUCTION

Trusting others is not simple. Knowing whom to trust and how far to trust them is a continuing problem for us all. A variety of factors are present in the relationship that may affect the level of trust in a given culture. Each may help or inhibit the exercise of trust.

Both trust and trustworthiness are closely related. The less trusting a person is, the less others trust that person. And the reverse is also true; the more we trust, the more others trust us. Trust is a learned capacity and the best teacher is example. The bottom line appears to be: if you want someone to trust you, you have to tell them the truth, act on that truth consistently, and then patiently wait for the relationship to mature. Several factors are critical in understanding how we develop trust, nurture it, and expand it (see Table 9.1). Among them are integrity, patience, altruism, vulnerability, action, friendship, character, competence, and judgment. We trust people who demonstrate these qualities more often than others who do not show a high degree of these qualities. These factors define the individual who is to be trusted, and they are also characteristics of an organization's culture that make it suitable for mutual trusting interaction.

## INTEGRITY

We tend to trust those whom we think have moral character. Many define high moral character in trust terms such as integrity. A person of integrity is honest, authentic, dependable. We know their motives. They

**Table 9.1**
**Critical Factors in the Trust Relationship**

| | |
|---|---|
| INTEGRITY | HONESTY |
| | AUTHENTICITY |
| | TRUTHFULNESS |
| | OPENNESS |
| PATIENCE | DURATION—RELATIONSHIPS OVER TIME |
| | REPEATED SHARED EXPERIENCES |
| ALTRUISM | TRUST IS VOLUNTARY |
| | IT IS A RESULT OF CARING |
| | IT IS A HELPING RELATIONSHIP |
| VULNERABILITY | IT IS A RISK RELATIONSHIP |
| ACTION | PROACTIVE |
| | REPETITION |
| | PREDICTABILITY |
| | DEPENDABILITY |
| FRIENDSHIP | SHARED VALUES |
| | COMPATIBILITY |
| | CREDIBILITY |
| | COMFORT WITH THE OTHER |
| PERSONAL COMPETENCE | KNOWN ABILITY |
| | KNOWN EXPERTISE |
| JUDGMENT | MAKES SOUND CHOICES |
| | MAKES CORRECT DECISIONS |
| | IS ETHICAL |

are open, exposed, even, about themselves. They level with others about themselves and about how the other person's behavior is affecting them. They communicate truthfully about who they are and what they think is important. They are also discreet, never violating a confidence.

Trust is always related to the ideas of morality and personal integrity. Leaders and organizations endure in proportion to the strength of their moral base. Shared ethical values are the foundation of cooperation (Barber, 1983). Leaders, like nations and organizations, stand or fall on the basis of their moral values.

Organized human life is founded on trust, trust in the authenticity of the people and ideas with which we interact. An authentic view of people and the ideas they project hold the organization and its programs and structured relationships together. Lack of trust in these moral imperatives lead to disintegration of the social culture.

## PATIENCE

It takes a long time to learn to truly trust someone else. While we may volunteer our trust on first meeting, a fully trusting relationship has to mature out of the cauldron of shared experiences. Trust rarely sprouts full-blown at the instant of our first contact with someone, but rather it is the result of a process of interaction that matures over time. This fact makes the development of trust at least partially dependent upon the environment of the person who desires to trust. The culture must be conducive to trust or the people in interaction will not take the risk.

## ALTRUISM

Trust is in part, at least, a gift from one person to another. We trust out of a concern for the well-being of another person, because we care, or out of our willingness to help others. We give our trust to another, and we can withdraw it also at will.

## VULNERABILITY

Deutsch (1949) defines trust as consisting of (1) action that increases our vulnerability to another person, (2) who has control of our behavior, (3) in situations in which the penalty we suffer if the other abuses our vulnerability is greater than the benefit we gain if the other does not abuse our vulnerability. Trust is a risk relationship and the risk increases as we increase our level and scope of trust in another person or thing.

## ACTION

Trusted people appear to be people who are willing to act even in risky situations. Leaders build trust, or tear it down, by the cumulative actions they take and the words they speak. They also trust others based on the developing record of authenticated reality built up in their interactions with followers. Building trust is an active process, not a passive one. Actions more than reputation ensure our trustworthiness or our willingness to trust others.

## FRIENDSHIP

Trusting people like the people they trust. Friendship is a composite of relationships. Ideas coming out of friendship relationships, such as shared values and experiences, compatibility, pleasure in associations with another person, and comfort in their company, contribute to the depth and scope of trust. Logic, as well as anecdotal evidence confirms that friends trust each other more than enemies do. Rogers (1964) suggested that friendship relations contribute to the helping relationship that is founded in large part on mutual trust.

## PERSONAL COMPETENCE

Trusted people place their confidence in the ability, expertise, and skills of those who trust them. They trust in the other's ability to work with people, and they value the other person's overall sense of the task and in their common sense.

## JUDGMENT

Trust also is a result of a person's ability to make sound choices. A leader's capacity to make decisions that are perceived to be right, correct, and appropriate by followers increases his or her trust quotient with them. Ethical judgment is affected by a wide variety of factors, including personal self-interest; organizational goals; friendships; larger societal norms; personal morality; and laws, rules, and regulations (Sims, 1992).

Judging what is ethical in a given context makes the task of ethical leadership complex, at best, and fraught with danger, at worst. Obviously, ethical judgments are seldom clear and direct. Introduction of formal codes of ethics may help, but we cannot expect a sterile, written document to be universally applicable. Leadership places the leader continually in the center of ethical controversy.

## BUILDING TRUST

A leader has a prime responsibility to create a culture in which trust and trustworthiness are integral parts of the definition of the culture. When leaders understand and appreciate a follower's efforts they are bestowing trust on that follower (Culbert and McDonough, 1985). For Culbert and McDonough, this kind of respect for individual differences is the key to the trust relationship. Trust is developed out of the context of shared respect for difference, not out of dependency.

Britton and Stallings (1986) suggested that people develop trust through a variety of behaviors and actions by both the person who trusts and by the person who is trusted. While the following list is long, the items help place the process of developing trust in the context of personal action. These actions affect individuals, those whom they want to trust, and the situation within which trust can take place.

### Actions Affecting Personal Behavior

Trusting self

Modeling trusting behavior

Making decisions that can withstand the scrutiny of objective critics

Understanding what is important to followers and response at that level

Modeling kindness, openness, and understanding even in crisis situations, or those of hostility, or nonsense

Constantly communicating

### Actions Affecting the Person Trusted

Never exploiting followers

Letting those affected by the decision have input

Working for consensus; avoiding voting

Delegating important tasks frequently

Recruiting people who are trusting

Providing training

Allowing autonomy

Nurturing follower's needs

Setting logical limits on behavior

### Actions Impacting the Culture

Promoting happiness (trust and happiness go hand in hand)

Improving levels of trust gradually

## FOUR WAYS TO DEVELOP TRUST

At least four approaches to developing trust has been identified: participation, helping, listening, and leadership. Each has something to offer in our overall understanding of trust, its development and maturation, and the ways people apply and use it in formal and informal relationships.

### Participation

Trust is encouraged and fostered by shared experiences, for example, through participative leadership styles. The sharing can be exclusively sharing organizational experiences, such as planning and decision making with other people, or it can be sharing our ideas or philosophies. Regardless of whether it is one, or the other, or a combination of both, the need for collaborative interaction is essential in developing and nurturing trust. Leaders acting out of an authentic participative leadership style provide a culture that encourages, among other things, trust in them and in the joint enterprise.

Characteristics of this participative leadership approach include the presence of open and free communication, shared decision making, open expression of feelings, and informal organizational structures and relationships. We associate participation with efforts made by the leader to increase support and commitment to organizational policies and goals.

Participation enhances the need for and the presence of trusting relationships. Where participation is low, followers reduce their trust in their leaders (Rosen and Jerdee, 1977). Alternatively, we encourage trust by being open, honest, and by talking freely with followers about the need for trust. Leaders who show a willingness to change if the facts warrant it attract trusting followers more than those who do the opposite.

## Helping

A helping relationship, according to Rogers (1964) is one in which one of the participants intends that another attain more appreciation of and use of his or her personal resources. Applied to leadership in organizations, this idea has merit. Leaders initiating helping relationships intend to help their followers discover their inner capacities and apply them in their mutual tasks.

Helping relationships require mutual trust. Rogers suggests that the more genuine one is in relationships with others the more they will establish a trust relationship. He also suggests that the more support leaders (or others) give co-workers, the deeper and more enduring the trust.

Leaders build helping relationships on a liking for other people. Supportive leaders are aware of their positive feelings for others and are willing to express them. The helping relationship also depends on understanding the other person's needs and capacities and accommodating them as much as possible.

We can summarize the main aspect of a helping relationship as non-judgmental—people are seen in terms of their potential. Leaders who are judgmental may find few opportunities to provide real, needed help to followers, and they may find that in judging they sabotage high trust.

In order to earn trust, a leader cannot be a threat to followers. Helping leaders avoid becoming a threat by not acting insensitively. They do not try to change another person into something they are not. Helping leaders allow the follower to be different from them.

Finally, helping leaders display attitudes of warmth, caring, liking, respect, and interest in followers. They try to see things as the other person sees them.

### Active Listening

Active listening is a process that asks the listener to see things from the point of view of the speaker. It is listening for total meaning, which involves listening for feelings, as well as content. It is a kind of naive listening (Fairholm, 1991) in which the listener listens as if he or she has never heard the communicated information before.

Naive listening is an active process of paying full attention to others to find out what they have to say. Naive listeners are not judgmental. They do not evaluate the speaker's words and ideas, at least initially, nor do they attach meaning to ideas prematurely. They are supportive, confirming, and encouraging of another's ideas.

### A Consistent Leadership Style

While the trend has been to use a participative leadership style in order to develop trust, leaders can use other styles of leadership to encourage trust, as long as there is consistency in application. As followers come to rely on the leader to behave in a consistent and predictable way, they can be free to extend their trust to that leader. Inconsistent, erratic, and unpredictable behavior by the leader results in distrust. When behavior is erratic there is no true foundation upon which to develop trust.

## STRATEGIES FOR DEVELOPING TRUST

Britton and Stallings (1986) noted at least four strategies for developing trust. First, make a commitment to people. Trust levels increase as we develop and implement positive organizational practices, such as values identification, visioning, commitment building, empowerment, and teamwork. In developing trust, successful leaders develop verbal and nonverbal patterns of behavior that encourage trust. They use positive phrases, model behavior that accepts criticism as developmental, and develop a pattern of giving advice before followers need it so that people do not see it as punitive.

Second, reward trust and penalize distrust. Trusted leaders develop policies, procedures, and merit systems that reward trusting behavior and discount distrustful behavior. Third, do not abuse power as a leader. This strategy for developing trust builds on an inner sense of fairness and caring for all followers.

Fourth, build cooperation and independence. This process involves leaders in showing and explaining what they want others to do. An important step in this process is building initiative, which is a process of teaching and then stepping back and letting others govern themselves. By building cooperation and independence, the leader and followers work together as a team to focus on the emotional and intellectual needs of each other. It is a process of communicating the mutual benefits of working in the organization, in addition to the organizational goals and benefits.

## THE FOLLOWER'S ROLE IN DEVELOPING TRUST

The astute follower can do a number of things to encourage a trust relationship (Gabarro and Kotter, 1980). Perhaps one of the most useful is to support the leader in what he or she does. Another is for followers to take appropriate action on their own initiative. Being proactive in moving the work forward is a demonstration of follower trust in the leader. Followers who realize that their relationships with their leaders is that of mutual dependence can trust more and be more fully trusted. Followers need to try to understand their leader and keep him or her informed. The payoff for the follower in this activity is a climate of trust in which there is higher productivity (Klimoski and Karol, 1976).

# 10

# Constraints on Trust Behavior

## INTRODUCTION

There is an apparent lack of impetus on trust issues in our organizations. Few organizations or larger social systems have precisely defined the aspects of trust behavior they expect of members. To complicate matters, trust issues in one social sector, for example, the family, may not be transferable to another segment of society, such as the government.

In this chapter, we introduce some elements in culture that may hamper the development of high trust relationships. Leaders need to recognize these potential problems so they can deal with them as they engage in the process of creating or changing an organization's culture to allow for a higher quality of trust in interpersonal relationships.

Among these elements constraining a fully trusting culture are the nature and quality of the communications system, the way the culture assigns authority among members, and general feelings of apathy and alienation in society. The overall decay of moral values now present in the larger society also affects people's willingness to trust other people or their work organization.

Development of a culture supportive of trust may also be hampered by the lack of effective accountability mechanisms to inform members about unethical conduct and punish it. The increased risk to leaders and followers associated with accepting a trusting relationship also restricts the establishment of high trust cultures. In shaping a culture, leaders must recognize that individual self-interest may constrain follower willingness to trust their co-workers.

Another constraint is time. Building trust cultures takes time, and while a situation conducive to high trust is being developed, group members may withhold their trust or parcel out its use. Finally, negative events have a powerful affect on our willingness to trust. So the history of events in a culture may impair current trust levels.

## COMMUNICATION

The level of trust in a relationship determines the quality and fidelity of communication (Timm, 1980). Trust permits one to accept information as accurate or useful. A working model of trust in communication is offered by Kanfer and Goldstien (1980). They said communications trust is a function of three ideas. First, the truster takes a risk by divulging information about his or her problems, feelings, attitudes, ideas, and behaviors. Second, the receiver responds with warmth, understanding, and cooperative attention. Finally, the receiver reciprocates the truster's disclosures by also being open and reacts to what is taking place in a helping way.

Berlo (1960) suggested that our nonverbal communications also affect the level of trust others have in us. If our nonverbal communications are congruent with our verbal messages, we increase trust. When they are incongruent, followers withhold their support, thus, diminishing trust. Thus, when trust is not present, evidence of defensive communications is.

Several human tendencies get in the way of trust (Culbert and McDonough, 1985). For example, people have an aversion to subjectivity because it is hard to control, and they see it as inefficient. Yet much of what we communicate in every day life is subjective, not fully supported by objective proof. Trust can be jeopardized when others in a relationship withhold trust because of our failure to provide desired proofs. Those we work with may interpret this as deception. The tendency to mislead is exacerbated in times of negative events.

People also honestly interpret the same event differently. They mistakenly assume others see the world as they do or would if the correct view was called to their attention. In this situation, little real communication takes place, since neither party is dealing with the fundamental trust element of the situation, only with their perceptions of that trust. Trust cannot develop in this kind of environment of artificial truth.

## AUTHORITY

People tend to resort to authority or politics in order to resolve differences in views. The actions of people in authority, therefore, becomes important in the development of a trust culture. The authority structures formed by the cumulative actions of leaders determines the internal climate and culture of organizations. Leaders may use their authority to foster and support a culture valuing high trust. They may also use it to create a nontrusting environment.

In a growingly complex world, organizations will not be able to function successfully without explicit internal interaction patterns that let worker and leaders know what to expect. The formal and informal structures developed will form the authority skeleton around which the character of the organization will be formed. The leader's role is one of structuring institutional authority in desired ways that lead to individual and group success.

## TRUST AND APATHY AND ALIENATION

The general trend in society today of depreciating our institutions and leaders has cultural implications. Acceptance of cultural values as our own lets us trust our leaders and their objectives for the organization. Similarly, rejection of cultural values fosters distrust. As members of our work force come to the workplace with alternative values either they change their values or risk alienation. Alienation reduces our willingness to trust the organization and its leaders to provide needed support and acceptance. And without a basic level of trust, leadership is impossible.

Workers' willingness to trust may come from their prior experience in the larger society. Or it may come from their experiences within organizations. Either—both—affect worker actions in the organization. As new members join our organizations, they bring with them perceptions of society and people generally that affect their organizational relationships. If the larger society's culture turns them off, these perceptions will shape their response in the work culture and vice versa.

The level of trust determines group member actions. On one level, high trust leads to complacency. On another, not enough willingness to trust can result in alienation of workers. And, by definition, alienated workers do not interact with their leaders or co-workers as much as engaged workers do. Leader actions to create trust cultures create alienated workers; they can also create committed workers. The key is in the nature of leader activity. Perhaps the most simple and direct actions leaders can take to reduce worker apathy—and build trust—include the following:

Understand worker needs and requirements

Understand the organization's role in the larger society

Infuse the organization with a values set all or most workers can accept

Be responsive to change from within and from outside the organization that builds, not diminishes success

Focus on team building to engage workers in accomplishment of organizational goals

Foster a spirit of cooperation

Promote interactive trust relationships

Encourage open communications systems

Place a high value on responsiveness to new demands and needs

Welcome interactive participation with leaders, workers, and customers

## THE GENERAL DECAY OF MORAL VALUES

The values present in the larger society permeate an organization's culture. The present breakdown of traditional values and morals are reflected in our work organizations. The decay of fundamental values such as honesty, integrity, dependability, and commitment can make difficult the leader's efforts to create a trust culture.

These core social values are also central to the idea of organization itself. As workers enter our organizations unprepared to be honest, or to accept the responsibility to do what they say they will do, or to commit to the organization's goals, methods, and structures, they jeopardize the integrity of the organization. Leaders cannot trust workers of this kind. Nor can they behave in trusting ways, nor create cultural systems that rely on trust.

## THE LACK OF EFFECTIVE ACCOUNTABILITY MECHANISMS

Trust is built on known, predictable, and continuing mechanisms that let customers or citizens know what unethical conduct is and that punishes it when it occurs. Achieving these kinds of control systems is, however, difficult.

The potential for unethical behavior is unlimited. It is impossible to design a system to counter every example of unethical behavior. Those who try find that they have built cultures that overcontrol and restrict ethical as well as unethical action. Such a system constrains trust relationships. Many accountability systems focus too narrowly on certain aspects of interorganizational relationships and exclude many others that can lead to ineffective conduct.

It is also true that some current cultural features have the effect of supporting norms that are counter to those described as supporting trust relationships. Many organizations focus on financial success as a primary goal and overlook the methods by which those goals are attained. This kind of end-result-only thinking can result in bribery, extensive negotiations, and sweetheart contracts. These types of behaviors detract from worker willingness to trust fully.

Finally, mishandling of a trust situation can weaken a leader's ability to be effective in subsequent similar situations (Bonczek, 1992). Whether the error is intentional or an honest mistake, the damage may be significant. In either case, the loss of trust in the culture is the same.

## THE RISK OF TRUSTING OTHERS

Some see trust as a simplistic belief in the goodness of others and in the benign nature of the world. They see trusting people as somehow less intelligent and more gullible than the rest of society. Rotter's (1980) work challenged this perception. He amassed evidence to suggest that high trusters are no less intelligent nor more gullible than others. His research did find that trusters are happier and more likely to be trustworthy.

In fact, the inclination to trust or distrust is not a function of intelligence or a willing acceptance of anyone. It is more experiential than intellectual. Trust develops over a long period of time and is a result of a person's cumulative experience. We can think of trust as a generalized expectancy that we can rely upon the word, the promise, the verbal or written statement of another person (Rotter, 1980).

One advantage of trusting others is that the truster is likely to be regarded by others as dependable and trustworthy. Trust is belief in the honesty of a communication, an interaction, or a relationship, not necessarily its correctness. High trusters have experience with trustworthy significant others, such as parents, teachers, and supervisors.

## PERSONAL SELFISH INTEREST

People use social relationships, including work organizational relationships, to compete with others for personal gain. This competition sets the stage for win-lose situations and highlights individual instead of group action. Development of high trust relationships is difficult in this situation.

Trust and focused self-interest are inimical. Values supporting high trust differ from those supporting a focused self-interest. Cultural leadership asks the leader to format a values environment that counters this natural tendency toward self-aggrandizement. It focuses the culture on values that foster trust.

## NEGATIVE TRUST EVENTS

While all of us hope for a positive, supportive culture in our work organizations, not all are totally positive. All organizations have a negative side. In the process of time, most organizational cultures develop a history of negative events that help define that culture. Negative events can have a powerful effect on our willingness to trust.

Many situations arise in organizations that deprive people of a trust context and create the need for office politics (Culbert and McDonough, 1985). For example, many workers worry about the boss finding a replacement for them. They react to this perceived negative relationship by, among other things, withdrawing trust. Also, it is hard for leaders to be consistent in all they do and say. Indeed, erratic behavior is common. This inconsistency produces unpredictability. Since predictability is essential to trust, the culture becomes a lower trust environment.

## ORGANIZATIONAL STRUCTURE

Structure affects human behavior in many ways. Too much hierarchy can defuse control so much that performing a task requires too much coordination. Too little hierarchy can result in uncontrolled anarchy. Highly structured bureaucratic organizations are slow to respond to individual needs of either internal or external stakeholders. They focus more on process and procedure than on responsiveness to the needs of their various stakeholders.

Trust flourishes in situations where individual workers are given freedom to control much of their day-to-day work lives. The structure that supports this independence will also support high trust relationships.

## MORAL VALUES

Values inspire and motivate us. America has a strong history of Judeo-Christian values that include happiness, freedom, faith, hard work, justice, doing our best, family, love, respect for life, and service to one another. These (and perhaps a few other) principles and ideals promulgated by the founders who formed our country not only form the basis of our society but are the rivets that hold it together.

Our cultural challenge today is about who we are and what we value. As a nation, we have defined ourselves in terms of these values and the ideals they represent. Unfortunately, there is a current tendency in America to challenge the historical and moral origins of these values. Our most widely accepted prejudice today is antireligion, antiethical, antimoral. The impact of most recent policy decisions in America has been to weaken our Judeo-Christian heritage. The result is a weakened culture.

The conflict in society today should not be between race, class, and gender, but between what is moral and what is not. Our real social struggle is about the order of the universe, the purpose of the state, and a focus for individual lives. These are essentially moral, religious concerns, but they impact on all we do as individuals and as groups.

Trust suffers when core moral values are ignored. This is true in the workplace as well as in other dimensions of life. Trust relationships are based on shared moral, as well as other, values. Limiting acceptable values on the job to those respecting shared work processes, methods, or goals can only go so far in building and maintaining trust.

The larger social trend toward rejection of traditional moral values and an unwillingness to substitute other moral standards is weakening the fabric of our society. Moral vacuum weakens our willingness to trust others. As moral decay enters the workplace trust levels must also deteriorate there.

## SYMPTOMS OF DISTRUST

Harvey (1983) identified several symptoms of trust and distrust in organizations. His symptomatic factors define aspects of the prevailing culture that sustain trust or, because of their absence in the culture, deter it. Harvey's listings are informative, if only illustrative of the kinds of features that support or detract from the development of a trust culture. His work suggests that we engender distrust by the absence of cultural elements noted in chapter 2 that support a trust culture.

For Harvey, the elements of the situation that lead to distrust include the following: ambiguity, caution, deceit, editing or screening, limiting channels, secrecy, indirection (grapevine), gimmicks, hostile humor, lack of emotion. Organizations displaying these cultural elements present barriers against trusting relationships.

Harvey's work also suggested that cultural features and the values supporting the trust culture are the essence of the organization. Clarity, openness, and honesty build trust; their lack fosters distrust. Loyalty to these organizational values encourages high trust levels. Leaders need to recognize prevalent values and include them into the vision statements before efforts to increase the level of trust in their organizations. Failure to do so inhibits the development of trust cultures necessary to stimulate higher performance.

## LEADER SENSITIVITY TO FOLLOWER NEEDS

Leader sensitivity to follower needs is an important element in developing trust relationships. Unfortunately, it is not a simple, easily learned skill. Differing perceptions between leaders and followers regarding leadership style hurts performance and reduces trust. These differing perceptions limit trust relationships.

Hunt, Skaren, and Schriesheion (1982) said that sensitive leaders develop a culture that demonstrates concern for individual follower needs. They become attuned to the climate of the group. Leaders also realize that the effects of their behavior on follower perceptions of the job, of them, and of work is powerful.

Sensitivity to another person's intrinsic needs is crucial in trusting relationships. Leaders need to acquire the ability to feel, perceive, and acknowledge a follower's moods. Smith (1972) suggests that the function of sensitivity is to enable the leader to predict the outcome of his behavior toward others in a given situation. Sensitivity is another way to demonstrate sincere caring.

## SUMMARY

In this chapter we reviewed some of the key forces that constrain the free flow of trust between the people in relationship. We see that trust permeates all of our interrelationships. It is a part of our formal and informal communications and authority networks. As such trust is a critical part of leadership of these systems.

The present low state of interpersonal trust in some of our social and work organizations attest to the need for leaders to pay more attention to the elements of trust including those that may hinder trust. The lack of focus on trust issues in our organizations complicates leadership and minimizes leader effectiveness.

Worker apathy and alienation is in part caused by a lack of trust. Apathy and alienation also causes distrust. The general decay of moral standards we see in the larger community are also reflected in our work cultures. Deteriorating moral standards mitigate against full trust. Trusting others today has become more and more risky and more difficult. One result is that some leaders are ignoring the advantages of maintaining a trust relationship and resorting to manipulation to get others to do what they want them to do.

Developing trust is a long-term problem. The present emphasis on defining success in terms of short-term results masks the need for long-term trust relationships. Nevertheless, the weight of experience suggests that leadership cannot take place in the absence of a trust culture. We may be able to manage successfully without trust but we cannot lead in a distrustful environment. Trusting the leader lets others accept the leader's ideas and methods. Trusting followers allows the leader to let followers perform work their way. While risky, in the final analysis, trust is the ingredient that lets leaders be leaders.

# PART V

# LEADERSHIP OF THE TRUST CULTURE

Leadership is a task of culture creation—of creating a culture of shared values, vision, and trust where people know what to expect and participate in because it is what they *want* to do. Leadership cannot take place in a culture where people distrust each other, doubt other's motives or sincere intent, and pursue independent action agendas. Pluralistic cultures are divisive; they mitigate against leadership and limit trust.

The role of the leader is to leave no doubt in the minds of followers and other stakeholders as to the organization's priorities and tasks. This role places two obligations on leaders. The first is to create a common culture where all members can trust each other to do their part to attain agreed-upon results. The second is to ensure that the trust culture created allows individual members to grow toward their personal self-development goals.

If these two obligations are satisfied, then a culture will have been created that is characterized by common values, customs, and traditions that celebrate the individual as part of a mutually beneficial symbiotic relationship.

The chapters in Part V elaborate on the details of such a concept of leadership action. Chapter 11 reviews the main tenets of values leadership (Fairholm, 1991) and places this new leadership philosophy in context of cultural leadership. It describes values leadership activities, principles, and results and relates these leader tasks to the need for mutual trust.

Many people once saw leadership as another aspect of management. Leaders were correct, in control, and in charge. This paradigm has dominated leadership theory and practice for a generation. Today, many are coming to see leaders in a different light. They are beginning to think of leaders as, at best, first among equals.

Today, we define the leader's job in part as seeking worker input for their skills, experience, and knowledge about doing the work. Many now see leaders as facilitators for these worker experts. This is a major shift in our paradigm—our rules about what a leader is and does and what it takes to be a leader. Similar paradigm shifts are discernable throughout the organization.

Chapter 11 defines the leader's role in cultural creation, change, and maintenance as primarily a values creation activity. Cultural leadership defines an intimate relationship between leaders and followers at the meaning level. It is only within this kind of culture that members can give their trust fully to another member of the organization. The basis for defining meaning is in the core values held in common by the members of the organization. They provide the basis for trust, for culture, and for collaborative action.

Leaders use values to define meaning for the group. They do this by focusing group attention on some values, programs, methods, or goals as opposed to potential alternatives. Leaders pay attention to some things and not others and encourage and persuade followers to behave similarly. The core values selected provide the measures of program and personal success. That is, a leader's core values are the measures of admission into the organization, of individual and group performance, and are the overall measures of ultimate success. In America, organizational core values are often reminiscent of founding values such as respect for life, freedom, happiness, justice, and unity.

Leaders make use of a variety of tools and techniques to accomplish this task and ensure interactive trust. They employ symbols to help focus group member attention. They set and enforce standards of performance and conduct, and they teach their followers these values and appropriate value-directed actions in direct and personal ways. The teaching approach most used is coaching, in which leader and follower are in intimate association defined and prescribed by the follower's needs.

Chapter 12 elaborates on team relationships: one cultural environment conducive to developing and using trust. The effective, functioning team is, perhaps, the most helpful culture within which trust can develop and take hold. It is in the cohesive team that members can participate most fully and most safely. Members know each other and share common values, visions, and operational approaches. These are optimum conditions to foster growth, quality, and mutual trust.

We characterize teams by their shared values, high commitment, loyalty, and cohesiveness. These factors in team cultures develop as leaders consciously pay attention to and foster these cultural features. Teams provide the best venue for empowering co-workers, for allowing them to develop multiple dimensions of their capacity, and for encouraging overall high-quality performance.

Effective team leaders develop a mutual trust culture in which they can empower members to take personal responsibility for the organization's programs and goals. Their role is to set a vision and then inspire team members to accept that vision as their own.

Chapter 13 introduces the idea of shared governance as a way to operationalize trust cultures in day-to-day organizational life. Shared governance is a new idea that seeks to change traditional organizational authority structures to make team relationships, self-governance, and member ownership easier to accomplish. This chapter also describes how leaders create worker councils and other forums to facilitate sitting in council with relationships in making organizational decisions and plans. These formal councils replace traditional hierarchical structures that have served to funnel decisions upward to top management levels.

Chapter 14 carries the idea of culture maintenance further by discussing how the leader's vision guides the culture. Leaders set a vision for the organization that serves to focus all member actions, goals, and approaches. Based on shared core values, the vision is a mental image of what the organization's goals and methods are and can become. The vision extends the organizational members into the future. It shapes their ideas and their ideals for self-in-the-organization.

The vision becomes the basis for leader action to plan, decide, and integrate individual and group effort. It also becomes the basis for follower actions as they shape their goals, actions, and mindset to conform. The vision inspires collective action and provides the emotional connection between the leader and all followers.

# 11

# Cultural Leadership

## INTRODUCTION

Culture is dependent on the actions of leaders. Their goals, vision, values, and behaviors provide important clues about what an organization will expect and accept. Many see cultural management as an essential leader action. The analyst can neither fully understand leadership nor organizational culture apart from the other. Leadership and culture are two sides of the same coin (Schein, 1985).

The total character of a culture, however, determines in large part the kind of leadership that is exercised. That is, the specifics of the cultural surround condition the kind of leadership actions that are acceptable to organizational members. Creating and maintaining a culture conducive to attainment of personal and group goals is, therefore, a hallmark of leadership. And the kind of culture conducive to effective leadership is one based on high levels of interpersonal trust.

The key to leader success is the values set established as the basis of cultural interaction. Leadership is founded on shared values. Cultural leadership, then, involves creating and maintaining the values basis supporting organizational culture.

## VALUES BASIS FOR CULTURAL LEADERSHIP

We can define values as broad general beliefs about the way people should behave or how they should relate to each other. Values connote desirability. They are, therefore, standards against which we measure and grade our performances. Values are the significant attitudes and beliefs developed by individuals about what is good or true or beautiful about the world. What is important about values from a leadership perspective is that everyone has values and they affect what we do and are. The leader's job is to create a values system, a culture of specific values that condition member behavior and shape their actions, intents, and results.

The values that we espouse come out of early conditioning, our experience, and significant events in our lives. Some of our values come from the people whom we decide to model. We also form values as a by-product of our training and experience. By the time we reach adulthood, most of us have internalized a value system that serves us throughout our lives. Values, therefore, come to define the "oughts" in our lives. We apply our values in our current practices and our interaction with others.

Some analysts suggest that we shape our values early in life and that they remain mostly stable throughout life unless a significant life experience intervenes. Others contend that values are more malleable, changing as situations change. In either case, at any given point in time, our values represent settled ideas we have about the way to measure experience and relationships. They are a significant element in any formulation of relationships among members of organizations.

Values are basic constructs. They undergird our rules of conduct. They are the criteria we use for selecting actions, goals, and methods. Some values are explicit, others are not. They, nonetheless, trigger some specific behavior and constrain behavior that contravenes the value(s).

We codify institutional values often in mission or vision statements. Leader created vision statements provide convenient frameworks for communicating and implementing behavior toward specific goals and results. They are useful in shaping group member behavior and in confirming institutional policy and mission. They determine acceptable actions, resolve conflicts, determine sanction systems employed, and are integral to reward systems.

When someone joins an organization, the organization's values can often take precedence over the individual's values. These new values prescribe subsequent behavior in that group. That is why management of organizational culture is such an important leadership tool.

When the organization is not in stress, its institutional forms can foster and respect both organization and individual values. When the organization is in stress, however, leaders often subordinate the individual's values. The relative power of organizational values vis-à-vis individual values is characteristic of today's organizations. This is one reason for the loss in member loyalty and commitment to the organizations they serve.

## LEADING CULTURAL CHANGE

Today, the situation in our organizational cultures is changing. The work force is typically more educated and more aware of social conditions and the work of their organization. Workers want to be a part of the decisions that shape their organizations and determine tasks, products, and impacts on the quality of life. As a result, today's workers are pushing for cultures that more closely align with their values and needs. This push reinforces the need for cultures that give priority to high levels of trust. Consequently, the old values favoring organizational survival and health are giving way to those that prize trusting people, serving them, and recognizing their rights. Research evidence supports a resurgence of values that eulogize the individual and that emphasize equality, trust, and mutual commitment.

Today, many organizations are resurrecting such values as freedom, liberty, justice, unity, and happiness as new truths of organizational relationship. These are the values upon which leaders are building current organizational cultures. These values guide leaders in their relationships with followers and provide the basis for interpersonal trust.

Both extant cultural values and a leader's personal professional values have relevance in our work life. Leaders prioritize traditional work and organizational values and they use these values as the basis for group action. A leader's work in creating and maintaining a culture-based value system allows followers to know where they are, how they fit in, and where they can expect to go.

Cultural leadership is, in essence, values leadership. Leaders can use any style they want within the confines of the culture they establish. If the cultural values are set and generally understood, leaders can be pleasant and still expect performance. They can compromise as long as it is done within the cultural values. They can change their mind, if the new direction is within the scope of the extant culture. It is only when the leader acts outside of the parameters of the culture and its values foundation that his or her leadership is in jeopardy.

### Impact on Effectiveness

Culture is a strong force in directing human energy in specific and desired ways. As such, it affects our ideas of organizational effectiveness and overall success. Workers are efficient or inefficient, productive or not, only as their cultures and traditions require them to be (Deming, 1986). In general, industrial societies evolve an efficiency criterion because of the need for time schedules, elimination of waste, and so forth. Nonindustrial societies value efficiency less. For example, padding payrolls via nepotism is illegal in the United States; however, it is a way to overcome killing poverty in some places—a form of welfare. Americans value business careers; they are less valued socially in other cultures.

Culture also defines and proscribes recruiting practices and job security. Merit is a criterion for continued employment in America, but not always a criterion elsewhere. Nepotism is a legitimate way of recruitment in some places. Friendship patterns also affect corporate operations in some countries. Strangers to these countries must learn to sense these friendship patterns and respond without being asked. Planning is second nature to American managers. In Egypt anyone who thinks ahead more than a week or two is considered a little crazy. Indirectness is a virtue in the Orient, not in the United States. Participatory leadership styles do not work where culture dictates deferment to senior people.

Organizational effectiveness, in essence, is a judgment we and others make about what we do and are responsible for doing. Effectiveness is a measure of the accomplishment of goals. The more our goals are accomplished, the more effective we are (Barnard, 1968). Stogdill (see Bass, 1981) identified three dimensions of leader effectiveness: productivity, integration (the vitality of the internal structure and process), and morale.

Wilkins and Ouchi (1983) connected an organization's culture and its effectiveness levels. They say many organizations are socially fragmented; that some organizations have an identifiable culture based on the larger social culture and others do not. They identify three alternative modes for governing interpersonal exchanges: markets, bureaucracy, and clans. Each of these is a kind of culture along a continuum of socially based cultural features.

The clan is the most closely aligned with the dominant culture as we now define it in the organizational cultural literature. Clan cultures are most effective since only members of clan cultures share general assumptions and values. Most American organizations operate under all three—markets, bureaucracy, clan—of these governing mechanisms. Only a few organizations will develop in-depth cultural values and social ties typical of the clan culture. Developing clan cultures is a problem of socialization and goal congruence. Such cultures, while effective, develop slowly and require time, stable membership, and the absence of institutional alternatives. Clan organizational cultures have a distinct technical advantage; they focus on the existing cultural assumptions.

### Intimate Nature

Life is a composite of events *and* their meanings for self. One's personal history—or the unique history of the individual group—is key to understanding group member action. We act out of our collective past.

Leadership must consider this collective past if it is to be effective in moving a group forward. Leaders need to approach their group's history in ways that inspire them. When a leader connects with the personal history—the culture—of a group, the following results are possible:

*Authenticity.* The leader's message gains authenticity because others see it as true to their personal history. Leadership needs to be based in familiar, recognized ideas. In effect, cultural leadership is telling followers what they already know. Making a leadership message, values, ideas, and programs familiar helps convince followers (Craddock, 1985).

*Identification.* The follower identifies with the leader, the message, and its implicit values. The key to holding commitment of others lies in connecting the leader's message directly to the past and present experience of the follower. A story about millionaires will not be significant to a follower group of ditch diggers.

*Institutional Memory.* This is a dominant force in the group's personal history. Leaders need to create positive memories in the personal experience of the individual and the group if they will form and maintain an inspiring relationship with followers.

Culture leadership is also personal. Erickson's (1974) studies of Ghandi and Martin Luther King, Jr., suggested that unsatisfied personal psychological needs propel individuals forward into a relationship with a leader. Groups also, he says, are attracted to leaders who fulfill some corporate psychological need. The basis of the leader-follower relationship grows out of the physiological need of the individual and a specific group.

Erickson's work helps us understand leader-follower behavior. Leaders address a group's needs for security, trust, esteem, love, and guilt. Symbols can become crucial in dealing with psychological needs. They affect the individual group member on a deeper level than consciousness. Stories also are an indirect technique for addressing psychological needs. Stories appeal to the right hemisphere of the brain—the center of picture, image, and gestalt.

Leaders need to articulate a group's collective dreams (Craddock, 1985), as well as their own. People are attracted to a leader's vision not because they may have helped develop it, but because the vision is an extension of their dreams for self and group. Participation in culture setting or vision setting within a culture is not as important as tapping the psychological needs of the group members. This requires a consensus of values. Followers must come to care about and trust a leader's vision. Diverse values jeopardize the group and the success of a possible vision statement.

## The Need for Follower Freedom to Accept the Culture

Some thinkers delude themselves into believing that culture is created by natural forces in the environment. Others describe culture creation as a birth, maturation, and death process—like plants or animals, or man. Free individual acts of choice, however, are the mechanisms for shaping an organizational trust culture, as well as for all cultures.

The decision to settle and not wander aimlessly creates culture. Our choices not to be alone and to live in concert with others is a culture choice. Stasis and proximity, not movement and distance, define human relationships. This choice requires individuals to live differently and become different. The choice to settle implies an agreement to live in a culture of similitude. Culture members must harmonize their lives with other members. They give up some uniqueness to accept the advantages of membership: mutual support, control over available resources, and protection from other cultural groups.

We, not some natural force, control the creation and quality of our organizational cultures. Our individual choices determine the nature and scope of the cultural constraints we impose on ourselves via our membership in organizations.

Organizational life is the sum of structure and human interactions— it is a sociotechnical system, not merely a technical one. The social element involves us in the whole array of cultural factors that we often ignore in our professional lives in the rush to theoretical wholeness and predictive accuracy. We need to remember that people run our organizations, and people are motivated by an array of internal needs. These internal needs do not automatically coincide with organizational goals or methods.

Indeed, organizations develop their own systems of mores, values, and personality characteristics that can promote member affiliation or hamper it. Leaders need to be alert to the climate they are building in their organization as well as the culture of the people who join it.

## THE DUAL LEADERSHIP FOCUS

Leadership traditionally has been defined in terms of the institutional leader or manager. These traditional ideas center around the manager's role in interpersonal relations, decision making, alignment of the individual with institutional (organizational) goals, etc. Aligning leadership with these tasks has merit. One part of leadership has to do with accomplishing organizational goals. Another part deals with the development of behavioral tools to get others to do the organization's work.

There is merit in understanding these tools. They are the strength— the hand—of leadership. Some behaviors, some tools are necessary in certain circumstances. Some work better than others in a given situation. Knowing how to use the tools to attain success in a given situation is important.

The most important aspect of leadership is the values center—the heart. This dimension deals with what a leader believes, values, dreams, focuses on, and commits to. It is the leader's personal and institutional vision. The heart of leadership defines the leader's "interior world" (Sergiovanni, 1990). This vision is the basis of the leader's individual or group's truth, its reality.

The head of leadership has to do with our theories of practice. It maps our intellectual, objective world. Over time each of us develops a "mind map" that catalogs and interrelates our cumulative experiences into patterns or theories that help us make sense of our experiences. This "head" aspect of leadership reflects life experiences and systematizes it into strategies for action.

The head of leadership is shaped and focused by the heart and drives the hand. The theories we have about life and leadership are given substance and meaning by an internal system of values. These values in turn, influence our behaviors, the hand, which reflect and reshape the heart and the head in an interactive, continuous, developmental dynamic.

The emerging literature on leadership is redefining the idea of leadership. Certain kinds of behaviors, specific values, attitudes of mind, and unique approaches are coming into focus as we consider leadership and leadership style. In one sense we can think of leadership as a mindset characterized by focus, symbols, standard setting, values, coaching, and love.

**Focus**

Part of leadership is paying attention to a few important programs, values, ideas, and ideals. It involves spending time and resources on one or a few items as opposed to others that could be focused on. Focus provides a professional and psychological direction, a values base, and a balance of competing ideas, values, and systems in the culture. When leaders focus clearly on the important aspects of the organizational experience, followers understand clearly what to expect. They can more easily find their place in the overall scheme of the organization.

Every leader has a focus. Often it is unconscious and unplanned. Effective leaders, however, are proactive focusers. They prioritize this activity and use it to move the organization closer to its vision, and in the process, they build a climate of trust. The act of focusing creates an intellectual and emotional balance integrating all that is done by the organization's members. It is an integrating function as well as a goal-setting one.

Leaders demonstrate focusing by certain behaviors. For example, they focus people's attention on what they repeat. Consistency in repetition builds predictability and trust. As followers observe leaders to behave in a given way, they come to see that behavior pattern as important. At least, they know how far they can trust the leader's behavior.

Similarly, consistent repetition of ideas, values, and methods, communicates the leader's interest and level of commitment. Consistency is especially forceful if followers observe this behavior in routine and crisis situations. Consistency in time of crisis or change helps trust develop as no other behavior can.

Leaders focus follower's attention and interest also in who they promote, which signals what behavior they value most. Promotions communicate what kind of follower behavior is valued. Focusing takes place in less dramatic activity as well. How leaders form their meeting agenda, the priority given to some matters over others on the agenda, who they invite, who speaks, what they allow people to say focuses attention on what leaders think is important.

Similarly, how leaders organize available space communicates what they pay attention to and value. Who gets offices, conference rooms, or functional work units says much about what people and what functions leaders have most interest in. Spacial relationships and relative percent of space devoted to each function communicates the leader's focus.

### Using Symbols

Every organization has its symbols—ideas, words, objects, or processes that represent aspects of its culture. Symbols include group traditions that define the organization, stories that color personalities, values, programs, visions, physical settings, seating arrangements, and meeting locations. Who gets invited to meetings has symbolic meaning, as does the order of the agenda and its content.

Leaders are symbols. Part of leadership, as noted in chapter 6, is creating a culture—including symbols—that is useful to the leader and the group in getting their joint work done. Another part of leadership is using these symbols to affect individual followers. Leadership is a symbol-creating, symbol-using activity.

Symbols can be anything. Language is symbolic. At Disney World, customers are called "guests." At People Express, every employee was a "manager." The symbolism in this kind of language use is obvious and effective in changing people's perception of themselves and their role in an organization.

The stories about an organization, its activities, and the people who compose it represent symbolically the organization and its culture, tradition, and history. At Perdue Farms, the story is told that Frank Perdue destroyed $50,000 worth of chickens because one had too many pin feathers after the cleaning process. This story of his decision to destroy profit to ensure his quality vision is a legend there. Whether it happened or not, it affects worker perception of the man and the organization he heads. It is a dramatic symbol that has focused his organization on that vision.

## Standard Setting

Kalman (1984) suggested that leaders maintain cultures through cultural norms. Norms are unwritten standards of behavior and conduct that group members accept. For example, organizational norms for one organization might be do not disagree with the boss in public, do not rock the boat, or do not reward people on the basis of merit, but on that of compliance. Violation of norms results in immediate and strong pressure to conform. The human need for acceptance by the group gives the group leverage to secure compliance.

Excellent leaders set organizational standards by teaching them, living them, and inspiring others to live them. Standard setting is a form of teaching, which communicates values, standards, and preferred method to followers who are then expected to internalize them in their work lives.

Teaching is a little recognized part of the tasks of leadership. Giving orders, instructing followers, relaying information of use to workers in their jobs, even the general demeanor presented by the leader teach and this action teaches the leader's standards.

Leaders also set and communicate standards via persuasion. The days when the manager ordered employees to do the work without questions and it got done are over, if, indeed, that ever was the case. Much more effective in transferring standards and values is logical argument or persuasion.

## Listening Creatively

Listening is a critical skill in leadership defined by Cronan (1989) as creative listening. Creative listening involves effort to understand and empathize with followers and to respond appropriately to follower comments. Listening helps a leader discover the strengths in followers as well as their driving needs. Only as leaders arm themselves with this kind of information can they be effective in moving followers to accept their lead.

Listening is also a foundation skill in trust building. It fosters trust cultures by helping the leader understand follower needs and shaping the cultural surround to help them. Listening increases the follower's sense of being appreciated and needed. By creatively listening, leaders can inspire confidence in their workers, understand when something is wrong, and meet their workers' true needs.

## Coaching

Coaching is a leadership style based on excitement, teaching, and encouragement. It is a personal relationship similar in many respects to coaching behavior. We can identify at least five roles of the coach-leader that have relevance here. Coach leaders are educators, sponsors, coaches, counselors, and comforters. Coaches are not tellers; they are teachers.

Coach teaching is a quintessential technique in leadership. The task of coaching is little known in leadership literature. Yet, Gardner (1990) suggested that those who do it well will be thrust into leadership roles whether or not they hold formal positions as leaders.

## Love

The literature is almost unanimous in defining leadership in terms of caring for others. Excellent leaders care about employees, services, clients, all people with whom they work. They nurture their colleagues and show a genuine concern for them (Clement and Rickard, 1992).

Leaders convey their concern for followers through multiple acts of caring. They care about the values followers hold, their beliefs, and their feelings (Cronan, 1989). Some analysts have cited unconcern, insensitivity to others, and disregard of the humanness of their co-workers as a major cause of professional derailment of leaders (Locke, 1991).

Leaders manifest their love for co-workers in many ways. Caring behavior comes from deeply held beliefs and perceptions about people, who they are, and their essential goodness. Much overt leader behavior shows caring, including listening to others, showing respect and trust, and allowing as much autonomy as possible. Leaders who care about their co-workers do not insult, intimidate, embarrass, or degrade.

Caring behavior also includes allowing others to function independently insofar as is possible within the organization. Most people want and need a degree of independence to perform their work on their schedule and in their way. Within the known constraints of the technology or organizational policy, workers will strive to show some independence on the job. Trusting leaders provides a guided autonomy that includes helping co-workers increase their capabilities.

# 12

# Team Building

## INTRODUCTION

Today, organizations are peopled with workers who are different in many ways than before. They have diverse backgrounds, personalities, training, and experiences. Welding them into effective teams becomes a major leadership task in the new century.

Because of the needs of today's organizations, we are reconceptualizing relationships, educational technologies, and work systems. Basic changes are occurring in function, work flow systems, operations and structure in most organizations. This restructuring produces questions about leadership and appropriate leadership technologies (Fairholm, 1991). One new structural format finding prominent place in today's organizations is team structures. Team building, team management, shared responsibility groups, and shared governance are becoming more and more common (Naisbitt, 1982).

A team is a group of people in which the individuals share a common purpose and the work done by each is coordinated and interdependent. It is a unified, cohesive, and interactive group. Team members function together in a culture of trust based on understanding of self and others and high communication and performance. Team relationships help the group identify and create a positive culture that is identified by high trust levels, broad communications, and enhanced opportunities. Team building increases member commitment to that culture and the purposes of the team.

We characterize excellent teams by such measures as high participation, shared responsibility, common purpose, high communication, a future orientation, a task orientation, use of the imaginative talents of members, and rapid response to opportunities.

Collaborative group action is a function of leadership. Only team effort can produce organizational effectiveness. The literature describes team work in terms such as alignment, common goals, mutual interaction, common language and symbols, joint problem solving, and shared decision making. It calls attention to the need for close interdependence in attaining excellent organizational performance.

## DEFINITION

Team building, as a technology, embodies the important values of participation and trust. Teams involve employees in some key decisions about what work to do and how to do it. Team building moves people and culture toward a common purpose or vision, excellence in group member performance, and people-oriented leadership. Team relationships help the group identify and improve leadership and create a positive culture identified by high trust levels, broad communications, and enhanced opportunities. It allows members to align with that culture and the purposes of the team. Team building increases member commitment to the culture and the purposes of the team. It leads to synergy in individual and subgroup actions.

Not all groups of workers are teams. Reilly and Jones (1974) identified four team elements: mutuality of goals or purposes, a perceived need for interdependence among team members, and a common commitment to coordinated group effort. Team members share understanding of self and others in the team. They are a cohesive, interactive group.

The group is more powerful and more permanent if it is imbedded in significant organizational life (Gibb and Gibb, 1969). Teams where individual members share the common organizational aims and values are stronger and more enduring than teams formed just to perform a one-time task. Similarly, teams whose members possess job skills that intermesh (Adair, 1986) and that relate to core organizational tasks are more permanent. Teams, while separate from the main organization have lasting utility as they relate in meaningful ways to the core tasks and purposes of the larger parent organization.

Two cultural principles undergird team leadership, which are participation and quality.

### Participation

Participation is the core element in a culture that fosters creativity, productivity, or satisfaction. Participation, for many, has come to be almost a right. Advocates say cultures that emphasize participation have greater flow of ideas, solutions, and results.

The participative process involves several elements. Participation engages the mental and emotional aspects of the leader and followers. It involves members' egos as well as their physical and mental capacities. Participation asks members to exercise their creative self to aid the team. Participation assumes a personal sense of responsibility through involvement. Team members need to recognize that the organization wants their total involvement. And, when given, involvement increases the members' sense of responsibility and ownership in the organization.

Participation produces an atmosphere that welcomes challenge and encourages input. It is one characterized by active listening and open discussion, and recognizes emotions as essential and legitimate.

### Quality Excellence

High quality applied to organizations means more as a description of an environmental surround than it does as a particular management or leadership skill (Peters and Austin, 1985). We attain excellence more easily when our attitude is right than through mere alignment with orders, policies, or procedures. Quality comes out of a work climate that fosters risk taking, creativity, challenge, and opportunity to participate and help.

Reference to the Japanese model is proper here (Ouchi, 1981). Everything important in Japanese life happens as a result of team work. For the Japanese nothing of value occurs as a result of individual effort. The foundations of the Japanese culture are the ideas of trust, intimacy, and subtlety. These same ideas produce quality teams in America.

## PRECONDITIONS OF TEAM RELATIONSHIPS

A key benefit in team relationships is participation (Townsend and Gebhardt, 1990; Sergiovanni, 1990). Teams form when (Fairholm, 1991):

The group is interdependent

Members believe that there are areas that can be improved

Members are motivated to change

Members have the power to change (see also Fairholm, 1993)

Members can see tangible results of their efforts

Members are willing to risk trying new ways to work together

Members are willing and able to diagnose their relationships

Teams exhibit high participation, shared responsibility, common purpose, and high communications (Buckholz and Roth, 1987). Team members can be most inventive in their teams, and they can be highly responsive. Adair (1986) says team members are self-understanding. They understand individual team members and the team as a unit.

## TEAM LEADERSHIP

Leadership is not so much the exercise of power but the empowerment of others (Bennis and Nanus, 1985). Adair (1986) said that team work is the by-product of this kind of empowering leadership. Team leaders are members of teams not outside the team. Teams do not emphasize normal rules of authority and hierarchy though the leader may legally have the last word. Team leadership involves setting and maintaining values and goals structures for the team.

While familiarity may interfere with a leader's ability to be impartial, becoming familiar with team members and their ways of thinking and behaving may make it easier to set and meet high standards. Without top level support, team leadership methods may be frustrated. Team leadership requires different skills of the leader, not the least of which is skill on sharing power. Communications are also critical in team leadership as is skill in values displacement.

Team member selection is critical to team success. Members need to be technically competent, have an ability to work with others, and have desirable personal attitudes.

## EMPOWERMENT

Pfeffer (1981) said that people want to achieve control over their environment. Many suggest that survival in the future is dependent on more empowered, self-directed workers (see, for example, Kotter, 1991).

The idea of increasing the self-control and self-direction of co-workers is a solid part of leadership literature. McGregor (1960) asked leaders to discover and make use of the unrealized potential in workers. Burns (1978) suggested that we can lift people out of mediocrity to fulfill their better selves through transforming leadership. And, Bennis and Nanus (1985) said empowering followers also enhances and strengthens leaders.

Leaders are coming to recognize this possibility and changing their behavior in order to share power with co-workers. Many leaders routinely engage in empowering technologies. This is a frequently used technology by leaders in helping followers to develop and use their talents on the job. Empowerment works because it supports deep psychological needs of people in groups. People want to make a difference, and if their leader lets them and teaches them to do it, it is to the leader's benefit.

Conger and Kanungo (1988) defined empowerment as a motivational construct aimed at enabling rather than delegating. Bennis (1982) said it involves helping people feel significant, aiding them in learning, involving them in the group, and making work exciting for them. Witham and Glover (1987) concluded that empowered employees respond with commitment in contrast with those who are treated as subordinate. These employees reciprocate with little or no commitment.

Anecdotal evidence suggests that empowerment adds to the power of co-workers by developing their talents. In developing, rewarding, and recognizing those around them, leaders are allowing the human assets with which they work to appreciate in value. The leader's actions to empower also involves sensitizing co-workers to their power and training them in its full use.

Leaders have the power to empower others (Reuss, 1987). It has been said that the only way in which we can lead is to restore to our followers a belief in their own guidance. Empowerment helps leaders capture the hearts of their followers. It makes followers feel strong, forceful, capable. The key to leader success in empowerment is trust. Leaders need to trust followers before they will delegate significant responsibility to them. This trust is encouraged by full and constant communication between leader and follower regarding techniques and vision.

For the leader empowerment is exercising control on the basis of results, not activity, events, or methods as managers do. Empowerment involves releasing the power in others through collaboration. It is endowing others with the power required to perform a given act and granting another the practical autonomy to step out and contribute directly to his or her job. It does not mean the leader gives away power. Rather it involves adding to the power of co-workers by development of their talents.

Empowered people are more self-confident, self-controlled, and self-motivated. The key is "self." People are empowered when they individually accomplish collaborative and participative efforts with a leader and co-workers. These accomplishments appeal to the innate values of independence, self-reliance, and individualism. Empowerment is allowing people to self-actualize on the job via interesting and challenging job assignments.

Empowerment involves the creation of job situations in which workers can be self-motivated instead of intimidated. It is not suppressing data about work. It is allowing room for co-workers to take risks without undue controls. In a real sense, it is helping workers find their niche, which would allow them to make full use of their strengths for their own benefit and for the organization.

Empowerment is intellectually connected with several values leadership ideas (Fairholm, 1991). Team, or participative management ideas imply empowerment, although few theories identify empowerment explicitly. Empowerment is also part of transformational leadership. The underlying idea behind this concept of leadership is to choose purposes and visions based on follower strengths and interests and create a structure to support them. Transformational leadership implies a changing of the individual as well as the group. It is self-actualizing and enables leaders and followers to reach higher levels of accomplishment and motivation. It releases human potential for the collective pursuit of common goals.

McGregor's (1960) Theory Y is another intellectual foundation of empowerment. People who fundamentally believe that others are good, want to work, and accept responsibility will give those others the opportunity to use those capabilities; this behavior is empowering. Several ideas underlie empowerment. First, people achieve more when they feel a job is worth doing and is challenging enough to arouse their interests. Second, people need to see their contribution to the final result. Third, people work harder and more consistently when they feel the result is worthwhile and morally valuable. Fourth, people work harder when there is mutual trust, respect, concern for each other, and integrity among the group members as human beings. These ideas are appropriate for a chief executive of an organization as well as the lowest worker.

Leaders empower people for three reasons. First, empowered people work harder. They work more independently when they can make use of multiple talents, capacities, and creative selves. Jobs that are fuller, more demanding, and more complex and that require more of the total self are attractive to employees. It increases personal motivation when leaders assign tasks that include some worker control over work environment and discretion about when and how the work is done.

Second, people who feel their leaders have concern for their development and maturation as a human being are more committed to that leader. They will follow a leader whom they feel shows concern for them apart from what they can do for the organization.

Third, empowered, committed people are more creative and innovative in their work. They produce new ways to do work that challenge past methods. Empowered people focus on their proven capacities and those of their co-workers. They are more open to change, more supportive of change, and more involved in determining the direction of changes made in the organization.

Empowerment illustrates leader trust in followers. It lets followers take responsibility for their actions and widens the scope of those actions. Notably, empowerment lets leaders do more than they could unaided. It multiplies the creative and innovative potential in the organization by bringing more people than the leader into creative roles (Nadler and Tushman, 1988). It is a sharing of roles that enlarges both parties.

There is some risk inherent in empowerment of others. It requires the leader to have faith in the essential goodness of followers. Leaders need to trust in their talent, commitment, and capacity to do work independently and in different ways than the leader would do the work. This is a different mindset from traditional leadership or management. It requires leaders to be teachers of others, communicating understanding of and commitment to a common vision of the organization's future. This kind of trust preceded by effective, appropriate training and values displacement ensures cooperative action even when the leader is not physically present.

## INSPIRATION

Inspiration means to enliven, exalt, and animate another person. It is similar to motivation in that when we feel inspired we want to act on that feeling. As leaders learn to inspire their followers, they can produce more directed, focused action directed toward accomplishment of goals. Inspiration goes beyond motivation by appealing to a collective need to be part of and engaged with others in lofty enterprise.

Inspiration grows out of the interchange between leaders and followers and the cultural environment in which leadership takes place. Inspiration is a particular relationship between a leader and a group of people, which enlivens the follower group and impels them with new insight, new emotions, and/or new directions. Inspiration is not so much a quality in the leader (the inspirer), as it is a function of the needs of the inspired.

To inspire someone the leader must appeal to the emotions. Inspiration appeals to the emotions, to the spiritual self, to the supernatural dimensions of personality. We are inspired when we are taken beyond our routine ways of thinking and behaving and led to another, higher, level of interaction and focus.

The host culture provides the climate and conditions within which the personal needs of the leader and the follower core can be juxtaposed in ways that they inspire the other. Culture provides a broad basis of consensus around core values, the mission guiding group and individual actions, and the ways group members can and should interact with each other. A central task of culture management then is to create the conditions in the organizational surround that ease the leader's task of inspiring followers to accept and act upon their vision, values, and strategic plans.

Inspirational leaders have high self-confidence, dominance, and a conviction of moral rightness. They transfer these qualities to followers (see Bass, 1981; Peters and Waterman, 1982; Maccoby, 1981; Nixon, 1982; Burns, 1978). Operationally, we define inspiration by several emotional results (Burns, 1978). Inspiration is the name of that influence that operates upon our minds under which we may be said to receive extraordinary guidance. This definition implies several ideas. First, inspiration involves a confirmation in the hearts of individuals that the common message of the group is true. Second, it connotes the idea of guidance to individuals in their group relationships. Third, inspiration is a means of full understanding of the inspiring vision. Fourth, inspirational messages are a way for individuals to have communion with other individuals. Fifth, inspiration impels one toward excellence. Sixth, it carries with it a feeling of rightness. Finally, inspiration has a teaching component.

Inspiration is a strong tool that can be used to re-energize followers and to commit and bond them together in a joint enterprise and has always been either an actual or potential tool in leadership. It is, however, a new concept in the leadership literature. This accounts, perhaps, for its infrequent mention as a legitimate leader technology. Nevertheless, leaders report inspiration is a tool in values leadership (Fairholm, 1991).

Craddock (1985) uses a clerical perspective in analyzing the factors in a cultural situation that facilitates inspirational leadership. Since inspiration is more a function of the readiness of the group member, than of the leader, creating a culture high in mutual trust is essential. The leader can only inspire others when they trust what the leader says and does to be true, right, and appropriate for them. For Craddock, this cultural foundation is a matter of shared history, mutually understood emotional needs, and shared vision.

Past joint relationships provide a history of shared understandings and a reservoir of group emotions. Just as our personal histories define us, so the shared past of the organization defines it. As leaders shape that joint history via culture creation and maintenance, they can help prepare for inspirational relationships.

Shared meanings developed from past associations and past events help the leader understand followers and appeal to them more directly and personally. From a cultural and an inspiration point of view, shared past events are most important for the meanings the group attaches to them than for their details. They define meanings, important values, and provide an integrating context that allows leader and followers to trust each other.

Awareness of followers' understanding of their joint past allows the leader to appeal to followers on an inspirational, more-than-rational level. Working from this shared past cultural base, the leader's vision and other messages have greater authenticity. Because of the common cultural experiences with their leaders, followers can more easily recognize the leader's vision and the meanings it carries. We enhance the strength of the vision or other message communicated to followers by references to the cultural meanings we attach to our shared experiences together.

Working from the base of a common history of shared cultural values and history, leaders are more aware of their followers' psychological needs. They can better develop programs and assignments that satisfy personal motives and needs of followers, while at the same time accomplish the leader's desires. The symbiosis thus achieved is advantageous for the leader and followers. Indeed, the connection between the leader's message and the psychological needs of followers is the essence of inspiration. One is inspiring precisely because what one says impels another to do something out of personal need.

Inspirational action or words by the leader are inspiring because they clarify and vivify what is already in the hearts of followers. We refer to leader's vision because that leader puts in words the hopes and dreams of followers. In visioning, leaders only articulate latent dreams that followers share. Visions become inspiring because of this and because leaders have touched powerful inner emotions and desires shared by others in the organization.

## CONFLICT

Conflict, while sometimes productive, often represents a negative effect on organizational interaction. Diversity sometimes intensifies conflict. Differing values, customs, and beliefs among employees provide the foundation for conflict. This kind of cultural diversity can produce negative results, confusion, and stress. While diversity produces more ideas, it also forces people to clarify their views. The resultant tension stimulates interest and creativity, but it also produces intense frustration in management and workers. It can cause waste of human energy and other resources. Potentially, diversity can cause more complexity in interpersonal relationships; can foster the continuing of longstanding, but implicit problems, and can cause people to suppress their differences.

Conflict resolution becomes a significant leadership task in which leaders become mediators of difference. They need to be power brokers to allocate influence and resources. Leaders often need to resort to any of the following strategies for dealing with conflict:

*Domination*—assuming the decision and rejecting dissenters

*Containment*—ignoring the issues, minimizing them, demanding rationality and objectivity in making the decision/dealing with the issues, maintaining control and confining the issues

*Capitulation*—getting one party to back down and surrender

*Compromise*—accommodating dissenters' positions insofar as is possible and asking each to give up some intractable positions

*Integration*—seeking a conclusion satisfying to parties involved

Several forces are driving us to adopt conflict resolution strategies associated with values integration: the move toward excellence and cultural diversity, changes in demographics, and increasing pressure for innovation and creativity.

## QUALITY

Quality is the driving force behind values creation, and values creation is the key function of all workers whether management or labor. The leader's job is to try to get employees to understand how important it is to adopt a quality imperative as part of their personal commitment to the organization's success. The problem is that we have committed too much to efficiency values and not enough to quality values.

Efficiency principles have been applied to the extent that they have dehumanized work and alienated workers. Adversarial labor-management relations are another negative characteristic of American work culture contributing to a decline in quality values. Managerial, as well as employee attitudes, which together compose a significant part of organizational cultures and mindsets, have played their part in the decline of quality in our social institutions. Danforth (1987) defines total quality in performance terms. He says quality is a function of shaping a culture in which doing the right things right the first time is the standard of quality.

Individualism and specialization in the American work culture once was important to high quality productivity. Today an overemphasis on specialization has undermined cooperation and teamwork and threatens the organization's ability to produce quality outputs. It is difficult in today's balkenized work systems to do things right the first time or any other time. Overspecialization has produced what Mroczkowski (1984–1985) calls the confederations of fractionated fiefdoms that now characterize our large-scale social and economic organizations. These fractionated fiefdoms work against the cooperation necessary to producing quality goods and services in today's complicated work systems.

The so-called quality imperative is also an organizational survival imperative in today's world (Danforth, 1987). Today, organizational success depends on cooperative relationships and interaction; not on independent action. This is also true in the quest for quality. Success in achieving high quality products and services depends largely on whether the whole organization is committed to quality and that that commitment is internalized by employees and groups at all levels. That is, quality results when the organizational culture strongly favors excellence (Cound, 1987).

These aspects of American work culture may be to blame for the decline in quality that appears common in most work institutions. This decline should be changed. That most people agree indicates an important shift in thinking about organizational change and management development. It signals a return to a quest for high quality work output. We must inevitably aim any programs of change at improving productivity and quality while reducing costs. The direction of this change, however, must be toward redefining organizational cultures.

Of course, we can improve quality through technology. Technological improvements, however, are only tools that will demand greater cooperation and teamwork, as well as greater organizational commitment. These are cultural issues. Leaders must incorporate them into a workplace characterized by values, ideologies, customs, and traditions of interpersonal relationships that will determine how we use technology and if quality will result.

Improving output or process quality involves the leader in altering culture. Cultures generate commitment and cohesiveness when employees believe in what they are doing. Excellent companies have a strong culture or philosophy. Attempts to change culture is profound and involves a primary reorientation in management as well as employee attitudes and in approaches to all stages of the work process. Improvements in working conditions, job design, and working environment have a profound impact on employee attitudes and organizational climate. At least four crucial elements are at work in any effective quality improvement program. First, orientation focuses on knowing what the customer needs and wants and successfully translates that knowledge into the operating requirements of the business. Second, human resource excellence is more than just attention to human needs. It deals with participation, continuing education and training, and motivation. Product or process leadership is the third element. Products are what is delivered to the customer, either hardware or a service. Processes include what is done to deliver them. Quality dictates that we pay close attention to products and services, as well as processes and procedures, information, and suppliers. Finally, quality depends on leadership. Organizational quality requires a vision for a new way for everyone to do his or her job. This requires planning, communications, and accountability.

## STRATEGIC PLANNING

Strategic planning is a mechanism for identifying critical issues that face organizations and that can serve as the basis for implementing the organization's vision. It is a tool for developing strategies to cope with these critical issues. Strategic plans operationalize the vision and the self-definition of what an organization is now and wants to be in the future. More and more, organizational leaders are being given strategic planning responsibility. The best planning is done by those people who are most intimately associated with the work of the organization. The idea that strategic planning can be done in an ivory tower is bankrupt. Many leaders now coming to power feel that they are strategic thinkers and can do the strategy development their organizations need.

Undoubtedly the quantitative, formula-mathematics approaches to strategic planning developed in the 1960s are out of favor. They focused on market share growth and underemphasized needed aspects such as culture, values, and goals. This kind of planning is also dangerously transparent to competitors. The tendency now is for leaders to plan strategically aided, if needed, by outside facilitators. The challenge in strategic planning is to turn leaders into strategic thinkers.

The purpose of strategic planning is to integrate organizational units and enable the headquarters unit to capitalize on the synergies so the whole organization is more than just the sum of its units. It applies the vision to each unique part of the organization. When we combine strategies with vision, they become the sources of "primary cohesiveness" in the organization (Eadie, 1983).

Strategic planning is not production of a detailed blueprint for action, nor is it a set of platitudes, nor organizational plans compiled and edited. It is not a surrender to the tyranny of numbers or to vague and fickle market forces. Strategic planning is a tool to operationalize a vision; a self-definition of what and who the organization is and wants to become (Fairholm, 1991). McLean and Weitzel (1991) suggested that leadership and strategic planning are inextricably linked. One without the other is a contradiction.

## INNOVATION

Innovation is a hallmark of excellent leadership. Peters and Waterman (1982) defined leadership in terms of innovation. Innovative leaders are especially adroit at continually responding to change of any sort in their environments. Innovation, for them, defines the indisputably excellent leader. Leaders use innovation to try to change the organization to fit the world. Managers often try to change the world to match the organization. Innovation is necessary to progress. It requires a willingness to risk failure. Innovation is experimentation.

Excellent leaders give everyone in the organization space for innovation. They create champions. An innovation seldom makes it to the marketplace unless a determined champion pushes it, and when they see an emerging champion, they encourage him (Peters and Austin, 1985). Some people are calling this aspect of leadership excellence "intrapreneurship." Intrepreneurs are people with entrepreneurial skills who work within the organization to move it into a position to compete in today's and tomorrow's world. Intrepreneurship requires "skunkworks"—small offline bands of mavericks that spend their time innovating.

## OWNERSHIP

Ownership means the employee's sense of commitment to the organization. It refers to the feelings workers have of being responsible, of owning the organization. Ownership comes from being in charge, from the ability to control one's work situation (Peters and Waterman, 1982). Owners typically perform at a higher level of quality than do mere workers or employees. To foster this level of quality, leaders must allow workers some control over their work situation and keep them continuously informed about the status, problems, and potential of the organization. So-called owners are personally involved in the organization and its survival and growth. They are more than workers. They are committed to the organization, its work, and its success. They feel a need to deliver because they are responsible, committed, and free to do the work their own way.

Ownership implies that every employee is a manager or wants to be (Myers, 1970). Owners make decisions that impact their lives and their organization in real ways. Fostering ownership is a key leader task. It usually asks leaders to create small problem-solving teams, ensuring that information goes to as wide an audience as possible. Leading worker-owners change the way leaders deal with followers. They seek solutions as low in the organization as possible, and they allow co-workers slack resources to do their job their way.

Leaders who foster feelings of ownership in followers decentralize to the maximum extent possible. They delegate to the limit of their authority and good sense. Such leaders create other leaders out of followers at several levels in the organization. As a result, there is a climate of personal satisfaction, individual dignity, challenge, and opportunity. Allowing others to share ownership in an organization, its work process, and products provides all with a stake in the outcome. It creates a sense of individual and organizational worth.

# 13

# Shared Governance

## INTRODUCTION

An emerging aspect of cultural leadership is the idea of self-governance, both as a goal of leadership and as a mechanism for empowering followers. The effect of modern cultural values, some say, is to initiate cultural norms, technologies, and performance expectations to produce co-workers who can and want to do an organization's work. The outcome is more competent, self-motivated, committed people who feel a sense of ownership in the joint enterprise.

A culture that fosters ideas of individual worker growth and development is one of shared governance. This idea of shared governance of a joint enterprise permeates trust cultures models. Shared governance, empowerment, and collaborative systems are the focus of the leader's work and the essence of the relationship between leaders and followers.

A small, but growing, body of research is available that deals with the process of helping co-workers gain the skills and desires to share in the governance of an organization. Porter-O'Grady (1984) centered his idea of shared governance in the values of participatory relationships. It is a process of educating co-workers to take more control over their work lives and empowering them to take ownership of the organization's goals and work process by including them in decisions that effect worker actions. Shared governance is a genuine sharing of the power to plan and decide with staff on the assumption that this collaborative effort between management and worker will increase satisfaction and performance.

This new leader-follower technology can be conceptualized variously as a framework of relationships, a strategy for managerial action, or a philosophy of life. In essence, shared governance involves the creation of worker governing bodies, or councils, to flatten the structural hierarchy and bring decision making closer to the workers. These worker-supervisor councils are typically charged with setting policies affecting work conditions. The idea is to include workers in such forums created specifically to share planning and decisions at the lowest organizational levels.

Shared governance gives workers increased autonomy. This freedom of action results in increased individual worker responsibility and accountability. It is a process of building partnerships among workers, clients, and managers to share decision-making power. It formalizes the rhetoric of participation. Shared governance builds individual investment in a worker-leader partnership. It is based on founding American values that prize freedom of action, individual responsibility, and respect for the individual.

Shared governance emphasizes the importance of broadly defusing information for decision making. It honors the value of the individual. It is built on the idea that when group and individual values are congruent, more productivity and satisfaction result. It places responsibility for organizational success equally on both leaders and workers.

## LEADING TOWARD SELF-GOVERNANCE

The technology for changing organizational culture to allow followers to assume more direct responsibility for the leadership of the organization is critical. Shared governance is a personal and institutional change process reminiscent of the theory of change, but applied in unique ways. The elements include assessing the situation, redefining worker and leader roles and priorities, altering expectations, changing information flows, and instituting new structural decision-making units or worker councils.

The first critical step in this cultural model is to accept the values implicit in this process and philosophy of collaborative leadership. Both the leader and those led must come to accept this values foundation that is centered in respect for the individual, regardless of role in the hierarchy. The second step is that of defining the level of staff involvement. Determining the extent of participation and specifying specific task assignments, duties, and responsibilities are important to final participant success.

The specific design is dependent on the needs of each agency. The use of formal decision committees and councils is critical here. They provide the necessary framework for the dissemination of power throughout the organization. They define the shared culture. This is the third step in implementing this technology. These mechanisms take the form of changes to structure, processes, and procedure.

A fourth step involves information dispersion. Effective participation depends on the skill and knowledge of participants. A key responsibility in moving an organization toward self-governance, therefore, is to keep all organization members informed. Leaders accomplish this information transfer in the normal ways and, significantly, in the behavior of leaders as they model desired behavior. Leaders need to reflect common values, methods, and results in all they do and say—both formally and informally.

The leader's role is to develop an atmosphere that expects individual accountability as well as responsibility for needed work. Accountability systems that include reporting, feedback, and quality evaluation are needed. The primary mechanism for their implementation and application, however, is in the attitude and behavior of the leader. As leaders model desired behavior, coach workers in the details of their work, and continually focus the group on the goals they have mutually set, shared governance leadership can be successful.

Finally, in self-governance systems, it must be accepted that no one person can or should control all organizational operations. The tasks of leadership in today's complex world requires the concerted effort of many people, not just a few managers. As staff members come to understand their contribution potential and participate actively in decisions made, they intensify their commitment to the organization.

Self-governance is a way to bring to bear the full impact of empowerment and team structures on organizational life. Effective followers who can manage themselves will be more committed to their organization. They will strive for maximum personal, as well as unit, output. And, they will apply honest, courageous, and credible effort to common tasks.

# 14

# Shared Visioning

## INTRODUCTION

We, as Americans, have been accustomed to a position of world leadership; however, recent political and economic trends place our premier position in jeopardy. The generalized feeling that American dominance in political and economic arenas is slipping has changed our quality of life and our national image. Causes for this decline range from apathy to resource depletion, but a prime reason is the loss of national integrity. We no longer know who we are or what we stand for. We are challenged on all sides by pressures to accept this or that philosophy or leadership and governance, for this or that political, social, or economic program. The solution to this confusion is integrating cohesive leadership that can refocus our national image and articulate a national agenda.

Cohesive leadership involves the important function of vision setting. It, perhaps as no other idea does, distinguishes leadership from management. Bennis (1989) suggested that we can summarize the differences between leaders and managers by saying leaders are involved with vision setting and horizon judgments and managers are concerned with efficiency and applied decisions.

Vision is the simultaneous understanding of history and of the future as one entity. It combines goals with energizing passion. History is full of examples of leaders with a vision. Alexander the Great envisioned the unity of all Greek city-states under Macedonian leadership and the restoration of national pride by overcoming the Persian empire. Alexander created the vision and lived it. He took his vision to his soldiers by living with them, eating their food, listening to their complaints and suggestions. He came to know them and let them know him and his vision for their country.

Once accepted by followers, the vision statement empowers leaders. Indeed, it makes leadership possible. Leaders can lead only when followers accept their leadership (Fairholm, 1991). Once accepted by followers, that vision becomes a concrete link guiding joint action. It establishes the basis for leadership, the boundaries of the possible (Fairholm, 1991). It becomes an integrating statement allowing followers to understand and take joint ownership of the organization's commitment to the future. This is the essence of leadership.

Creating a vision engages the leader in a variety of tasks (Bennis and Nanus, 1985). One is foresight for achieving a vision that fits the environment. Another is hindsight to ensure that the vision is compatible with tradition and culture. It also asks the leader to have institutional depth perception to delineate the vision in detail and scope so the vision can respond to the aspirations of all stakeholders.

Creating a vision asks the leader to create a cultural world view that interprets current developments and trends affecting not only the local community but also other communities. It is both global and specific. Finally, visioning asks the leader to engage in periodic revision so as to change the vision according to environmental changes. The leader needs the qualities of balance and perspective for vision setting.

The vision the leader creates becomes the basis for all other interactivity in the organization. It is the repository of values, the future anticipated, and the measure of interim activity. It is the basis for interactive trust and the foundation of the culture.

## CREATING THE VISION

The vision is the guiding principle of an organization (Fairholm, 1991). It is central to culture management. A leader's success in large part depends on his or her ability to institute a base of loyal, capable, and knowledgeable workers. The leader's task is to generate momentum among these workers and then to maintain that momentum. Much of this momentum comes from the leader's vision of what the organization ought to be. Of course, strategy, structure, and system are important, but the guiding process is vision. Vision articulates a realistic, compelling view of the future of the organization. It is the bridge between now and tomorrow.

Creating a vision involves leaders in several specific activities and tasks. Perhaps the most important task is self-preparation. Self-preparation to be competent in these kinds of activities and attitudes asks the leader to be optimistic, confident, assured, and to know what exactly the organization should become. Setting visions is a risk activity, one requiring an assured, confident leader who finds the vision, the tasks, and the organization as an extension of self. The task is to define from all possible futures the one that fits the leader at this time. It also should fit the organization, which can be seen as an extension of the leader's personality, goals, and values.

Visions are an amalgam of past, present, and future but prioritize the future. They take from the cultural traditions of the leader and the organization. They reflect the combined talents and capacities of the organization, including the leader's. On this base, vision creation assimilates features of the present situation including present capacities, constraints, and limitations, as well as new cultural values, standards, and resources.

The future focus of visions builds on the present and past and probes, tentatively at first, the possibilities for the future. Small pilot changes in system or process or program can help lessen the risk of implementation of a new vision for the organization. These experiments begin the new vision culture. They allow for controlled application of the vision in ways that let the leader make midcourse corrections and refine long-term forecasts.

The genius of leadership visioning is in the leader's ability to assemble a variety of information and form a coherent, values-laden statement of the future "being" of the organization. Leaders realize this goal as they answer questions (following Bennis and Nanus, 1985) about who has a stake in the organization, possible results of continuation of present or alternative actions, possible value indicators of performance, and actions needed to realize vision goals. Answers to these kinds of questions reveal patterns that may suggest a possible vision(s).

Vision setting is a process where leaders integrate both internal and external cultural factors affecting the organization (Pascerella, 1984). It is a process of bridging past and especially the present and future potential of the organization. It is an integrating process of uniting cultural values with present interactions among stakeholders. It is making those values driving forces moving both leader and led to the same future, employing the same methods and measures of success along the way.

Leading on the basis of vision does not come naturally to people. Vision leadership takes a specific mindset, specific skills, and specific knowledge. Bennis and Nanus (1985) identified four skills leaders need to lead on the basis of vision: management of attention, meaning, trust, and self. Gaertner and Gaertner (1985) described the vision leadership process as intention setting. Vision setting is a strategic change technology (Gioia and Chittipeddi, 1991), using both cultural foundations to alter current work processes.

## ARTICULATING THE VISION

A key task is communicating the vision to all stakeholders. Communication requires judgment, intuition, and creativity. We communicate the vision by metaphor and models with enthusiasm, emotion, and passion. Leaders set and articulate the vitalizing vision of an organization. Group members need more than just task instruction or goals. They need a central, guiding purpose toward which they can mutually work. Visioning is comparable to setting the superordinate goal that Pascale and Athos (1981) discussed or what Bradford and Cohen (1984) called overarching goal setting. It is, at heart, a challenging, unifying, unique, and creditable statement of what the organization is and can become.

Visioning engages the emotions and the mind. Visions are value laden statements, not rational statements. The leader's vision carries the strong message that the future will be different. It is a flexible, overarching tool for harnessing change and making it work for leaders and their organizations. The strategic vision ideally should encompass the whole organization, but wherever the leader is in the organization using a strategic vision can help play his or her role better.

Most vision statements are articulated in a few words that summarize what is unique and special about the organization. It is a guideline all employees can use to focus their collective attention on what the organization stands for. For example, one personnel department decided to focus on providing training and procedures that would enable managers to "manage humanely in a growing organization." A payments department manager selected a vision to "work with clients with an attitude of solving their problems with imagination."

By themselves these statements can be meaningless; it is only when the leader believes in and constantly talks about them and uses them in all his or her interactions with followers that they come to life and become inspiring visions of the present and future for organization members.

## COMMUNICATING THE VISION

Vision setting is a process of intention setting, specifying the leader's intention (Gaertner and Gaertner, 1985). Vision intentions are activated by proactive decision choices. There are three levels of intention setting. The visionary level is one. This level is simply one of definition of what is important, what the leader expects, and how to do the work. The second, the strategic level, communicates the global picture; it is strategic rather than tactical thinking. Use of institutional memory is part of this phase. The final level is that of goal setting. This is translating the strategic vision into short- and midterm goals and purposes.

Bennis (1982) studied organizational leadership to find out how organizations translated intention into reality and sustained it. According to Bennis, before we can translate an intention into reality, we must express it convincingly enough to attract and motivate participants. It must be compelling. Leaders express their vision in ways that achieve two goals: to take an organization to a place it has never been and to have the capacity to permeate all levels and divisions.

Vision is the compelling intention or plan to build creative, long-term problem-solving linkages from the present to the future, so as to transform an organization's culture in ways that positively affect its productivity for the future (Bennis and Nanus, 1985; Sashkin, 1986). The compelling vision is made up of symbolic forms expressing a tapestry of intentions that give what goes on in organizations a sense of importance and, notably, connects the organization with the larger world. Leadership is truly effective when individuals place symbolic value on these intentions and their expressions. This kind of involvement with the whole world motivates and empowers others.

The vision, once articulated, must be communicated. Leaders sell the vision by acting on what they talk about and believe. They use their vision as the primary motivating force for self and others, and they must communicate it often. A vision becomes the basis for all leader action. It is, in effect, an internal contract with employees to encourage trust, commitment, and innovative effort to realize the shared vision.

Vision setting is most easily done in entrepreneurial rather than bureaucratic settings. The entrepreneurial setting is one that assists in establishing personal authority and responsibility. It encourages enlightened self-interest. It allows individuals to hone and use behaviors that increase personal and organizational interests. Entrepreneurial organizational cultures emphasize authentic tactics and living by example. Bureaucratic organization, by contrast, emphasizes organizational, as opposed to individual, self-interest and use manipulative tactics and political behavior.

Visioning involves seeking and understanding the forces for change in the organization, community, and broader cultural environment. It seeks answers to questions about individual and organizational roles; service fields; and legal, moral, and social constraints from the extant and possible future cultures. Developing an effective vision requires that leaders know and understand complex economic forces and technological advances, and be conversant with applicable political policy and processes. Vision setting also asks leaders to be futurists, molders of opinion, and teachers. The task also challenges leaders to create trust cultures in which organizational members feel free to expose something of themselves without undue risk of attack.

The vision thus created from the ferment of these tasks becomes the basis for the organization's mission statement. It is a clear statement of what leaders and followers wish to be the purpose of an organization.

Vision statements stretch one's perspective, insight, scope. The leader must secure member understanding and then tie it to member's specific work tasks. It is a process of securing member trust and commitment to the common goals, processes, and values supporting both goals and methods.

The vision setting task takes time, thought, and creativity. Preparation is necessary to ensure effective, directed action. Leaders need to prepare by being clear about the purposes of a vision statement and have ideas in mind *before* they begin to develop an organizational vision statement. They need also to prepare the members of their leadership cluster and other members of the organization who may participate in the vision setting process.

The process involves identifying what the organization does for its employees, clients, the total organization, and society. Selection of the central activity of the organization is not always easy. Even current mission and goal statements may be misleading—often they tell us what we want to do or be, not what we are. We need to look beyond routine activities to focus on the nature of the organization's tasks, the technology used, the technical proficiency needed, and the relative abundance or scarcity of resources.

Assessment of personal interests, skills, and areas of commitment is part of this process, as well as identifying the organization's clients/customers, and matching external client needs and internal personal capacities and interests. Preparation of a formal, written vision statement must await this preliminary assessment work.

A final step in the visioning process is to determine the relationships of the vision statement to various interest groups. Members need to see all relationships and how important the statement is to the organization, its customers, and individuals and teams before they will personally adopt it as their own.

## USING THE VISION

Making a vision statement is one thing, using it another. The vision is only valuable as leaders work toward the vision continuously after they introduce it to the group. Leaders need to use the vision by giving it continuous attention in their words, pictures, speeches, training, promotion decisions, pamphlets, posters, plans, and by their every action to help realize the vision aims. Leaders enhance group trust by being faithful to their vision.

Sharing the vision unleashes the discretionary power of the workers. Visions bind leader and those led to a common future, but leave the follower free to decide details of realization of the vision. Acting to make real the vision and not another goal, object, or purpose is the final test of visioning. Visions focus leader and worker attention on shared goals, methods, and values. The vision is successful when leaders reflect the vision in every choice and action of the entire leadership team and the larger work force.

# PART VI

# OPERATIONAL ASPECTS OF A TRUST CULTURE

The new key words for the 1990s are leadership, values, vision, trust, transformation, change, innovation, quality, team building, and inspiration. These key process characteristics of our organizational cultures are integrated in the idea of culture. And, the key characteristics of organizational cultures today are change, transformation, and continuing change. They deals not so much with structure or system, but with interpersonal trust, individual values, team unity, perceptions of quality, innovative change, and evolving patterns of behavior.

Organizational culture acts as a paradigm (or cluster of paradigms). A paradigm is a set of known and accepted rules and regulations that define truth for culture members. Paradigms map the route to present and future institutional success. Cultural paradigms define and delimit the world for group members. They provide the context within which group members interact and the measures of both individual and group success. Cultural paradigms support organizational values, traditions, and customs. Paradigms evolve slowly, which is why organizations are so difficult to change (Kiechel, 1984).

The key to paradigm shifting is trust. The cultural leadership task is to learn how leaders induce others to trust them and then do it. The challenge of leadership now and for the future is to find answers to questions such as the following: How do leaders build enough trust to get followers to change creatively, to innovate? How do leaders get followers to trust them enough to accept their system of priority values? How can we learn to define quality in a leader's terms? What elements of culture are most important in building and sustaining high trust levels?

The thrust of cultural leadership is individual and organizational change to higher levels of trust and other desired values. Leaders use culture creation and maintenance as part of their overall strategy of change. Part VI focuses discussion on some specific ideas that may help leaders operationalize strategies they might consider in the process of cultural change. We can view each of these ideas as present or emerging cultural paradigms that leaders need to change or shift to better accommodate their desires for a trust culture to meet their needs.

Change is difficult and fraught with risk, but it is a central task of leadership. Leaders are future-oriented change makers. Leaders need to focus on changing the culture, altering the values and the guiding vision for the future and the climate of trust within which members can individually commit to each other enough to work together to attain both personal and organizational development goals. The leader's vision defines a desirable future state, and their values and culture supports member action to make that vision real. The chapters in Part VI also introduce some potential problems in creating a unified trust culture.

Chapters 15 and 16 raise the issue of an increased cultural diversity among our work force. They chronicle some effects of multiculturalism on developing a trust culture. Chapter 15 deals with the overall issue of a growingly diverse work force and places this societal trend in context of the study of leadership.

Chapter 15 also identifies some present myths about cultural diversity in the literature and among practicing professionals and counters them. For instance, many people believe that fully accepting diversity among members of its work force is not only morally right, but organizationally helpful. They believe that encouraging diversity will generate more creativity. The facts are that full acceptance of everyone's values, ideals, and methods requires that the organization forego a unifying vision. Blind acceptance of all values means leaders cannot develop a congruent, unifying values system to guide co-workers. This situation leads to weakness, not strength. The overriding leadership task is to mold diverse values, ideologies, and paradigms into a new synthesis that unites workers with each other and their leader.

Chapter 16 deals with leadership issues in diverse cultures. In this chapter, we discuss the benefits of removing cultural factionalism from the workplace. The chapter focuses on ways to create a new culture that is broad enough to accommodate the useful elements of the diverse cultures represented in the work force, yet specific enough to let members focus their energies and their interests on tasks and programs. This chapter suggests the use of standards, values, and wide dissemination of information throughout the organization. It notes the need to manage stress and the need for workers to align themselves with leader-created values and visions. This chapter also speaks to the ethical dimension of cultural leadership.

Chapter 17 deals with quality and culture. A common thread in leadership studies has to do with the need for excellence and high quality performance by both leader and follower. This chapter traces contemporary quality-enhancing programs to their origins. The sections in this chapter discuss Total Quality Management (TQM) and other quality programs and places them squarely within the purview of culture theory and leadership.

Chapter 18 is a discussion of the principal human and institutional barriers that leaders may face in forging a trust culture from the present, implicit, sometimes vague, and often multidifferentiated subcultures making up our organizations. The sense of this chapter is that leaders must be sensitive to the organizational and personality pathologies potentially present in their organizations and develop appropriate response strategies. Indeed, culture management defines a unifying process of molding different people into a working whole.

# 15

# Leadership and Multiculturalism

## INTRODUCTION: THE CHALLENGE OF DIVERSITY TO CULTURAL HOMOGENEITY

The character of our work force is changing, becoming more diverse and less homogenous. The labor pool of workers for our organizations now include people from many nations, with widely varying educations. The people coming into our organizations enter with different values, mores, and customs. These cultural differences in the people making up American organizations pose major problems in developing a trust culture. Indeed, diversity makes the task of developing leadership more difficult.

Obviously, the organization is the locus of the leader's exercise of leadership. Unless the organizational group is homogeneous, leadership cannot take place (see chapter 1). Diversity in skill, knowledge, and ability is valuable, but diversity in core values works against leadership and is anticulture.

Leaders act in the stream of history and in an arena of multiple, sometimes divergent, forces. Nevertheless, the leader's role is to build unity out of diverse individuals. Indeed, we distinguish leaders by the values and vision they provide around which group consensus can be sought. Leaders can lead only united, compatible, colleagues who, in essence, volunteer to accept the leader's leadership.

This is contrary to the prevalent view that vision and values can be ascertained by a consensus-seeking process. Common visions and values do not often come out of a sifting of good ideas or values. They result from articulating one (or a small group of) ideal(s) that the larger group can accept and around which they can coalesce. The essential leadership task is to first set the vision and values and then seek consensus; this is becoming more difficult in these times of growing diversity in the workplace and in the larger community. It is also made more important, even critical, by these work-force changes.

History suggests that formerly the workplace was culturally homogeneous. The "melting pot" idea—where all races are melting and reforming into one culture—is our historical, political, social, and economic organizational, standard. Indeed, the ideal of organization connotes people in coordinated, formally structured interaction around a common goal or methodology.

This idea is losing acceptance as race, gender, and economic groups living within the United States act to keep their cultural ties inviolate. They are opting to keep separate their subgroup values at the expense of social continuity. The idea of subordinating individual goals into a new group goal has lost some appeal. It, nevertheless, is the basis of leadership. Leaders can only lead in situations where one set of values becomes the group value system.

The obvious positive benefits of adding to the wealth of values, skills, and points of view of a diverse population are significant: creativity, added scope, and new methods. Leaders should encourage innovation and change for enlightened self-interest, if for no other reason. But, the positive payoff as leaders build cultures characterized by trust, common values, common customs, and work systems is of even greater potential. The growing diversity in the workplace challenges our ability to lead at all unless leaders can induce increasingly diverse people to accept common values, one vision, and similar perspectives.

### The Scope of Diversity

Operationally, the world is becoming smaller. Now workers are more knowledgeable, more skilled, and more wanting than ever before, and they are demanding the right to participate directly in decision making that affects their work and their immediate environment.

Today, many observers and analysts of American corporate life are equating America with multicultures. On one level, they say American is not one culture, but many occupying the same territory. On another level, these analysts are describing an evolving situation where more and more people are immigrating to America. On a third level, they say our workplaces will soon be populated by more minorities, women, and ethnic immigrants. There is a natural compulsion to accept each group's culture and make it automatically a part of American culture. To do otherwise is to meet with challenges of racism. While laudable, this compulsion to accept unreservedly fuels the debate over diversity in America today.

Once, the workplace was made up of mostly white males. Females and minorities in traditional organizations, if present in numbers, were in certain kinds of jobs and specific roles. The facts are that today's worker is becoming more diverse physically. For example, today white men account for only over half of total workers. The United States Labor Department projects that white males will, by the turn of the century, represent only 25 percent of the labor pool entering the work force. Forecasts suggest that before long more than 75 percent of *new* workers will be minorities or women. And Asians and Latin Americans make up the largest portion of new immigrants to the United States.

In-migration (moving from rural to urban areas) is also a factor in making our work force diverse. In-migration amounts to about 34 percent of each group (Hoyt, 1987). Dreyfuss (1990) forecasted that these numbers might reach as much as 45 percent by 2005. The white male-dominated work force is becoming smaller and smaller as a percentage of total workers. The obvious implication of this is that diversity among workers will increase in the years ahead.

The work force is also getting smaller in real terms. Naisbitt (1982) said that the work force is shrinking rapidly. By the end of the twentieth century, there will be 4 to 5 million fewer entry level workers than in 1990. Trend analyses agree that the nature of this smaller work force will be more diverse. Brown (1990) and Dreyfuss (1990) and others suggested that the modern worker is different from past workers. They are better educated; better trained; and more socially, politically, and economically aware than in any former time. Today's worker is more technologically sophisticated and involved.

Our organizational leaders have always sought the best people to hire, promote, and retain. It is plain that in the future, many of these workers will come from other than the ranks of white males. Indeed, many organizations are actively seeking minorities and women now to satisfy not only personal fairness values but legal requirements as well.

## SAMENESS AMID DIVERSITY

The changes noted have led to a conclusion that unrestrained acceptance of all other cultures is desirable, and a goal leaders should actively seek. It can be said, however, that an implicit purpose of the so-called multiculturalism movement in society is cultural balkanization or cultural relativism, not true openness and fairness. In this light, multiculturalism is merely a politically correct policy, not a useful socioeconomic managerial or leadership concern.

On the surface, multiculturalism is attractive. After all, who wants to be bigoted? But, significantly, the literature extolling cultural equality largely ignores the costs of uncontrolled enthusiasm in this regard. For our purposes, a key cost is leadership. Trust and diversity for diversity's sake are not a viable formula, nor is effective leadership in culturally balkanized organizations possible.

Fortunately, a leader's task in this growingly diverse world is not as daunting as it may first appear. There are some underlying unifying forces also at work. While more cultural difference is a fact in our organizations and in the general culture, there is also an extant culture already present. Our organizations are characterized by an identifiable and strong culture. This cultural foundation forms a viable base for mutual action, trust, and support.

We do have a common culture based on shared ideas developed in ancient civilizations and matured in Western Europe. Our political traditions are Roman and Greek and Anglo-Saxon, not Asian or Apache or Nigerian. Our ethics come from the Bible, not Confucius. Our aesthetic ideals come from a variety of sources: Shakespeare, the Dutch masters, the classical musicians. These are the facts about our culture. Leaders need to use both the old and new values in shaping tomorrow's organizational cultures.

American culture is not strictly speaking any ethnic group's culture. It is our unique collective culture. It is not Anglo-Saxon culture, biologically. It is not black culture, biologically, nor is it solely a Native American culture. It is not the culture of past immigrants from Western European nations. It is, rather, an amalgam of these sources and much, much more.

These and many other diverse features of culture, noted in chapter 2, are present in each workplace. Analysis of present cultural forces must consider both the competing and complimentary features of our traditional culture along with any new cultures represented by new workers. As leaders form new cultures, they must do so in context with the overarching American umbrella culture. Only in this way can leaders form an organizational culture capable of developing enough interactive trust to perform necessary work effort effectively.

The cultural relativists reject the idea that any culture is better than another. The effect of this mindset is to accept all people's values and their resultant behavior, whether or not they thwart needed productivity. The unbiased facts lead to an opposite conclusion: cultural relativism results in organizational disaster. Leadership, on the other hand, is an integrative activity that proposes one value system, one culture, around which many people can gather to accomplish socially useful results.

There are many cultures that include values, ideals, or behavior that work against effective, coordinated performance. American society typically does not accept cultural values that regard punctuality as unimportant or that condone nepotism. Neither do they sanction values based on bribes or child labor. These examples of unacceptable values are inimical to efficient interpersonal relationships and are normally not accepted in American organizations. We do not value them equally with values like cooperation, hard work, effective use of time, and so forth. The leader's job is to create other values that supersede inappropriate ones introduced into the organization by diverse people and replace them.

Of course, all Americans should be open to new values and alterative ways to behave. But we need to match these alternative prospects with what we now have and change only when we are sure the change will add to civilization, not take us back to our uncivilized, heathen past, despite whether or not it is politically correct.

### Diversity and Organizational Unity

Most ethnic cultures in America today are resisting the "melting pot" idea prominent in our past culture and are struggling to keep their ethnic identities. Our work cultures must find ways to accommodate these ethnic drives for identity. Simultaneously, they must also build cultures characterized by trust, sharing, common values, and coordinated, cooperative joint action. Leaders in culturally diverse situations have the difficult task of maintaining as much of the diversity found in their workers as possible as well as molding those diverse values and customs into a new culture, one that asks members to trust each other and cooperate according to specific organizational values.

The task is to unify, even homogenize, disparate co-workers with mismatched cultural values. Adherence to these new unifying organizational cultural values may require that organizational members reduce full adherence to some of their former values that may be inappropriate given their particular organization. But this requirement has always been a function of membership. Members of any group are distinguished by their acceptance of a specific set of standards and rules of conduct to the exclusion of all others.

Each culture represented in the work force, and that of the larger community within which the organization operates, reflects cultural values that, while often addressing similar values, attach different levels of importance to each. Each organization's unique cultural values mix represents a challenge to leaders. A few examples may help illustrate the nature of the challenge facing cultural leaders today.

*Time.* Many people from urban cultures follow rigid time schedules. Those with less urban roots are more natural clock (sun) oriented. The problem of tardiness, for example, becomes one of discrimination unless decisions are made based on a common value respecting this cultural trait.

*Space.* Many organizations have formalized rules about who gets what space in the organization: 50 square feet for a secretary, 75 for a senior clerk, and so forth. Space for many is a status symbol. Others treat it as inconsequential. Both quantity of space and layout of work spaces have important cultural connotations that the leader in a diverse organization must consider in creating a space policy (Orstein, 1989).

*Tenure.* Some, such as the Japanese, see life tenure as important. Others see mobility as valuable. Still others ignore this aspect of work life in their values. The leader of workers from different cultures will have a difficult time developing one tenure system to meet all workers' value concerns based on technical considerations alone. Leaders must concentrate first on shaping a specific tenure value to which all can adapt.

*Motivators.* Independence motivates some; dependence others. Weber (1958) said the Protestant work ethic was instrumental in producing behavior conducive to industrialization. Others suggest a bureaucratic work ethic is more descriptive of today's situation (Jackell, 1983). As diverse values respecting motivation for working proliferate, the complications of leadership in multicultural organizations increase exponentially.

*Heros.* Are workers or leaders more honored in an organization? In the former Soviet Union, workers were theoretically more important. Is business or government more honored? Is the military person honored?

*Age.* Age commands more respect in Europe and the Middle East than in the United States. How a given organization views it is another part of the leader's values integration role.

*Authority.* In Japan, leaders are part of the social life of workers. Are our leaders higher in the social "pecking order" or on the same level with workers? What about other organizations to which we belong (church, family, club)?

## Diversity and Leaders

Many of today's leaders and employees are unprepared for diversity. Most of us have little experience with polyglot cultures. Our education systems have not prepared us for diverse cultural relationships. Minorities also lack training, education, and experience in dealing with diverse cultural situations.

The benefits of diversity are not automatic. Working with people different from ourselves can be difficult. Different values, perceptions, expectations, and approaches can cause misunderstanding, reduce trust levels, take more time, cause stress, and result in poor performance. We need something more than just close working arrangements.

Without the integrating effects of leadership based on shared values, organizational work effort is bound to deteriorate. Present trends showing waste, low productivity, and anomie in the work place attest, at least anecdotally, to the negative impacts of the increasing cultural diversity.[1]

The implications for the individual leader and worker is that their success in the future may depend on their learning to work and excel in organizations characterized by multiculturalism but using techniques geared to more than just acceptance of difference. Along with the trend toward workplace diversity, more emphasis is needed on unifying values. Each of us needs to examine ourselves, develop collaborative approaches, and spend thoughtful effort in order to deal successfully with workplace diversity. Building trust cultures demands this kind of action. Building accepting cultures that accommodate diversity as far as possible also require this mindset of our leaders.

## LEADING A CULTURALLY DIVERSE WORK FORCE

In such a culturally diverse context that has been described, leaders will have to be more effective in working with superiors, peers, and subordinates. They also will have to meet clients', customers', and suppliers' needs and those of the average citizen, all of whom are different from themselves. And, they will need to keep their focus on progress, innovation, and excellence. The benefits, however, can be enormous:

A more open corporate culture

Better business decisions

More responsiveness to diverse customers

More loyalty as workers feel they are valued

Competitive advantage

### Barriers to Diversity

As noted, diversity is not all positive. The mere fact of difference alone creates artificial barriers for some minorities and women in today's work cultures. Reflective of the glass ceiling syndrome, many minorities and women "top out" at levels below their white male counterparts. One problem often used to excuse this phenomenon is the lack of experience. This problem may, however, result from lack of opportunity because of their difference from the traditional norm expected of past leaders. Reluctance to promote someone may stem more from lack of comfort than from lack of abilities. Some leaders do not even "expect" to see contributions from workers who are different from themselves. Solomon (1988) identified four barriers to diversity:

Stereotypes and assumptions

Actual cultural differences

The "white male" club

Unwritten rules and double standards

Other barriers include:

Low acceptance of other cultures

Lack of managerial sensitivity to diverse people

Lack of role models

Inadequate evaluation systems that include diversity factors

Lack of networks for people outside the norm

Job descriptions or organizational structures that do not allow for diversity

Leaders must recognize that equality (treating everyone uniformly the same) is not always fair. Color blindness alone is not the prime goal. Leading in a culture of diverse followers will tax leaders' ingenuity. They must learn to create new cultures, not just try to meld available cultures into a unified whole.

### Limiting Unrestrained Diversity

Importantly, we may have to subordinate some features of a given worker's cultural values and customs to the larger needs of the organization. Total acceptance of each worker's individual value system may lead to inefficiency and waste, not productivity; to license, not trust. Indeed, we see some evidence of this potentially negative result of unrestrained cultural acceptance even at this early stage of the diversity push.

In fact, all organizations are diverse and always have been. What is new is that we have *focused* on diversity as a social and organizational good. Of course, leaders (as they always have) need to be sensitive to the potential for enhancement of individuals and the organization in the plethora of values and customs represented by our increasingly diverse labor pool. They need also to recognize that diversity by itself is not indispensable to the organization. Indeed, the opposite is most often true.

The leader's task is to create a new organizational culture that may accept some values in individual member's cultural past but creates a new cultural synthesis that binds workers and leaders together. The task is to create new trust relationships characterized often by entirely new values and customs, but that support the organization at this time in its history. Perhaps in doing this we will have to ignore or limit some otherwise useful cultural values in worker cultures.

Leading culturally diverse workers is not an exercise in mere acceptance. It is an exercise in creating new values to which we can induce diverse people to align for their individual benefit and the benefit of the organization. Leading culturally diverse workers asks the leader to be culturally innovative, not just culturally inclusive.

Of course, diverse workers may resist the new culture. Indeed, some causes of the explicit statements of racism/sexism in the workplace may be due to other factors than race (Enos, 1992). Some reasons for singling out a minority worker may be genuine misconduct common to any person. Other reasons may include the unusually high levels of scrutiny to which we subject most new workers. We can attribute some other causes to a natural American tendency to bring down a high-ranking individual. None of these latter causes are racially motivated. They happen whether the incumbent is male or female, white, black, red, yellow, or brown. Members of cultural groups may attribute conduct as racism and not to the true or alleged mistake or normal attitudes of someone. Some minorities, like some in the majority, do screw up. Development of a culturally diverse workplace asks leaders to ensure that members base relationships within the organization on known, accepted, and fair values, exhibited behavior, and trusting interrelationships systems.

### Valuing Diversity

An individual's performance and career advancement often depend on working relationships with others. As the "others" become more dissimilar, all members of our organizations must become more sensitive to cultural factors and to the culturally based actions of their co-workers.

Understanding the differences in co-workers helps in developing effective work teams. The potential benefits of appropriately leading diversity are many. Besides promoting team relationships, a culture that effectively and accurately considers the diverse needs and capacities of its people can expect improvement in the quality of work life. Other advantages might include a work force willing to take more risks to succeed or one with more creativity, innovation, and initiative. The potential for increased productivity, as group members use new ideas and methods and the new management skills of multiculturalism, is also enhanced.

Leaders need to develop skill in accepting and using difference to add to the organization's capacity to survive in a growing and increasingly complex world. They also need to suppress their feelings of fear and antagonism and increase their capacity to accept difference. And, they need to be proactive in gaining education in leading in situations of cultural diversity.

### NEGATIVE RESULTS OF DIVERSITY

While diversity is becoming more and more common, not all results are positive. One study, reported in a local newspaper (Kendel, 1992), suggested that many minority children are at least one grade level behind their classmates. This may, in part, be a result of separation from other classmates. In another instance, the development of Afro-centric education programs, as a way to enhance minority self-esteem and improve achievement, may have laudable results. They have, however, also served to differentiate African Americans from other students. Sometimes this effort has focused them into academic programs that are full of undocumented assertions and dubious sources to emphasize the uniqueness of their culture. They are also, on occasion, politically divisive in their larger communities.

One could make a case that ethnic- or gender-centered education is not multicultural but, rather, the opposite. It often separates, rather than integrates, diverse subcultures. Using ethnicity to organize such things as academic studies can encourage separatism and cause distrust and tension between groups. Building a trusting organizational team in such a situation of diversity is impossible.

## NOTE

1. Recent studies suggest a rise in overall productivity statistics in the United States. These numbers reflect more the effects of downsizing in middle management jobs more than they do true increase in per-worker output.

# 16

# Leading for Cultural Unity

## INTRODUCTION

Each organizational culture displays different attitudes and values that define what is important and required for success. That is, organizational culture consists of a complex of values and resultant rules governing member behavior and defining successful performance. These cultural values define how organization members are to behave and how much people are trusted, respected, controlled, or rewarded. Organizational cultures build up a complex of values, expectations, and rites and rituals (Deal and Kennedy, 1983). They act as control systems to tell people what to expect and accept from others and define the basis of the organization's support and sanction systems. They define the level of trust, the quality of the relationships fostered, and the measures of group success.

In most, if not all, organizational cultures, many of the most important rules are unwritten. They are obvious to insiders, but often obscure to all others. Typically, they take on the character of rites or rituals. Examples include office etiquette, how and with whom to socialize, and how to recognize individual performance.

Other, often unwritten, cultural norms also define acceptable group attitudes. They proscribe attitudes toward punctuality and hours of work, who gets consulted, who gets information, dress codes, and office or work-station appearance. Cultural norms define appropriate language standards, the level of formality or informality expected, and the formats for written communications. Norms determine the acceptable ways for people to compete, the degree of openness about compensation matters, and relationships between managers and subordinates. They define the quality of trust relationships. These important factors about organizational life and much else are all constrained and delimited by cultural values, expectations, rite, rituals, and customs.

The organization's cultural rituals may pose problems for the newcomer. They represent the sense of the organizational office politics (Fairholm, 1993). They serve the important purpose of introducing the newcomer to the organization (Deal and Kennedy, 1983). These rites and rituals work well for the traditional employee who is similar in most ways to the existing work force.

In the past, the pressure to change has been on the new employee coming into the workplace. Now more people are entering the workplace with different cultural backgrounds and the pressure is on the organizational culture to change. The established expectations, rites, and rituals may have to be altered for the new but different worker. And, some of the present cultural systems may need to be discarded, changed, or modified.

The goals for the leader are still the same, however. The leadership role and function in leading a diverse work force is first to define the common values and customs. The second role is to integrate and acculturate workers into the organizational culture, its value systems, and its operating practices. The process is to set a vision and seek consensus on that vision and then legitimize that vision in the culture.

The challenge is to ensure that the organization's culture is continually open to new, different, and appropriate practices in dealing with its various stakeholders, while maintaining focus on the common vision. This is critical. Also critical is that leaders clearly define and install a culture and operating values so members can accept this unique vision as an alternate or supplement to their own.

The leader's role today is to provide leadership in managing culture to integrate needed changes while maintaining the necessary unifying features that allows coordinated and cooperative action from willing followers. The aim is to develop a work force that is compatible with and supportive of the organization's avowed vision, mission, and work goals. The leader needs to ensure that every employee is working toward the same organizational goals in ways that are conducive to their accomplishment. New employees have an equal responsibility to align their behavior and goals with those of the organization. Cultural diversity complicates this task; it does not change it.

## PROBLEMS AND CHALLENGES IN LEADING DIVERSE GROUPS

In a diverse culture, leaders must manage a wide variety of internal and external forces and operating systems to be effective. Managing culture to develop interpersonal trust is fundamentally a task of values change. The change needed is to match worker performance with organizational need while resolving a variety of operating system problems. The organization's system of communications is one example.

Managing communications systems is really managing understanding of meanings. When leaders translate verbal and written materials into understandable values, purposes, policies, and procedures, they are managing a cultural feature as well as the technical information flow system. Unless workers perceive the information flowing to them as appropriate, useful, and "right" for them, the mechanical process of passing information to them will be sterile and useless.

Similarly, organizational training programs are as much culture creation tasks as a simple skills building ones. Whether the training program concentrates on job-related skills, organizational philosophy, remedial reading and writing, English as a second language, or problem-solving skills, the goals sought also must include transfer of ideology, values, and context. Without these cultural features, the training will not be complete, nor can we expect to serve fully the organization's needs. These communications and training examples are typical of those many leaders face in their work. They are cultural more than they are technical problems.

## MANAGING CULTURE

Most cultures are not intrinsically good or bad. They are merely different. The task is to accept the best from those cultural features represented in stakeholder groups. Leaders can resolve some problems via culture management, but not all, by any means. A new idea in leadership practice and theory is that some can respond to cultural leadership. Failure to respond to problems on a cultural level, as well as a technical one, is risky. It leads to cultural factions—a kind of balkanization—which is detrimental to trusting relationships.

Cultural factionalism in the organization costs leaders time and resources. Dealing with special interests and advocacy groups and responding to such things as charges of bias takes considerable time and resources. Organizational factionalism also contributes to lost time in directing a diverse work force which does not respond equally to an instruction, order, or policy. Poor morale is also a frequent result, as well as a loss of productivity.

The unfettered organizational factionalism that some say will reduce bias may, in fact, produce more conflict based on bigotry. For example, as we allow members of organizational subcultures to behave in nonconforming ways or receive different treatment, we can expect those not similarly treated to react in nonhelpful ways. Trust cannot exist in this kind of situation, nor can high quality, productivity, or excellence.

Good leaders have always recognized that prejudicial differences are sometimes present in our organizations. They have acted to ameliorate them, at least somewhat, by values and culture management technologies. Most accept the fact that prejudice exists, whether we condone it or not. This recognition is one issue. Understanding that other reasons for aberrant behavior may be present in a situation that triggers conflict is also a necessity. The challenge is to separate bias based on class, race, sex, or ethnicity from real cultural differences and to deal with each cause differently.

To allow people to be recognized for their uniqueness, leaders need to offer multiple reward systems that recognize the different values of a culturally diverse work force. Leaders need to articulate consciously their organization's value system and educate newcomers to accept and act within that value system. They also need to accept the challenge to constantly alter organizational member's values to accommodate positive values coming from their new multicultural co-workers.

### The Leader's Role

Organizational values, rites, and rituals may conflict with new employees' values. Managing cultural diversity is one of acculturating the new culturally diverse worker into the current organizational culture. The problem is to do this fairly, recognizing that the new worker may bring approaches, methods, and ideas that may help the organization. The difficulty is to integrate the new employee quickly so he or she comes to trust co-workers and share in the advantages the organization offers to all.

Also, leaders need to be aggressively open to new ideas, methods, and approaches that may help the organization survive and prosper in an increasingly diverse world. This requires the leader to be proactive in reshaping the culture. They must integrate the best of the values, customs, and traditions of the incoming workers.

Leaders need to give attention to setting work and accountability standards that consider the diverse nature of their work force. They need also to be willing to alter them as the situation demands. These standards should be reflected in organizational design—shared responsibility, teams, matrix organizations, quality circles, and so forth. The culturally responsive organization will embody appropriate job standards in job structure and content and merge them into position descriptions that reflect interchangeability of skills, working hour schedules, use of flex time, job sharing, and other systems. These standards become the means of allocation of authority and of encouraging employee involvement and participation.

Standards set to match the level and nature of the cultural diversity of the work force help in determining unit goals, work processes, and work scheduling. They are basic to devising motivational strategies, compensation plans, training opportunities, and promotion or transfer systems. And, such standards are, or should be, the foundation of disciplinary and corrective action processes, feedback systems, and affirmative action policies. They are the foundation of any culture characterized by trust, whether formed from a single cultural system or from many different cultures.

### The Worker's Role

Succeeding in the multicultural workplace requires the worker to behave differently. As the workplace becomes multicultural workers can no longer assume that work will be done as it was in the past. Tasks may change as new methods are introduced by incoming workers from other cultural backgrounds. Old measures of performance and standards defining success may also change as new values are introduced by new workers. Communications patterns, reporting formats, even leisure activities (lunch and breaks) may change. Indeed, workers' conception of career itself may need to be altered.

The entry of new workers into the workplace will require employees to manage their careers on different levels. Others may help them do this, but the weight of experience supports the idea that the individual is primarily responsible for his or her own career progress and professional development. The task is to find out what the organization demands of a new worker and do it.

Managing the stress of being bicultural is another new skill needed. The organization the newcomer joins also has a culture. The new worker's task is to align with that culture or change it, or some of both. Newcomers need to learn the new culture and behave accordingly while the change process is ongoing. A key to personal comfort in this acculturation process is to value self in the process. As the individual becomes bicultural—adopting values, behavior patterns from both personal and organizational cultures—he or she can reduce or, even, eliminate stress.

Multiculturalism is new for many organizations, and newness is by definition stressful. Learning to manage stress in socially acceptable ways reduces the tension of working with culturally different people. For example, action of any kind often relieves stress. So does finding other than work-related outlets to release energies triggered by interpersonal relations. Educating colleagues about your needs also can help defuse a potentially stressful job situation.

The following ideas may serve to illustrate features the culture group members should be sensitive and responsive to in shaping their work goals to accommodate the stress of diversity on the job. For example, observing what values and behaviors are rewarded in a given organization is key. So is determining which jobs lead to where you want to go. Knowing the influential people in the organization is also helpful in planning and implementing a personal career betterment plan in the midst of diversity.

New upwardly mobile organizational members should strive also for full information about the organization, its programs, goals, methods, and approaches. Careful reading of the organization's newsletters, annual reports, bulletins, and other formal publications may be helpful in this regard. So, too, might be talking candidly about success requirements with supervisor and peers.

The burden of change is not entirely on the culturally diverse new individual. Nevertheless, they have a prime job to become personally useful and accepted. Newcomers often need help to become useful. Since performance is central to individual and organizational success, the newcomer should become a contributor as soon as possible. The key is to focus on efforts that supervisors value and to excel in ways that are obvious.

Managing the supervisor is another gate to advancement. New workers need to consider their managers in their career plans. Managing the boss involves the worker in a proactive task. Many managers like a proactive employee, especially if the proaction results in success. Adapting relationships to the particular needs of the supervisor, realizing that every leader is different, is also a sound strategy (Fairholm, 1993).

Employees who know their supervisors' proclivities intimately are more assured of a favorable relationship with that person than those who ignore this area of worker success. Some employers are readers; others are listeners. Some are political; others are not. Some are team players; some work independently. Some are results-oriented, others are process-oriented. Some are people-oriented; others are task-oriented. Knowing details of your boss's style can ease a follower's stress and minimize the negative effects of an apparent difference.

Employees who share their needs and aspirations with their leaders often are better off. Since multicultural leadership is an emerging technology, employees who share their insights about multiculturalism and about their own cultural needs and orientation may prosper more than those who obscure these needs. Letting the supervisor know why we behave as we do may be helpful to both parties.

Managing even further up the organization than the immediate supervisor is often also useful. Being known several layers up the organization can result in increased attention and recognition. It also lessens the potential loss due to changes in management. Visibility is the standard.

Part of successful cultural management for the individual worker involves managing the system. Initiating relationships outside the group spreads the risk of loss of an immediate superior. Clustering with other like-minded co-workers can be good and comfortable and can provide a kind of networking, support group. Clustering may, of course, also be nonproductive. Clustering can be exclusionary and may lead to undervaluing some co-workers by decision makers, cause conflict, and/or constrain free communication. Nevertheless, it is natural to cluster with like-minded people. People build trust relationships in this way. Newcomers who cluster with others who also share specific organizational values find it easier to conform to these shared values.

Clustering is one way an individual can avoid isolation in the system. Demonstration of one's willingness to participate also is shown by joining social events such as taking lunch with colleagues. Making an effort to secure a mentor is increasingly effective in this regard. Networking is also often effective. It allows minorities to get support from like-minded people and can be a tool to help the organization prosper as well. This kind of office politics is common. Newcomers need to engage in this legitimate and ubiquitous process.

Members of the majority can learn also from newcomers. New members bring new language, symbols, approaches, and skills that the organization may profitably use, if its leaders are open to difference. Until the newcomer has conformed to the organization's culture (or has introduced a change in that culture), leaders must understand that equality does not always mean uniform treatment. Their treatment of newcomers may need to be different from how they treat others. Each group is internally different. To relate to others stereotypically endangers cultural understanding. We base stereotypes on assumptions, and sometimes cultural assumptions are wrong.

## MANAGING ETHICS IN DIVERSE ORGANIZATIONS

The tendency toward a multicultural work force raises serious and difficult issues of ethics. Increasingly, people are asking for a return to our founding values and ethics (Hart, 1988). Concurrently, other voices are being raised suggesting that ethical diversity is a new good. They say diverse values outweigh traditional values and social relationship models. These voices forget that America's values foundation was forged in a very diverse community. They found acceptance because of their general applicability to people from many nations and cultural backgrounds.

A multidifferentiated work force compels strong leader action to set an ethical groundwork for an organization. Too many people relegate ethics to an academic cubbyhole. Many others assume that organizational members share ethical views. This is unsubstantiated in practice. Individual ethical behavior is a function of many forces. But, in essence, our ethics flows out of individual values and the strength of those values. The ethical standard of an organization is a function of shared values and the relative strength of those individually honored values.

Diversity raises new ethical issues and presents both leaders and followers with new situations that may challenge established ethics. People are tempted to act outside an organization's ethical standards when their own values conflict with the organization. They also might act unethically by organizational standards when the rewards and sanctions implicit and explicit in the organization's culture respecting violation of accepted norms of behavior are not compelling to them.

Diversity fosters erosion of traditional standards of moral and ethical behavior. Ethical conduct requires a common basis of shared values that not all participants may share in the present situation of multiculturalism. Nevertheless, we cannot ignore the need for clearly defined ethical foundations (Fairholm, 1991). Ethics, and the values they support and operationalize, provide an important standard guiding individual conduct and measuring individual and organizational success.

A culture that emphasizes ethics produces high trust and a deeper commitment in both leaders and followers to the organization and its programs, values, and goals. Promoting ethics asks the leader to convey basic information about ethical positions. This effort may take the form of vision statements, codes of ethics, and mission statements.

In promoting ethics, leaders may use formal or informal orientation programs to introduce newcomers to the organizational codes of ethical conduct. Ethical leadership also may include sponsoring training seminars for key leaders to define and promote ethical conduct throughout the organization. Increasingly, all stakeholders are participating in decision making involving ethically charged issues. But at its heart, ethical leadership is setting and then living by values and standards of conduct that honor freedom, justice, and individual dignity (Fairholm, 1991; Clement and Rickard, 1992). Leadership cannot take place separate from a commitment to ethical behavior and action.

Discussion of ethical issues in management meetings and in other forums is a way for leaders to sensitize the group to ethical needs. Such discussion often helps to define and contextualize ethics within the organization. Another effective method leaders may choose to follow is to provide an open door policy that promotes a climate of trust and high ethical conduct. Periodic ethical reviews of performance of the organization make sense.

# 17

# Integrating Quality

## INTRODUCTION

There was a time when "Made in America" was the standard for quality in the world. This is now no longer the case. Gitlow and Gitlow (1987) described our current state of focus on quality as being adrift without a rudder. Their solution to a return to high quality is to alter our overall approach to managing our work systems and organizations. Using the model of the Japanese under W. Edwards Deming's comprehensive quality approach, they predict a similar rise in quality for American organizations. They and many others have proffered plans to raise America to its former greatness by using various systems of quality improvement.

This interest in quality is not new to the latter decades of the twentieth century. A focus on high quality performance has always been a part of leadership and management. Lammermeyer's (1990) research, reviewed briefly here, pointed out that quality has been a factor in even the earliest management systems. He reports that many so-called new management systems and processes actually have their origins in ancient rules, guild standards, trade agreements, and formalized standard practices. This is the case with our current interest in quality. Most so-called innovations are really revisiting older quality systems.

## HISTORICAL THREADS OF THE QUEST FOR QUALITY

Many older civilizations valued quality in individual and group performance long before our current interest (George, 1968). For example, in 2150 B.C. a quality standard in housing construction was written into the Code of Hammurabi. According to Lammermeyer, part of item 229 relating to housing construction standards stated: "If a builder has built a house for a man, and his work is not strong, and the house falls in and kills the householder, that builder shall be slain." Even our most rabid advocates of high quality have not yet reached this level of priority. The Phoenicians, too, used a very effective corrective action program to maintain quality. To eliminate nonconformance, Phoenician inspectors cut off the hand of the person responsible for unsatisfactory quality.

Guilds in the Middle Ages were the first counterparts of the modern quality circle. Guild members had the practice of eating the midday meal together to discuss projects, methods, and progress. Quality was a hallmark for the guilds, since guild members signed their work with the guild seal or symbol.

The Industrial Revolution reconstituted the way work was done in America and much of the Western world. Its main contribution was to bring the benefit of increased quantity to large-scale manufacturing and processing tasks. Quality was initially a priority in industrialization. The focus of the scientific management movement of this period was initially on quality, but quantity issues soon predominated and reduced the focus on individual unit quality. Nevertheless, early scientific managers introduced such technologies as time and motion study, statistical quality control, reliance on jigs and standard patterns, and similar techniques to focus worker and managers alike on quality performance.

According to Naisbitt and Aburdene (1985), our present business-oriented society has evolved from an industrial society to an information society. They suggest that people—the human resource—are more valuable in today's work world than money was in the industrial age. If we have a competitive advantage in America, it is in our people. The American work force traditionally has been committed, motivated, and prepared educationally and psychologically to produce at high performance levels and quality levels. This advantage, however, is lost if we accept workers with all types of standards, work values, and personal commitment to the joint enterprise.

The pressure is still present to provide more and more gadgets to a growing and demanding population. As a result, much of the responsibility to secure high quality is built into organizational structures and systems, not in the attitudes and values of the organizational culture. Today, we delegate the problem of increasing quality to third parties who examine worker product after the fact. Now inspectors, behavior modification experts (who use psychology to induce workers, often via threats and bribes, to produce at predetermined levels), and quality control units have responsibility for quality. The results have been the continued increase of quantity, but at the expense of quality.

There has been, however, a renewed interest in making quality a value in contemporary American business and government cultures. Spurred by the success in post–World War II Japan of quality control techniques coupled with participative structures, some American organizations moved into this technology. Current systems typically focus on a commitment to organizationwide quality, a customer service orientation, and measurement of performance effort.

## DEFINING QUALITY OPERATIONALLY

The dictionary definition of *quality* includes ideas of excellence. George Edwards defined it as existing when successive articles of commerce have their characteristics more nearly like its fellows and more nearly approximating the designer's intent (Lammermeyer, 1990). Crosby (1984) defined quality as conforming to requirements. He said that the best way to obtain quality is for the task to be done right the first time. Juran (1989) defined quality as freedom from waste, trouble, and failure. Others suggest that quality is meeting and exceeding informed customer needs.

Quality can also be defined in global terms. As such, it is a composite of all the organizational components, such as design, engineering, manufacture, marketing, and maintenance, that a given product and service receives. Defined this way, quality is a function of process. Customer satisfaction also is a factor in defining quality. Today, many organizations place a strong emphasis on customer satisfaction when defining quality. They see quality as a way of managing, not as a task of management.

W. Edwards Deming is a founder of the so-called Third Wave of the Industrial Revolution. He also defines quality in customer satisfaction terms. Quality is the result of forecasting customer needs translated into product characteristics to create useful and dependable products. Quality is, in effect, creating a system that can deliver a product at the lowest possible price and consistent with both customer and producer's needs. Deming produced a 14-point philosophy of quality (Walton, 1986) dealing with quality enhancement rather than a system of techniques to produce quality.

Attaining quality performance today requires the concerted effort of all levels in the organization. Quality is a part of the actions and attitudes of all members. The first step is to recognize that a quality improvement process can be of benefit to the organization, individual members, and all other stakeholders. Other steps involve specific training in improved techniques and institution of measurement systems to evaluate progress.

The movement toward increased quality throughout the organization is a cultural challenge more than a technological one. While both are important, the prime need is to develop a culture that supports continuous improvement in customer service through accomplishment of cultural shifts. This task is one of education of the heart rather than just training of the hand. It is a task of leadership more than of managerial control over resources. It is a values-change task.

Once quality was a major element in organizational management, now it is the key to leadership. An organization's effectiveness in quality terms is more a function of the attitudes and style of the leader and the culture he or she creates than it is a function of a specific managerial control system. Quality is more than ensuring that systems of work include an inspection component; it is a part of the values, purposes, and goals of leaders and their followers.

In the following sections, some currently used quality improvement systems are described in terms of their value elements. Their success is a function of their capacity to induce stakeholders to accept the values underlying quality enhancement, not as discrete tools or systems to control worker performance.

### Quality Circles

One way to get improved quality performance is to instill in employees a desire for quality. Another is to place prime responsibility for and a mechanism to attain high quality in the hands of workers. Quality circles (QCs) are the fad of choice to accomplish this. Quality circles are small groups of about 10 people, including a supervisor. They meet regularly to identify, analyze, and solve problems experienced on the job. Dr. W. Edwards Deming is a pioneer in QC methods, which he developed while working in Japan.

The secret of success for many quality circle programs is the change of values in the members of the circles (teams). Quality circles reshape the attitudes of the people who actually do the organization's work. They become a small in-house consultant team tasked to improve conditions and results. In effect, a quality circle program makes the members mini-leaders, each with the same goal of change to improve current performance. Typically, QC teams make suggestions on how to enhance the quality of goods or services, solve workplace problems, and improve organizational communications. They also install agreed-upon suggestions. These are all tasks that would normally be assigned to managers and leaders.

The quality circle members are volunteers. Experience has shown that workers cannot be forced into accepting the attitudes, values, and tasks of leaders. They must individually agree to adopt this role in their work unit. The key to success in quality circle programs is in the willingness of workers to take on these tasks. Of course, each circle has a leader who most often is the workers' supervisor. The key role of the supervisor, however, is not to supervise the team, but to promote its work. Circles and their leaders often have a resource expert to aid them in their work. These resource people are also facilitators.

Circles typically meet weekly at or near the work site. The circle leader conducts the meeting. The circle selects a list of problems and begins by discussing the top priority problem. The resource person provides a communication link between the group and higher management or other units in the organization. Facilitators also can help teams through training and in the acquisition of in-house technical staff or other helpers. These in-house experts are on tap, not on top, in this technology. They support the work of the QC. They do not dominate. Circle leaders and resource people work to ensure that the experts do not take over.

The success of quality circles are dependent on the members' willingness to accept change in the organization. They take personal ownership of their part of the organization. Quality circles help improve productivity and improve employee morale. They improve interpersonal problem-solving skills and can improve the level of service to customers. These are all functions and goals sought by leaders.

Quality circle programs are a kind of philosophy of worker self-governance more than they are a program of action. To be effective, the quality circle must be an integral part of the organization's management philosophy. Circle programs aim at improving productivity by changing the way people work together, what they value, and their processes of interaction for problem solving and goal accomplishment. They ask us to treat employees as adults, trusting them, respecting them, and helping them become their best self. This quality program asks leaders to be obsessed with quality and requires all group members to be involved in the quest for quality (Peters, 1987).

## Deming's Management Philosophy

Mention has been made of the contributions of W. Edwards Deming to the development of a culture of quality enhancement in our organizations. Deming's philosophy is summarized in his now famous 14 points. Each of these 14 points, or principles, help define the process of quality creation in an organization. These principles address the need to create constancy of purpose toward improvement of product and service and advocate adopting a philosophy of quality, rejecting the idea that the group can accept delays, mistakes, defective materials, or faulty workmanship.

Deming suggests that organizations end the practice of awarding business based on component price alone. He assigns managers the task of working continually to improve the system by instituting modern methods of training and different methods to supervise workers. He says the responsibility of the supervisor must change from numbers to values about quality.

Deming's program goals include the elimination of fear so that everyone may work effectively for the company. Leaders need to break down the barriers between departments and to abolish numerical goals and slogans for the work force, asking instead for new levels of productivity without providing detailed methods, which employees can better supply. The intent of the Deming philosophy is to remove barriers that stand between workers and pride of workmanship. The focus of his 14 points is on creating a new culture that values quality.

A summary of the 14 points follow:

1. *Begin to require constancy of purpose.* Develop and promote a long-term, firm commitment to the goal of changing the workplace to make it better.

2. *Improve constantly.* Adopt a philosophy that we can no longer deal with the commonly accepted levels of delays, mistakes, defective materials, and defective workmanship. Adopt the idea of the Deming wheel which defines an ongoing process of plan-do-check-act-analyze.

3. *Cease dependency on mass production.* Require, instead, statistical evidence that quality is built in. Abolish numerical goals and focus rather on improving the process of work, not just its results.

4. *Find problems.* It is management's job to work continually on the system. Create a structure in management that will push every day for high quality.

5. *Inaugurate modern methods of leadership.* The responsibility of leader—from supervisor to top management—must change from numbers to quality. Remove barriers that stand between workers and their right to pride of workmanship.

6. *Drive out fear.* Take the fear out of bad news so all workers can use the information to improve the process.

7. *End the practice of awarding business on the basis of lowest bid.* Strive for lowest product price, not lowest component unit price.

8. *Break down departmental barriers.* Unite all units in organizational mission accomplishment and quality improvement.

9. *Inaugurate training on the job.* Training with the work group fosters teamwork. Install a vigorous program of education and self-development.

10. *Foster employee pride.*

11. *End the annual merit rating;* it is unfair and harmful. If good employees are selected, there will be little variation in performance. Measuring individual performance fosters jealousy and destructive competition. Base compensation on experience and responsibility.

12. *Eliminate slogans and exhortations.* They foster an adversarial relationship, since employees alone cannot change the organization.

13. *Cease dependence on mass inspection*—it plans for defects. Rather, design processes that identify faults early and prevent production of defective materials.

14. *Create a structure in top management that will support the previous 13 points.*

In every essential respect, Deming's philosophy is a prescription for culture change. Adoption of a quality value requires a change in the essential culture of an organization: a change in its values, ideals, relationships, and approaches. It is also a call to move from management to leadership.

A central aspect of Deming's quality system centers on the special knowledge leaders need to attain high quality performance. Called *profound knowledge* or knowledge for the management of transformation, this knowledge is about the work flow system and how to shape it to attain high quality. Deming's principles of statistical control of quality, by which he means detailed knowledge about common and special causes of work activity and results, focus on the details of the work system and supervisory practices. Both are critical to developing a continuously improving organization. Perhaps the most important from a leadership point of view is applying statistical quality control in the management of people.

## Juran's Quality Philosophy

Another pioneer in the quality movement is Joseph M. Juran. Juran was chief of the inspection control division of Western Electric and a professor at New York University. He taught a 10-step method for implementing quality that is similar to Deming's 14 principles. Juran's philosophy centers on building awareness of the need and opportunity for improvement. He suggests leaders set goals for improvement and organize to reach the goals. Juran supports establishment of quality councils to identify problems, select projects, appoint teams, and choose facilitators.

Juran's quality councils represent a new form of organizational structure based on values of quality, sharing, and participation. It is a version of shared governance, which was discussed in chapter 13. The councils provide training in quality techniques to workers, who then carry out projects to solve problems. His approach includes elements of accountability via regular progress reporting.

Other elements of his philosophy involve giving recognition for quality performance, communicating broadly quality enhancement skills developed by one council, and keeping score, that is, recording progress routinely to ensure that all workers know and understand the organization's priority on quality performance. The bottom line of the Juran philosophy is making improvement part of the regular values, work systems, and processes of the company.

## Total Quality Management

The recent emphasis on total quality management (TQM) is an outgrowth of the work of Deming and Juran and their students. It integrates the central quality-based philosophy of these pioneers and their main operating principles and values. TQM is an attempt to apply the Deming-Juran philosophy to an American work culture setting. The basis of the TQM system is cultural change. In TQM, products or services possess quality if they help somebody and enjoy a sustainable market.

TQM implies something other than zero defects. Traditional definitions of quality (automation, computerization, best efforts, more inspection, zero defects, MBO, a quality manager) ignore the responsibility of leaders and places responsibility on workers or equipment or suppliers. Quality is the responsibility of the leaders of the company working with customers. It is made by top management, by leaders. It is determined, shaped, and given meaning at the top.

TQM proposes that our best organizational efforts must be guided by knowledge developed by leaders, not customers. The organization's customers, contrary to popular myth, do not provide useful information about what they need and the level of quality required. Often customers do not know what is possible or what options may be open to them respecting new or higher quality products or services. Leaders have this knowledge. They have created and sold most of today's new products and services. Beyond doubt, this is the case with computer software houses. It is also the case for most innovations in automobile manufacture and other service and product industries. The manufacturers/suppliers develop new products and then induce customers to see their value.

Most customers expect only what leaders have led them to expect. In TQM, the leader's job is to teach workers and customers what they need in the way of quality products and to value high quality products or services. A wise customer will listen and learn from a supplier.

The central problem in TQM is development of a culture that puts value on this kind of learning. Part of the leader's job is to keep asking what product or service will most help customers. Quality demands a culture conducive to this kind of learning and dissemination. Several aspects of quality learning are central to understanding TQM. The following statements are brief explanations of these key TQM learnings.

> We must innovate to predict customer's needs and to give them what they need, not just what they say they want. Leaders that create a culture conducive to innovation and who are lucky will take the market.

A culture supportive of continuous improvement is more important in attaining quality than the mere goal of better quality products.

Costs are not causes of loss due to poor quality, they are the results of poor quality. The cause of loss is in the system, the culture, and the formal and informal relationships it fosters. No amount of skill or care in workmanship can overcome integral faults of the system.

Much of quality improvement comes from improvements that may be hard to measure precisely. It is wrong to suppose that if it cannot be measured, it cannot be managed. This is a costly myth about attaining quality.

The values and style of the leader is key in producing quality. Depending on the leader's style, it is the foundation of either total quality actions or the biggest cause of waste. Faulty leadership more than anything else affects organizational quality performance.

Inspection after the fact does not guarantee high quality. A lot of unnecessary and wasteful paperwork, for example, begins in the leader's supposition that the cure for repetition of mistakes or fraud is more audit or inspection.

## SUMMARY

Leaders that focus on tight control will fall short of attainable high quality performance and can expect failure, even destruction. Tight control precludes innovation, testing of alternative methods, and creatively altering work systems. Tight control forces leaders and workers to continue to perform their work according to standard operating procedures. Tight managerial controls will thwart quality improvement inputs from workers and make change to improve quality difficult.

Attaining high quality requires total employee involvement at all levels in the organization. It is a matter of cultural change to give high priority quality values and methods. It requires effort by workers, middle managers, and top leaders. Each needs to play a role in changing the culture to value quality and performing to attain it.

Producing high quality products or services also implies quality of work life factors that are difficult to attain. Leaders need to create a culture that meets the needs of all stakeholders both within and external to the organization. Leaders need to give employees something meaningful to commit to before they will commit themselves to quality goals (Pascerella, 1984). Ludeman (1989) suggested, rightly, that we need to replace the old Protestant work ethic with a "worth ethic."

High quality will come only as we move from a situation where workers work because they fear economic deprivation, to a situation where they work because they want to improve themselves and make a difference in the world. It is an empowerment idea.

# 18

# Barriers to Shaping Trust Cultures

## INTRODUCTION

Much of the current attention given to cultural maintenance focuses on creating cultures that empower organizational workers. The conventional wisdom says that an appropriate cultural environment lets workers trust each other enough to take responsibility for their jobs and for realization of their goals, along with those of the organization. The thrust of much of the power literature (Fairholm, 1993) is also toward empowerment of individuals and work teams so they will accept the organization's goals and purposes. The outcome is expected to be work system improvement—what the Japanese call *kaizen,* or "constant striving for improvement."

Unfortunately, organizations, like people, do not always act in the ways our theories—or common sense—would suggest. Sometimes a group's actions produce the opposite result. Individual or collective behavior is sometimes counterproductive. Berkley (1984) called this kind of self-destructive behavior pathological. He identified several organizational pathologies that hamper interactive trust and, therefore, effective individual or group action. That is, some—often widespread and common—individual and group behavior act on the organization as a system to bar attainment of stated goals and purposes. Whether or not Berkley's list of aberrant behaviors fit exactly with common medical definitions of pathology, at least they are barriers to effective group success. They act to stifle, not empower, group members. Some of these behaviors are identified below.

## BARRIERS TO BUILDING TRUST

There is some support in the literature for thinking about cultural factors in terms of their negative or unintended effects. The literature describes this inappropriate behavior as pathological, as barriers, rather than aids, to success (see, for example, Simon, Smithburg, and Thompson, 1950; Katz and Kahn, 1966; Berkley, 1984). These research findings give us some understanding of system- and/or human-based barriers that hinder group and individual success. The TQM focus on continuous improvement of the system is a current example in which experts recognize failures in the situation—for example, the tasks of leadership, the presence of fear, unclear or inappropriate organizational aims as the root of dysfunction.

We can find other examples of these organizational system or personality barriers throughout the literature. The following summary of the most common cultural system and human barriers to a trust relationship may help place the problem of inappropriate human behavior in perspective. This discussion points up potential problem areas leaders may need to consider as they go about creating and managing appropriate cultures that support a trust relationship.

### Organizational System Barriers

A trust culture is a delicate construct composed of people in informal and formally structured relationships, work processes, physical facilities, and institutional goals. Failure in any of these subsystems can affect the whole. Unfortunately, failures in organizational systems can happen when we do too much of the right thing as well as when we do things incorrectly. Some organizational barriers to creating or maintaining an effective trust culture flow out of these overdone actions. Berkley (1984) suggested that we hamper development of an effective trust culture when the organization or one of its components survive beyond their normal effective life. We also hamper development of effective trust cultures when traditional behavior patterns dominate the need for change. This is also the case when the tendency toward bigness becomes counterproductive. Trust cultures suffer also when some organizational components seek status vis-à-vis their peers. A review of these system barriers follows.

**Survival beyond effective need.** Berkley (1984) suggested that the natural tendency for all things to persist can become a barrier to effective organizational interaction. Naturally, organizations want to survive over time. Some organizations, however, survive beyond their effective, useful life. These obsolete organizations, or parts of larger organizations, develop a culture that can become a burden on the larger organization or on society. While the organization endures, those people and other organizations who deal with it find it difficult to act from a position of trust toward the obsolete organization or its members.

Organizations that continue beyond their useful life span become barriers to overall social or institutional trust building. In effect, they are unnecessary links in the organizational chain that forms the fabric of the culture. These obsolete organizations ask their members to perpetuate an institutional fraud on themselves and on those with whom they interact. They clutter up the organizational landscape and hamper free-flowing communication and idea and material exchange. They also use valuable resources of time, energy, and material, which could better be used elsewhere in the system.

**Traditionalism.** Organizations have not only a natural tendency to survive, but they have a tendency to maintain traditional ways of thinking and behaving. This tendency, like survival, can be either positive or negative.

Past practice often becomes the basis for present activity. The idea that if "it ain't broke don't fix it" is rampant in organizational life. This mindset is a part of organizational culture maintenance and often is a positive tool to perpetuate desirable organizational interaction and activity patterns.

Overreliance on past practice, however, can narrow the organization's vision and cause leaders and followers to fail to see future targets of opportunity. Unfortunately, too much of a good thing can become dysfunctional for the organization and forestall effective change to keep the organization up to date.

Organizational rigidity often comes as the organization matures. Once new systems and procedures become entrenched, they can mask the underlying values that formerly tied people to the organization's vision and work systems. In these organizational cultures, change becomes a problem of shifting long-standing paradigms that have prescribed rules and regulations and have assigned values within the organization.

Instituting a new cultural paradigm in an entrenched organization can be difficult. Established patterns of interaction, traditional values, and known structural relationships can thwart a leader's efforts to alter that culture. Importantly, it can thwart the organization's efforts to accomplish its own goals as the drift of society places different pressures on the organization to conform. Trust in this kind of entrenched organizational culture becomes an issue of conformity that stifles innovation and limits trust to narrow behavior standards.

**Uncontrolled Growth.** Another institutional barrier that may hamper development of a trust culture is growth. There is a tendency among organizational leaders and followers toward growth—in the size of the organization, in product mix, in market share. Many equate success with growth. It is rare to find a leader or a group who values stability in growth, the small-is-better philosophy or "right-sizing," without compelling outside pressures.

Of course, there are valid reasons for growth. It adds strength, vitality, opportunity to the institution, to its people, and to the larger society. But, increased size adds to the problems of creating and maintaining a trust culture. As more people are added to the work force, more complicated interpersonal relationships result. This causes an increase in leadership problems. Leaders need more time to train and interact intimately with more people. Growth requires more layers of leadership, which requires even more training and contact.

Growth sometimes brings with it a tendency toward personal and institutional self-aggrandizement. Berkley (1984) referred to this tendency as an imperative for territory. Growth can become dysfunctional as individuals of subgroups contend with others to gain more control over more territory—be it geographical or institutional. American society is enamored of bigness, but bigness can reduce trust relationships and add unnecessary layers of supervision and control mechanisms.

**Office Politics.** Everyone uses their personal and positional power to help them be personally successful on the job and in relationships with other members of their groups. The world calls this behavior office or organizational politics (Fairholm, 1993). Organizational politics can be good and bad. They can be a bar to the close cooperation needed for trusting relationships and can cause well-laid plans to come to nothing.

Some organizations can be characterized as Machiavellian (Grifin, 1991). This organizational culture type is characterized by negative power plays, rigid hierarchy, intrigue, internal strife, and distrust. Mutual fear is the operative psychology, and it, more than any other barrier is antithetical to development of trust. The technology employed by members in this kind of organization is negative organizational power politics. Turning around these organizational cultures is difficult. The solution is to use power tactically to support trust values, goals, and action (Fairholm, 1993).

### Personal Barriers

Several distinct personality types can be identified as possible barriers. They are discussed below under headings emphasizing the chief features of personality that may be bars to trust. Uncontrolled and uncompensated for, these personality types hinder team and, therefore, leader success. They can become dysfunctional and thwart development of a viable trusting culture capable of serving both individual member and group needs.

Despite a leader's best efforts to empower co-workers, sometimes they act in ways that are detrimental to the organization and themselves. Leaders need to identify these psychological and sociological obstacles that may hamper development of a trust culture. Without intending to be comprehensive, the following elements in the social relationships between leaders and followers may become organizationally unhealthy barriers to positive, trusting cultures.

**Power Usage.** The need for personal power is strong in most healthy adults. Some say the pull of power is instinctual. Machiavelli said the desire to control our fellows is so strong that it dominates the minds of kings and commoners (Grifin, 1991). As followers come to demand more freedom to make their own work-related choices, the issue of the proper distribution of power becomes a central culture creation issue.

Properly allocated and properly used, power is a tool to help leaders build a trust culture. The pressure for leaders to share their power with others, nevertheless, can be a barrier to development of a trust culture. Giving up our craving for power in favor of empowering others goes against longstanding leadership traditions and, maybe, psychological forces.

Analysis of the idea of power use in an organizational context leads to the interesting conclusion that power use is a critical factor in determining leader dominance in a given situation (Fairholm, 1993). That is, the most influential person in the group can attain domination over others, called power targets. Powerful people become leaders.

Observation can identify a few simple tests of a leader's willingness to share power. When leaders are unwilling to share power:

They make all decisions, no matter how trivial

There is no excitement about work

Everyone works at an adequate level, not beyond

They take acceptance for success but spread blame

They, along with workers, fear change as a potential harm to the power structure

On the other side of the power question, a leader may have difficulty in getting others to accept power. The presence in the organization of people who resist empowerment efforts offered by their leaders in some or any situation can also diminish overall success. We can classify this situation as dysfunctional, a barrier to development of a desired level of trust in the culture.

The problem with empowerment is that it is powerful. Giving power to workers allows them to be more productive in group goal accomplishment. This power can also be used to move the organization away from desired goals. Also, not everyone wants, or is prepared to, receive power and use it wisely or effectively. Sometimes, people do not or cannot exert power because they fear it. People are flawed, and the systems people create are flawed. Rather than helping, sometimes what leaders (or followers) do become barriers rather than gates to progress.

There are physical, psychological, and sociological system barriers to empowerment that leaders often ignore in their rush to create a trust culture based on worker empowerment. These factors sometimes play out in dysfunctional ways in organizational relationships. Despite the leader's best efforts, characteristics of the people worked with or the character of the current culture can sometimes dissipate collective energy. This can cause the leader's explicit goals to become fuzzy and unclear and direct the work effort toward harmful, not helpful, activity.

These factors can be conveniently thought of as cultural pathologies; barriers within the situation itself that contribute to unhealthy, rather than healthy, organizational relationships or processes. These system-based, personal, or situational barriers can thwart accomplishment of intended goals. These organizational cultural barriers can frustrate leaders' attempts to focus group energy on needed results, even as they "apply" the latest theory of leadership technologies.

**Status.** Membership in an organized group is a psychological need. It is also common that once a part of a larger social grouping, people want to have a special place in that group. The quest for status among our fellows is a common activity seen in organizations. As with the other barriers, some seeking for special status is a part of personal and organizational growth and maturation. It can, however, become a problem and lead to wasted effort, conflict, and diminution of trust.

The quest for status can blind individuals to goals and values other than their own and can become dysfunctional as the individual turns from the institutional goal of customer service to personal need satisfaction. Many customers feel that leaders create social and work organizations to serve the members, not the customers. Many organizations place in service times of opening, complex requirements, and detailed procedures to ease the tasks of the leaders and co-workers, not to meet the needs of clients and customers. In this eventuality, the quest for status degenerates into a dysfunctional search for personal ease.

**Dysfunctional Sociopathic Behavior.** McClellend (1975) suggests that some people have an inner need to use power. If, however, someone who desires power becomes psychologically stressed, this need can become dysfunctional and, pathological. Used this way, power reduces trust and fractionates the culture.

A psychopath can be defined as a person who determines behavior based, not on society's standards, but on her or his own desires. Psychopaths typically behave according to their own rules, not those of the community, and they constantly change these rules at their convenience. They often feel little guilt or anxiety about their behavior or its impact on others, no matter how aggressive, dominating, or demanding. They feel no close bonds with others, lacking the psychological and social ties to the values basis supporting the rest of the group. The presence in a culture of these organizationally functional psychopaths reduces the likelihood of development of a trust culture.

These so-called "functional psychopaths" follow the culture's rules only so they can attain their desires, not because of any moral obligation or feelings of responsibility toward others. Controlling others makes the functional psychopath feel superior. We can see similar behavior in both leaders and followers.

When we see this behavior pattern in leaders, the results are predictable. Such leaders will rarely give up their power over others to satisfy followers or organizational or system requirements. Functional psychopaths do not concentrate power to accomplish a group vision or to promote accomplishment of the organization's goal. They do it to achieve dominance over other people for personal reasons. Trust is *not* present in this situation.

**Cynicism.** Some group members see a problem in any assignment. Cynical behavior, or the inability to believe in or care about what one does, can disrupt group action, reduce trust levels, and lessen potential group results. While cynics can be passionate, they express their caring in negative terms (Carr, 1990). Some cynics are open about their negativity (e.g., "we've never done it this way before"); others are less obvious. Cynical behavior is contagious (Carr, 1990). We can find cynics in the ranks of both leaders and followers.

Leadership of cynics is difficult, as it is with any dysfunctional behavior. The key to reorienting the cynic is motivation. The goal is to find common experiences, values, and purposes; break down suspicions; and develop trust in the leader and in his or her goals for the group. Dialogue with the cynic is key to reordering his or her values foundation.

**The Enemy Within.** Unlike the open cynic, members of some groups direct their negativity toward the group or its program(s) in subversive ways. Their purposes may be legitimate disagreement with plans, program, or methods or revenge for a past insult, or attack. They undermine the organization and its leaders and programs in covert ways. Either the leader or followers can be subversives.

Sometimes the enemy within has a personal agenda to remove or discredit the leader (Grifin, 1991). At other times, the goal may be to stop some intended change. The typical techniques of this dysfunctional behavior is innuendo, slander, and rumor mongering (DuBrin, 1978). The motive may be personal dislike or professional ambition. Development of a culture of trust is the best antidote for this organizational pathology.

Leaders need to address the identified problems to the degree they are legitimate. Left unaddressed, these organizational subversives can destroy a culture and eradicate trust entirely.

**Burn Out.** Sometimes in some work groups, we can identify persons who are unwilling any longer to perform at expected levels. The colloquial term is *burn out*. The causes for this condition vary. Among the various causes are the following:

1. Lack of interest in work

2. Inadequate or inappropriate incentives

3. Boredom

4. Emotional exhaustion

5. Indifference

6. Feelings of helplessness

7. Stress

8. Alienation

9. Lack of trust in co-workers of the system

The leadership strategy for turning around this kind of group member is to create a trust environment capable of inducing the burned-out member to accept empowerment. Sitting in council with the follower is one way to build trust and guide the direction of empowered action (Fairholm, 1991). This approach to counter burn out is indicated in some cases. This is more intimate than just delegation of responsibility and authority to the burned-out employee. Of course, professional help is sometimes necessary for severe burn-out cases.

### Office Romances

A new challenge in organizational culture management is managing the office romance. On-the-job romance between co-workers has always been a minor part of the organizational dynamic. It has more currency today and is a reflection of changes in the demographics of most of our offices and workplaces. This change in organizational life reflects normal male-female relationships in the general society.

The rapid addition of women in the workplace performing the same jobs men perform has exacerbated the potential for workplace romantic involvements. Many leaders have little experience in dealing with it. Nevertheless, emotional alliances between co-workers is a growing phenomenon in the workplace and affects the character and the quality of the culture developed in a given organization. It can change the trust dynamic in an organization and if not considered, office romances can get out of hand and hamper group effectiveness.

Because of the newness of this interpersonal relationship type, there is little experience to help guide leaders in dealing with the involved group members. While sexual issues are difficult to deal with in any context, it is an especially difficult issue on the job. At its base, the problem lends itself to only two responses. Leaders can either ignore the romantic involvement and hope it will end without disruption, as some do, or they can do something about it. The affair should be considered as private in the absence of a job-related impact, such as a potential impact on participants' careers, on co-workers, on job performance, or on accomplishment of shared goals.

In any effort to ameliorate the negative impacts of an office romance, issues of sexual discrimination should be considered and guarded against. Guidance may be obtained from the organization's conflict of interest rules or from rules regulating nepotism. Some traditional rules of thumb may not be possible today, given the general litigiousness of our society. Many of these rules are being challenged in court. At least the organizational leader should insist on honesty and no special favors. Obviously, any rules or policy should apply equally to all employees, not only to those involved.

Leaders need to be wary of the dynamics of male-female relationships. They should be cautious of sexist stereotypes carried over from their earlier lives. They are also many fuzzy distinctions between romance and harassment. Most leaders need training in how to handle these kinds of situations. But, because of the newness of this phenomenon and the complexity of direct action, training by itself is not a cure-all. Creating and shaping a culture that considers this potentiality is a more effective and longer-term strategy. The task is to accommodate this prospect within an overall culture of mutual support, encouragement, and opportunity for individual improvement and collective success. The culture leaders create must recognize this dynamic and set values and other parameters to guide individuals in this intimate and emotional relationship. They must also use these guidelines to protect others who may be caught up in this dynamic.

# Bibliography

Adair, John. *Effective Teambuilding.* Brookfield, Vt.: Gower Publishing, 1986.

Adler, Alfred. *The Individual Psychology of Alfred Adler,* ed. H. L. Ansbacher and R. R. Ansbacher. New York: Basic Books, 1956.

Aguayo, Raphael. *Dr. Deming: The American Who Taught the Japanese About Quality.* New York: Carol Publishing, 1990.

Alfano, Sal. "Commitment in America." *Psychology Today* (June 1985).

Argyrus, C. *Intervention Theory and Method: A Behavioral Science View.* Reading, Mass.: Addison-Wesley, 1973.

Bailey, Stephen. "Improving Federal Governance." *Public Administration Review* (November/December 1980): 548.

Bain, David. *The Productivity Prescription: The Manager's Guide to Improving Productivity and Profits.* New York: McGraw-Hill, 1982.

Barber, Bernard. *The Logic and Limits of Trust.* New Brunswick, N.J.: Rutgers University Press, 1983.

Barker, Joel. *Future Edge.* New York: Morrow, 1992.

Barnard, Chester. *The Functions of the Executive.* Cambridge, Mass.: Harvard University Press, 1968.

Barnes, Louis B. "Managing the Paradox of Organizational Trust." *Harvard Business Review* (March–April 1981).

Bass, Bernard M. *Stogdill's Handbook of Leadership.* New York: The Free Press, 1981

Batten, Joe. *Tough Minded Management.* New York: American Management Association, 1989.

Beattie, John. "Ritual in Social Change." *Man* 1 (1966): 60–74.

Beck, Arthur, and Ellis Hillmar. *Positive Management Practices.* San Francisco: Jossey-Bass, 1989.

Bennis, Warren. "The Artform of Leadership." *International Management* (May 1982): 21.

———. *Why Leaders Can't Lead: The Unconscious Conspiracy Continues.* San Francisco: Jossey-Bass, 1989.

Bennis, Warren, and Burt Nanus. *Leaders: Strategies for Taking Charge.* New York: Harper & Row, 1985.

Berger, Peter L., and Thomas Luckman. *The Social Construction of Reality.* Hammondsworth, England: Allen Lane, Penguin Press, 1966.

Berkley, G. E. *The Craft of Public Administration.* Newton, Mass.: Allyn and Bacon, 1984.

Berlo, David K. *The Process of Communication.* New York: Holt, Rinehart and Winston, 1960.

Blake, Robert R., and Jane Srygley Mouton. *Productivity: The Human Side.* New York: AMACOM, 1981.

Bocock, Robert. *Ritual in Industrial Society.* London: Allen and Unwin, 1972.

Bolman, Lee G., and Terrence E. Deal. *Modern Approaches to Understanding and Managing Organizations.* San Francisco: Jossey-Bass, 1987.

Bonczek, Stephen J. "Ethical Decision Making: Challenge of the 1990's—A Practical Approach for Local Governments." *Public Personnel Management* 21, 3 (Fall 1992): 75–87.

Bradford, D. L., and A. R. Cohen. *Managing for Excellence.* New York: John Wiley & Sons, 1984.

Brassier, A. "Strategic Vision: A Practical Tool." *The Bureaucrat* (Fall 1985): 23–26.

Britton, Lester R. *The Nine Master Keys of Management.* New York: McGraw-Hill, 1972.

Britton, Paul, and John Stallings. *Leadership Is Empowering People.* Lanham, Md.: University Press of America, 1986.

Broder, David. "On Crisis of Family Values, Dan Quayle Was Right." *Richmond Times-Dispatch,* March 24, 1993, p. A11.

Brown, Luther. "Should Blacks Fight an Influx of Foreign Labor?" *Black Enterprize* 20, 11 (June 1990): 59–60.

Buckholz, Steve, and Thomas Roth. *Creating the High Performance Team.* New York: John Wiley and Sons, 1987.

Burns, J. M. *Leadership.* New York: Harper & Row, 1978.

Carr, Clay. *Front-Line Customer Service.* New York: John Wiley and Sons, 1990.

Cartright, D. "Influence, Leadership, Control." In J. G. March, ed., *Handbook of Organizations.* Chicago: Rand-McNally, 1965.

Cavalari, S. A., and R. A. DeCormier. "The Microskills System for High-Speed Leadership." *Leadership and Organization Development Journal* 12 (1988): 9–12.

Clark, Burton R. "The Organizational Saga in Higher Education." *Administrative Science Quarterly* 17 (1972): 178–84.

Clement, Linda M., and Scott T. Rickard. *Effective Leadership in Student Services: Voices from the Field.* San Francisco: Jossey-Bass, 1992.

Cohan, Abner. *Two Dimensional Man: An Essay on the Anthropology of Power and Symbolism in Complex Society.* London: Routledge and Kegan Paul, 1974.

Cohan, Percy S. "Theories of Myth." *Man* 4 (1969): 337–53.

Conger, Jay A., and Rabindra N. Kanungo. *Charismatic Leadership: The Elusive Factor in Organizational Effectiveness.* San Francisco: Jossey-Bass, 1988.

Cound, Dana M. "A Call for Leadership." *Quality Progress* (March 1987): 11–14.

Craddock, Fred B. *Preaching.* Nashville, Tenn.: Abington Press, 1985.

Cronan, Thomas E. "Thinking and Learning About Leadership." In W. E. Rosenbach and R. L. Taylor, eds., *Contemporary Issues in Leadership*, 2nd ed. Boulder, Colo.: Westview Press, 1989.

Crosby, Philip B. *Quality Is Free*. New York: McGraw-Hill, 1979.

————. *Quality Without Tears: The Art of Hassle-Free Management*. New York: McGraw-Hill, 1984.

Culbert, Samuel A. "The Invisible War: Pursuing Self-Interest at Work." *Journal of Applied Behavioral Science* 6, 1 (1970): 45.

Culbert, S. A., and J. J. McDonough. *Radical Management: Power Politics and the Pursuit of Trust*. New York: The Free Press, 1985.

Danforth, Douglas D. "The Quality Imperative." *Quality Progress* (February 1987): 17–19.

Dasgupta, Partha. "Trust as a Commodity." In Diego Gambetta, ed., *Trust: Making and Breaking Cooperative Relations*. Cambridge, Mass.: Basil Blackwell, 1988.

Davis, Stanley M. *Managing Corporate Culture*. Cambridge, Mass.: Ballinger, 1984.

Deal, Terry E. "Deeper Culture: Mucking, Muddling, and Metaphors." *Training and Development Journal* (January 1986).

Deal, T., and A. Kennedy. *Corporate Cultures: The Rites and Rituals of Corporate Life*. Reading, Mass.: Addison-Wesley, 1983.

DeCormier, R. A. *Counselor Selling: A Presentation and Test of Three Constructs of Counselor Selling: Personal Microskills and Techniques and Sells Process*. Doctoral thesis, Bradford, England, University of Bradford Management Center, 1991.

Deming, W. Edwards. *Out of the Crisis*. Cambridge, Mass.: Massachusetts Institute of Technology, Center for Advanced Engineering Study, 1986.

Denhart, Robert, James Pyle, and Allen Bluedorn. "Implementing Quality Circles in State Government." *Public Administration Review* 47, 4 (1987): 19.

de Tocqueville, Alexis. *Democracy in America*. New York: The New American Library, 1956.

Deutsch, M. "An Experimental Study of the effects of Cooperation and Competition upon Group Processes." *Human Relations* 2(1949): 199–232.

Dreyfuss, Joel. "Get Ready for the New Work Force." *Fortune* 121, 9 (April 1990): 165–81.

Drucker, Peter F. *Managing The Nonprofit Organization: Principles and Practice*. New York: Harper & Row, 1990.

DuBrin, Andrew J. *Winning at Office Politics*. New York: Van Nostrand Reinhold, 1978.

Dunn, John. "Trust and Political Agency." In Diego Gambetta, ed., *Trust: Making and Breaking Cooperative Relations*. Cambridge, Mass.: Basil Blackwell, 1988.

Dyer, W. G. *Team Building: Issues and Alternatives*. Boston: Addison-Wesley, 1987.

Eadie, Douglas C. "Putting a Powerful Tool to Practical Use: The Application of Strategic Planning to the Public Sector." *Public Administration Review* (September–October 1983): 447–52.

Ehrenhalt, Alen. *The United States of Ambition: Politicians, Power and the Pursuit of Office*. New York: New York Times Publishing Co., 1991.

Enos, Gary. "Cries of Racism Surround Probe of Mayor." *City and State*, February 10, 1992, p. 1.

Erickson, Eric. *Dimensions of a New Identity.* New York: Norton, 1974.

Etzioni, Amitai. *A Comprehensive Analysis of Complex Organizations.* New York: The Free Press, 1961.

Fairholm, Gilbert W. *Values Leadership: Toward a New Philosophy of Leadership.* New York: Praeger, 1991.

————. *Organizational Power Politics: Tactics of Leadership Power.* New York: Praeger, 1993.

Feder, Don. "All Cultures Are Not Created Equal." *Richmond Times-Dispatch,* April 16, 1992.

Fiedler, Fred E., and Martin M. Chamers. *Leadership and Effective Management.* Glenview, Ill.: Scott Foresman, 1974.

Follett, Mary Parker. *Dynamic Administration: The Collected Papers of Mary Parker Follett,* ed. Henry C. Metcalf and L. Urwick. New York: Harper & Brothers, 1942.

Frederick, Bill. "Government by the People: A Prescription for Florida's Future." *Youth Policy* 14, 8 (November/December 1991): 7–17.

Frost, Peter J., and David C. Hayes. "An Exploration in Two Cultures of a Model of Political Behavior in Organizations." In Peter J. Frost and David C. Hayes, eds., *Organizational Functioning in a Cross-Culture Perspective.* Kent, Ohio: Kent State University Press, 1979.

Frost, P. J., V. E. Mitchell, and W. R. Nord. *Organizational Reality: Reports from the Firing Line.* New York: Scott Foresman, 1982.

Gabarro, John L., and John P. Kotter. "Managing Your Boss." *The Best of Business* 2, 2 (1980): 18.

Gabor, Andrea. *The Man Who Discovered Quality.* New York: Time Books, 1990.

Gaertner, Karan M., and Gregory H. Gaertner. "Proactive Roles of Federal Managers." *The Bureaucrat* (Fall 1985):19–22.

Gambetta, Diego. "Can We Trust Trust." In Diego Gambetta, ed., *Trust: Making and Breaking Cooperative Relations.* Cambridge, Mass.: Basil Blackwell, 1988.

Gardner, John W. *Self-Renewal: The Individual and the Innovative Society.* New York: Harper Colophon Books, 1964.

————. "Leadership and the Future." *The Futurist* 24, 3 (1990): 8–12.

Garfield, C. *Peak Performers.* New York: Avon Books, 1987.

Geertz, Clifford. *The Interpretation of Culture.* New York: Basic Books, 1973.

George, Claude S., Jr. *The History of Management Thought.* Englewood Cliffs, N.J.: Prentice-Hall, 1968.

Giamatti, A. Bartlett. *Take Time for Paradise.* New York: Summit Books, 1989.

Gibb, Jack R. "Defense Level and Influence Potential in Small Groups." In L. Petrillo and B. M. Bass, eds., *Leadership and Interpersonal Behavior.* New York: Holt, Rinehart and Winston, 1961.

————. "Climate for Trust Formation." In L. P. Bradford, Jack R. Gibb, and Kenneth D. Benne, eds., *T-Group Theory and Laboratory Method.* New York: John Wiley and Sons, 1964a.

————. "Defensive Communication." *Journal of Communications* (1964b): 141–48.

————. *A New View of Reason and Organizations Development.* New York: Guild of Tutor's Press, 1978a.

————. *Trust: A View of Personal and Organizational Development.* Los Angeles: Guild of Tutor's Press, 1978b.

Gibb, J. R., and L. M. Gibb. "Role Freedom in a TORI Group." In A. Burton, ed., *Encounter*. San Francisco: Jossey-Bass, 1969.

Gioia, A. D., and Kumar Chittipeddi. "Sensemaking and Sensegiving in Strategic Change Initiation." *Strategic Management Journal* 12 (1991): 433–48.

Gitlow, Howard S., and Shelly J. Gitlow. *The Deming Guide to Quality and Competitive Position*. New York: Prentice-Hall, 1987.

Golembiewski, Robert T., and Frank Gibson. *Readings in Public Administration*. Boston: Houghton Mifflin, 1983.

Good, David. "Individuals, Interpersonal Relations and Trust." In Diego Gambetta, ed., *Trust: Making and Breaking Cooperative Relations*. Cambridge, Mass.: Basil Blackwell, 1988.

Greenleaf, Robert K. *Servant Leadership*. New York: Paulist Press, 1977.

Grifin, Gerald R. *Machiavelli on Management*. New York: Praeger, 1991.

Hafen, Bruce, "These Bonds Are Our Liberation." *Brigham Young Magazine* (February 1993): 28–33, 59.

Hall, Edward T. "How Cultures Collide." *Psychology Today* (July 1976): 66–102.

Hampton, D. R., C. E. Summer, and R. A. Webber. *Organizational Behavior and the Practice of Management*, 5th ed. Glenview, Ill.: Scott Foresman, 1987.

Handy, Charles B. *Understanding Organizations*. Middlesex, England: Penguin Books, 1976.

Haney, William V. *Communication and Organizational Behavior*. Homewood, Ill.: Richard D. Erwin, 1973.

Hart, David K. "Life, Liberty, and the Pursuit of Happiness: Organizational Ethics and the Founding Fathers." *Exchange* (Spring 1988):2–7.

Hart, Vivian. *Distrust and Democracy: Political Distrust in Britain and America*. New York: Cambridge University Press, 1978.

Harvey, Jerry B. "Trust and Organizational Effectiveness." *Technology Review* (May/June 1989):271–77.

Havelock, R. G. *The Change Agent's Guide to Innovation in Education*. Englewood, N.J.: Educational Technology, 1973.

Hawthorne, G. "Three Ironies in Trust." In Diego Gambetta, ed., *Trust: Making and Breaking Cooperative Relations*. Cambridge, Mass.: Basil Blackwell, 1988.

Hertzberg, Frederick. *Work and the Nature of Man*. Cleveland, Ohio: World Publishing, 1966.

Hitt, William D. *The Leader-Manager*. New York: Battelle Press, 1988.

Hodgkinson, Christopher. *Toward a Philosophy of Administration*. New York: St. Martin's Press, 1978.

Hoffer, Eric. *Working and Thinking of the Waterfront*. New York: Perennial Library, 1969.

Homans, G. *The Human Group*. New York: Harcourt Brace Jovanovich, 1950.

Hoyt, Kenneth B. *The Changing Workforce: 1986–2000*. Lawrence, Kans.: University Press, 1987.

Hult, Karan M., and Charles Walcott. *Governing Public Organizations*. Pacific Grove, Calif.: Brooks/Cole Publishing, 1990.

Hunt, James G. *Leadership: A New Synthesis*. London: Sage, 1991.

Hunt, James G., Uma Skaren, and Chester A. Schriesheion. *Leadership: Beyond Established Views*. Bloomington: Southern Illinois University Press, 1982.

Jackell, Robert. "Moral Mazes: Bureaucracy and Managerial Work." *Harvard Business Review* (September–October 1983): 113–30.

Jones, Allen P., L. R. James, and J. R. Bruni. "Perceived Leadership Behavior and Employee Confidence in the Leader as Moderated by Job Involvement." *Journal of Applied Psychology* 60, 1 (1975).

Juran, J. M. *Juran on Leadership.* New York: The Free Press, 1989.

Kalman, Ralph H. *Beyond the Quick Fix: Managing Five Tracks to Organizational Success.* San Francisco: Jossey-Bass, 1984.

Kalman, Ralph H., Mary J. Saxton, and Roy Serpa. "Issues in Understanding and Changing Culture." *California Management Review* 28, 2 (Winter 1986): 87–94.

Kanfer, Frederick, and Arnold P. Goldstien. *Helping People Change.* New York: Pergamon Press, 1980.

Kanter, Rosabeth Moss. *The Change Masters.* New York: Simon and Schuster, 1983.

Kats de Vries, Manfred, and Associates. *Organizations on the Couch.* San Francisco: Jossey-Bass, 1991.

Katz, D., and R. L. Kahn. *The Social Psychology of Organizations.* New York: John Wiley, 1966.

Kelley, R. E. "In Praise of Followers." In W. E. Rosenbach and R. L. Taylor, eds., *Contemporary Issues in Leadership,* 2nd ed. Boulder, Colo.: Westview Press, 1989.

Kelman, H. C. "Compliance, Identification, and Internalization: Three Processes of Attitude Change." *Conflict Resolution* 2 (1958): 51–60.

Kendel, Ruth. *Richmond Times-Dispatch,* July 1, 1992, p. B6.

Kiechel, Walter, III. "Sniping at Strategic Planning." *Planning Review* (May 1984): 1.

Klaus, Rudi, and Bernard M. Bass. *Interpersonal Communication in Organization.* New York: Academy Press, 1982.

Klimoski, Richard J., and Barbara L. Karol. "The Impact of Trust on Creative Problem Solving Groups." *Journal of Applied Psychology* 61, 5 (1976): 630–33.

Kostenbaum, Peter. *Leadership: The Inner Side of Greatness.* San Francisco: Jossey-Bass, 1991.

Kotter, John P. *A Force for Change: How Leadership Differs from Management.* New York: The Free Press, 1991.

Kouzes, James M. "When Leadership Collides with Loyalty." In W. E. Rosenbach and R. L. Taylor, eds., *Contemporary Issues in Leadership,* 2nd ed. Boulder, Colo.: Westview Press, 1989.

Kouzes, J. M., and B. Z. Posner. *The Leadership Challenge.* San Francisco: Jossey-Bass, 1987.

Kozlowski, S.W.J., and Mary L. Doherty. "Integration of Climate and Leadership: Examination of a Neglected Issue." *Journal of Applied Psychology* 74, 4 (August 1989): 546–53.

Kroeber, A. K., and Clyde Kluckholm. *Culture: A Critical Review of Concepts and Definitions.* New York: Vintage Books, 1952.

Krueger, Cathleen. "Shared Governance: The Challenge of the Early Phases of Implementation." *Nursing Administration Quarterly* 13, 4 (1989): 11–16.

Lagenspetz, Olli. "Legitimacy and Trust." In D. Z. Phillips, ed., *Philosophical Investigations* 15, 1. Oxford, England: Blackwell Publishers, 1992.

Lamb, Warren, and Elizabeth Watson. *Body Code: The Meaning of Movement.* Boston: Routledge and Kegan Paul, 1979.

Lammermeyer, Horst. *Human Relations: The Key to Quality.* New York: ASQC Quality Press, 1990.

Lasswell, H. D., and A. Kaplin. *Power and Society.* New Haven, Conn.: Yale University Press, 1950.

Lee, Chris. "Followership: The Essence of Leadership." *Training* 28, 1 (1991): 27–35.

Lincoln, James R. *Culture, Control, and Commitment.* New York: Cambridge University Press, 1990.

Lipset, Seymour, and William Schneider. *The Confidence Gap: Business, Labor, and Government in the Public Mind.* Baltimore, Md.: The Johns Hopkins University Press, 1987.

Locke, Edwin A. *The Essence of Leadership: The Four Keys to Leading Successfully.* New York: Lexington Books, 1991.

Lorsch, Jay W. "Managing Culture: The Invisible Barrier to Strategic Change." *California Management Review* 28, 2 (Winter 1986): 95–109.

Ludeman, Kate. *The Worth Ethic.* New York: E. P. Dutton, 1989.

Luke, R. A. "Matching the Individual and the Organization." *Harvard Business Review* 53, 3 (May–June 1975): 17–34, 165.

Lundin, Stephen C., and Lynne C. Lancaster. "The Importance of Followership." *The Futurist* 24, 3 (1990): 18–22.

McClellend, David C. *Power: The Inner Experience.* New York: Irvington Publishers, 1975.

Maccoby, Michael. *The Gamesman.* New York: Simon and Schuster, 1976.

———. *The Leader.* New York: Simon and Schuster, 1981.

McGregor, Douglas. *The Human Side of Enterprise.* New York: McGraw-Hill, 1960.

McLean, J. W., and William Weitzel. *Leadership: Magic, Myth, or Method.* New York: AMACOM, 1991.

Manz, Charles C., and Henry P. Sims, Jr. "Superleadership: Beyond the Myth of Heroic Leadership." *Organizational Dynamics* 19, 4 (1991): 18–35.

Maynard-Moody, Stevens, Donald D. Stull, and Jerry Mitchell. "Reorganization as Status Drama: Building, Maintaining, and Displacing Dominant Subcultures." *Public Administration Review* 46, 1 (1986): 301–10.

Meadow, A., S. J. Parnes, and H. Reese. "Influence of Brainstorming Instructions and Problem Sequence on a Creative Problem-Solving Test." *Journal of Applied Psychology* 43 (1959): 413–16.

Milgram, S. *Obedience to Authority: An Experimental View.* New York: Harper and Row, 1974.

Mitchell, T. R., and W. G. Scott. "Leadership Failures, the Distrusting Public and Prospects of the Administrative State." *Public Administration Review* (November/December 1987): 445–52.

Morgan, Garath. *Images of Organization.* Newbury Park, Calif.: Sage, 1986.

Mroczkowski, T. "Productivity and Quality Improvement at GE's Video Products Division: The Cultural Change Component." *National Productivity Review* (Winter 1984–1985): 1.

Myers, Scott. *Every Employee a Manager*. New York: McGraw-Hill, 1970.

Nadler, David A., and L. Tushman. *Strategic Organization Design*. Glenview, Ill.: Scott Foresman, 1988.

Naisbitt, John. *Megatrends: Ten New Directions Transforming Our Lives*. New York: Warner Books, 1982.

Naisbitt, John, and Patricia Aburdene. *Reinventing the Corporation*. New York: Warner Books, 1985.

"The New Breed of Strategic Planner." *Business Week,* September 17, 1984 (cover story).

Nixon, R. *Leaders*. New York: Warner Books, 1982.

Novak, Michael. "Ridicule of Cultural Values Undermine Nation's Social Foundations." *Richmond Times-Dispatch,* September 1992, p. A10.

Odom, Randall Y., W. Randy Boxx, and Mark G. Dunn. "Organizational Cultures, Commitment, Satisfaction, and Cohesion." *Public Productivity & Management Review* 14, 2 (1990): 157–69.

Orstein, Suzyn. "The Hidden Influences of Office Design." *Academy of Management Executive* 3, 2 (1989): 144–47.

Ott, J. Steven. *The Organizational Culture Perspective*. Belmont, Calif.: The Dorsey Press, 1989.

Ouchi, William G. *Theory Z: How American Business Can Meet the Japanese Challenge*. New York: Avon Books, 1981.

Pascale, R. T., and Anthony G. Athos. *The Art of Japanese Management: Applications for American Executives*. New York: Simon and Schuster, 1981.

Pascerella, Perry. *The New Achievers*. New York: The Free Press, 1984.

———. "Visionary Leadership Will Design the Future." *Industry Week* 238 (August 21, 1989): 48–49.

Peters, Tom. *Thriving on Chaos: Handbook for a Management Revolution*. New York: Knopf, 1987.

Peters, Tom, and Nancy Austin. *A Passion for Excellence: The Leadership Difference*. New York: Random House, 1985.

Peters, Thomas J., and Robert H. Waterman. *In Search of Excellence*. New York: Harper & Row, 1982.

Pettigrew, Andrew M. "On Studying Organizational Culture." *Qualitative Research* (1979): 87–103.

Pfeffer, Jeffrey. *Power in Organizations*. Marshfield, Mass.: Pittman Publishing, 1981.

"Politician, Heal Thyself." *Newsweek,* June 10, 1991, p. 27.

Porter-O'Grady, Timothy. *Shared Governance for Nursing: A Creative Approach to Professional Accountability*. Rockville, Md.: Aspen System Corporation, 1984.

Posner, B., and W. Schmidt. "Values and the American Manager." *California Management Review* (Spring 1988): 202–16.

Pye, Lucian. "A Psychoanalytic Approach to Charismatic Leadership: The Case of Mao Tse-tung." *Political Science Quarterly,* 91 (Summer 1976): 219–35.

Randolph, W. A., and B. Z. Posner. *Getting the Job Done! Managing Project Teams and Task Forces for Success*. New York: Simon and Schuster, 1992.

Reilly, A. J., and J. E. Jones. "Team Building." In J. W. Pfeiffer and J. E. Jones, eds., *The 1974 Annual Handbook for Group Facilitators*. San Diego, Calif.: University Associates, 1974.

Reuss, L. E. "Catalysts of Genius, Dealers in Hope." *Vital Speeches of the Day* 53, 6 (January 1, 1987): 173–76.

Reynolds, P. D. "Organizational Culture as Related to Industry, Position, and Performance: A Preliminary Report." *Journal of Management Studies* 23, 3 (1986): 334–45.

Rogers, Carl B. *On Becoming a Person*. Boston: Houghton Mifflin, 1964.

Rosen, Benson, and Thomas H. Jerdee. "Influence of Subordinate Characteristics on Trust and Use of Participative Decision Strategies in a Management Simulation." *Journal of Applied Psychology* 62, 5 (1977): 628–31.

Rosen, Benson, and Kay Lovelace. "Piecing Together the Diversity Puzzle." *HR Magazine* 36 (June 1991): 78–82.

Rossiter, Charles M., Jr., and Barnett W. Pearch. *Communicating Personally*. New York: Bobbs-Merrill, 1975.

Rost, Joseph C. *Leadership for the Twenty-first Century*. New York: Praeger, 1991.

Rotter, Julian B. "Generalized Expectancies for Interpersonal Trust." *American Psychology* 26 (1971): 651–65.

———. "Trust and Gullibility." *Psychology Today* (October 1980): 35–41, 102.

Salikis, J. T. "Ethical Beliefs, Differences of Males and Females." *Journal of Business Ethics* 9 (1990): 509–17.

Sashkin, Marshall. "True Vision in Leadership." *Training and Development Journal* (May 1986): 58.

Sathe, Vijay. "Organizational Culture: Some Conceptual Distinctions and Their Managerial Implications." Working paper, Harvard Business School, Division of Research, July 1983.

Savage, Doris. "Trust as a Productivity Management Tool." *Training and Development Journal* (February 1982): 54–57.

Schein, E. *Organizational Psychology*. Englewood Cliffs, N.J.: Prentice-Hall, 1980.

Schein, Edgar H. *Organizational Culture and Leadership*. San Francisco: Jossey-Bass, 1985.

———. "Coming to a New Awareness of Organizational Culture." In David A. Kolb, Irwin M. Rubin, and Joyce S. Osland, eds., *The Organizational Behavior Reader*. Englewood Cliffs, N.J.: Prentice-Hall, 1991.

Schmidt, W. H., and B. Z. Posner. "Values and Expectations of Federal Service Executives." *Public Administration Review* (September/October 1986):447–54.

Schneider, Benjamin, ed. *Organizational Climate and Culture*. San Francisco: Jossey-Bass, 1990.

Scott, Dow. "The Causal Relationship Between Trust and the Assessed Value of Management by Objectives." *Journal of Management* 6, 2 (1980):157–75.

Scott, William G., and David K. Hart. *Organizational America: Can Individual Freedom Survive Within the Security it Promises?*. Boston: Houghton Mifflin Company, 1979.

Selznick, P. *Leadership in Administration*. Evanston, Ill.: Row, Peterson, 1957.

Senn, Larry. "Corporate Culture." *MW* (April 1986):16–18.

Sergiovanni, T. J. "Adding Value to Leadership Gets Extraordinary Results." *Educational Leadership* 47 (1990):23–27.

Shaver, Phillip. "The Public Distrust." *Psychology Today* (October 1980).

Sholtes, P. R. *The Team Handbook: How to Use Teams to Improve Quality*. Madison, Wis.: Joiner Associates, 1988.

Shonk, James H. *Working in Teams.* New York: AMACOM, 1982.

Simon, H. A., D. W. Smithburg, and V. A. Thompson. *Public Administration.* New York: Alfred A. Knopf, 1950.

Sims, Ronald R. "The Challenge of Ethical Behavior in Organizations." *Journal of Business Ethics* 11 (1992):939–48.

Sinatar, Marsha. "Building Trust into Corporate Relationships." *Organizational Dynamics* (Winter 1988):73.

Smircich, Linda. "Concepts of Culture and Organizational Analysis." *Administrative Science Quarterly* 28 (1983):339–58.

Smith, Henry C. *Sensitivity to People.* New York: Abbey Press, 1972.

Solomon, Charlene. "The Corporate Response to Work Force Diversity." *Personnel Journal* 67, 1 (January 1988): 46–51.

Steers, R. M. "Antecedents and Outcomes of Organizational Commitment." Ph.D. diss., University of Iowa, 1985.

Stewart, Debra W., and G. David Garson. *Organizational Behavior and Public Management.* New York: Marcel Dekker, 1983.

Swartz, Marc, and David Jordan. *Culture: An Anthropological Perspective.* New York: John Wiley, 1980.

Taylor, Edward B. *Primitive Society.* New York: Holt, 1877.

Taylor, Sylvester, and Luke Novelli, Jr. "Telling a Story About Innovation." *Issues and Observations* 11, 1 (1991):6–9. Greensboro, N.C., Center for Creative Leadership.

Thompson, D. F. "The Possibility of Administrative Ethics." *Public Administration Review* (September/October 1985):555–61.

Timm, Paul. *Managerial Communication.* New York: Prentice-Hall, 1980.

Tosi, Henry L., John R. Rizzo, and Steven J. Carroll. *Managing Organizational Behavior.* Marshfield, Mass.: Pittman Publishing, Inc., 1986.

Townsend, P. L., and J. E. Gebhardt. *Commit to Quality.* New York: John Wiley, 1990.

Trist, Eric. "Socio-technical Systems." Address, University of Cambridge, November 18, 1959; referenced in Henry Leavenson, *The Exceptional Executive.* Cambridge, Mass.: Harvard University Press, 1968.

Ulrich, Wendy L. "Why Culture?" *Human Resources Management* 23, 2 (1984):117–28.

Uttal, B. "The Corporate Culture Vultures." *Fortune* 108, 8 (1983):66.

Vanfleet, David D., and Gary A. Yukl. "A Century of Leadership Research." In W. E. Rosenbach and R. L. Taylor, eds., *Contemporary Issues in Leadership.* Boulder, Colo.: Westview Press, 1989.

Wallach, E. J. "Individuals and Organizations: The Cultural Match." *Training and Development Journal* 37, 2 (1983):29–36.

Walton, Mary. *The Deming Management Method.* New York: Dodd, Mead, 1986.

Weber, Max. *The Protestant Ethic and the Spirit of Capitalism,* trans. by Talcott Parsons. New York: Charles Scribner's, 1958.

Weiss, Joseph W., ed. *Regional Cultures, Managerial Behavior, and Entrepreneurship.* New York: Quorum Books, 1988.

Westoff, Leslie A. *Corporate Romance.* New York: Time Books, 1985.

Wheatley, Margaret J. *Leadership and the New Science: Learning About Organization from an Orderly Universe.* San Francisco: Berrett-Koehler Publishers, 1992.

Whitley, D. *Winning the Innovation Game.* New York: Berkeley Book, 1989.

Wildavsky, Aaron. *The Nursing Father: Moses as a Political Leader.* Birmingham: University of Alabama Press, 1984.

Wilkins, Alan L., and William G. Ouchi. "Efficient Cultures: Exploring the Relationship between Culture and Organizational Performance." *Administrative Science Quarterly* 28 (1983): 468–81.

Witham, Donald C., and John D. Glover. "Recapturing Commitment." *Training and Development Journal* 4, 4 (April 1987):42–45.

Zand, Dale E. "Trust and Managerial Problem Solving." *Administrative Science Quarterly* 17 (1972):229–39.

Zelznick, Abraham. "Managers and Leaders: Are They Different?" *Harvard Business Review* (May–June 1977): 67.

# Index

## About the Author

GILBERT W. FAIRHOLM is Associate Professor of Public Administration at Virginia Commonwealth University. He is the author of *Values Leadership* (Praeger, 1991), used by several institutions of higher education as part of executive development and academic programs, and *Organizational Power Politics* (Praeger, 1993), a *Choice* Outstanding Academic Book.

ISBN 0-275-94833-1

90000>

EAN

9 780275 948337

HARDCOVER BAR CODE